RADICAL *Review*
HISTORY

Issue | 144

Historicizing the Images and Politics of the Afropolitan

Theorizing the Afropolitan Past and Present

Rosa Carrasquillo, Melina Pappademos,
and Lorelle Semley

The evocative cover for this issue, by the Nigerian photographer Emeka Okereke, features the participants in the Invisible Borders Trans-African Project during their trip to Bangladesh in 2019.[1] We were drawn to it because it reflects and transcends so many of the ideas associated with the ideal and the challenge of the Afropolitan. Par excellence, the term *Afropolitan* signals mobility, but one often connected to the Global North or to the largest cities on the African continent. Without any context, it is not possible to know that the image is of Bangladesh from the landscape—a low seawall, a busy road, the speeding car rendered motionless. The viewer can only search the expressions of the people standing together and apart, facing and turned away from the camera, for clues. It is also not entirely clear who is from the Trans-African Project and who is from the Bangladeshi Drik Network partnered with them.[2] The viewer is put in the uncomfortable situation of assuming who might belong and who might not, raising a central question about the Afropolitan who seeks to transcend such borders.

The photograph appears on the cover of the *Trans-Bangladeshi*, a newsletter that Invisible Borders published in Dhaka as part of its project. From the newsletter's essays, poems, and photographs, we learn some of the stories and interests of the participants. Next to the cover image is the opening reflection, "Let's Try On New Clothes," by the Nigerian writer Kay Ugwuede. The short essay uses the metaphor of "trying on clothes" to reflect on how countries can outgrow their colonial borders. She also describes the initial meeting with their Bangladeshi counterparts

Radical History Review
Issue 144 (October 2022)   DOI 10.1215/01636545-9847774
© 2022 by MARHO: The Radical Historians' Organization, Inc.

as a fraught moment when they "try each other on like clothes," wondering if their cross-border collaboration will "fit."[3] Indeed, Okereke, who took this particular image, themes the series of photographs from his trip—featured as a coauthored Curated Space in this issue—as a "search for intimacy." In discussing the images with his colleague and friend Mathangi Krishnamurthy, he notes the paradox, as an "Afropolitan in Asia," of being seen and not seen in encounters "full of warmth" that simultaneously "deflect[ed] intimacy." The cover image evokes this duality. At the same time that the idea of a group of artists traveling and creating in Bangladesh suits the common image of the globe-trotting Afropolitan, the unexpected context and the ambivalent emotions around mobility, encounter, and borders complicate the narrative.

This photograph is a fitting introduction to the different set of questions this issue asks about what Achille Mbembe described in 2007 as the fundamental "paradigm of itinerancy, mobility, and displacement" shaping African and African diaspora history.[4] Rather than only thinking of Afropolitanism in the present or as part of "Afrofutures," we asked contributors also to explore and theorize the potential for Afropolitan pasts.[5] In his essay in this issue, David Schoenbrun analyzes the quotidian "rhythmed mobility" of the Afropolitan in his story of *vashambadzi* (Shona for travelers) in fourteenth-century southern Africa. He suggests ways to get at the stories of mobile Africans before the explosion of slave trades that would carry away millions, and before the formal imposition of European colonialism. The afterlives of both processes still shape how the continent and its histories are seen today, and some proposed the concept of the Afropolitan precisely to disrupt those powerful narratives. But the contributors to this issue suggest that Afropolitanism can be a useful framework of historical analysis in a much broader time and space. Their articles analyze the Afropolitan from itinerant artisans in fourteenth-century southern Africa to a sixteenth-century outpost in Latin America, West African kingdoms and port cities in the waning decades of the Atlantic slave trade, a hair salon in twenty-first-century Paris, and a busy roadway in Bangladesh before the world knew COVID-19.

Afropolitanism: Origins, Uses, and Opportunities

To date, much of the focus on Afropolitanism, as a present-day phenomenon, has occurred in literature, sociology, philosophy, and popular culture.[6] The strongest critiques of Taiye Selasi's original short musing in *LIP Magazine* in 2005 object to how the ideals of transnationalism and mobility inevitably refer to Western models of leisure and style that commodify a jet-setting African experience.[7] Scholars who have attempted to reclaim and redefine the Afropolitan still often only debate their activities in the twenty-first century. In his essay "We, Afropolitans," the literary scholar Chielozona Eze lays out a manifesto defining an Afropolitanism rooted in a universalism that does not extend from the European Enlightenment but from an ethos in African communities that recognizes the interconnectedness between mobility and home. For Eze, mobility is not in the physical movement but in the mind and fabric of the self: "We, Afropolitans, believe in the ever expanding universe in which we are the centres; . . . We are fitted not just with double-consciousness; we possess multiple consciousness, for we perceive the world from multiple perspectives."[8] But the "we" Eze is referencing is unclear, perhaps purposefully. Eze's Afropolitans may be women and men of some means, but they are defined by their interiority rather than their upward mobility, making for the possibility for a much more expansive "we."

Many scholars have continued to evoke the term despite the backlash, seeing in it a shortcut to allude to transnationalism or to a cosmopolitanism that at least claims to move beyond the Western trappings of the term.[9] Though historians of Africa and the African diaspora have not shied away from debating and theorizing about transnationalism and cosmopolitanism, the term *Afropolitan* has mostly remained a domain of literary scholars, theorists, and, occasionally, sociologists. The historical work in this issue takes a more interdisciplinary approach even when using archival and primary sources. In engaging the Afropolitan as a historical as well as contemporary subject, our contributors tend to coalesce and overlap along three key lines of critical inquiry: visual culture, narrativity, and intersectionality. Their approaches to these themes are diverse yet very much in dialogue. For example, the authors critically examine images occurring in historical art, photography, and mixed media but also create powerful images through their own texts. Narrative can offer a mode of analysis and also raise questions about the politics of knowing. Contributors to the issue propose innovative, transnational, and intersectional theoretical frameworks that recognize race, place, and gendered Black life. We follow our thematic discussion of the articles with an overview organized by their order of appearance in the issue. While the order of the articles follows a certain narrative arc, the juxtaposition of the different texts also disrupts chronologies and geographies, just as Afropolitans often have.

Theorizing the Visual in Images and Texts

The scholar Nicholas Mirzoeff observes that "the emerging global society is visual."[10] Indeed, the politics of the Afropolitan are often connected to imagery, whether in visual media or conjured in literary and, here, historical texts. The idea of the Afropolitan may be most readily evoked in fashion and consumer culture, but the term also evokes a powerful visual aesthetic associated with urbanized landscapes both within and beyond the African continent, past and present. In her study of eighteenth- and nineteenth-century Dahomey, Elizabeth Fretwell analyzes images and descriptions from traveler accounts to show how Dahomean kings and elites used multiple kinds of cloth, styles of dress, and accessories to establish status, legitimacy, and power. In a very different setting in sixteenth-century

Latin America, Antonia Carcelén-Estrada reveals how the famous painting *Los dones de Esmeraldas* refers to a complex history of local Indigenous trade networks, maroon communities of fugitive slaves, and colonial politics, though many observers may misunderstand the iconography behind the dress, gestures, and politics of the Indigenous artist who painted it. The global visual society that people see in the present had precedents in the past that operated on a different scale.

Similarly, Patrícia Martins Marcos deconstructs the Portuguese national imaginary as white and male through the study of art, performance, and photography in what she calls countervisual *quilombismo*. Mirzoeff defines countervisuality as "the assertion of the right to look, challenging the law that sustains visuality's authority to suture its interpretation of the sensible to power, first as law and then as the aesthetic."[11] Martins Marcos focuses on the ways Black artists and activists transform and resignify space in Portugal, where the long history of a Black presence is often forgotten. Her essay resonates with Dawn Fulton's discussion of Francophone African women writers in Paris and how they create written and visual portraits of themselves in different areas of the city. Discussing the mundane—including food, fashion, and hair—the women claim space and belonging for themselves and their families, countering another European imaginary that often elides its colonial past and history of diversity.

The articles that include images differ from the Curated Spaces and Afterword by visual artists, who center the image as the story and forcefully evoke Mbembe's discussion of the Afropolitan as worlds-in-movement. Héctor Mediavilla shares a collection of photographs from the International Fashion Festival in Africa (Festival International de la Mode en Afrique, or FIMA), which started in Niger in 1998. Through contextualization with behind-the-scenes imagery and interviews, Mediavilla reveals fashion pieces that reflect different African sensibilities and Western influences. Emeka Okereke and Mathangi Krishnamurthy take us to a very different setting in Bangladesh in the discussion of the photographs Okereke took during the Invisible Borders Trans-African Project, a collaboration between African and South Asian artists. The discussion between Okereke and Krishnamurthy frames their own movements in the world as very different postcolonial subjects, as they reflect on Okereke's photos of people embracing, a child being held, and a bird perched on the side of the road as part of his theme on the "search for intimacy." The photos and conversation remind the reader and viewer of the reality of postcolonial subjects in movement across national borders that are artificial dividers from colonial times. In "Does Afropolitanism Apply to the Americas?," Aniova Prandy also plays with the ideas of forced mobility, the implied lack of mobility of slavery, and fugitivity through the use of sugar, satin cushions, and iron collars—all of them open, save one. Her work demands the use of all the senses to engage the different textures, colors, and even the bittersweet taste.

As the sensory nature of Prandy's visual art reminds us that texts can also incite the senses, David Schoenbrun's sample of creative nonfiction set in fourteenth-century southern Africa does similar work through text. The descriptions in the story of the young couple Mma and Tswan provide a visceral portrait of Afropolitan mobility. The smell of burning grass, the taste of water flowing from a stream, the feel of the foot on the landscape, the stories told in rock art, and the sight of a stone-built walled city all bring to life a different sense of space in the distant African past. As many of our contributors suggest, the limits of the archive can partially be remedied through creative narratives, unusual sources, and artifacts we encounter and struggle with to move historical narratives forward.

The Politics of Storytelling

The theoretical framing by the visionary literary scholar Saidiya Hartman has been a crucial source for historians engaged in the practice and politics of storytelling about the past. Hartman's scholarship on African American history has posed interlocking theories of critical fabulation and narrative restraint to trace not only the stories found in the "mortuary archive" but also Black life in the fugitive, radical freedom dreams of young Black women.[12] Her theory of "critical fabulation" calls for the scholar to paint as full a picture of Black lives as possible to recuperate, if not the details, then the moods and experiences of lives consumed by the archive, in other words, "to displace the received or authorized account, and to imagine what might have happened or might have been said or might have been done."[13] But, struggling with the potential violence of even this creative act, Hartman also insists on the author's use of narrative restraint and refusal to fill gaps and provide closure for what has been lost.[14] With these kinds of frameworks in mind, our contributors both theorize narrative as a tool of historical analysis and create new narratives that evoke the Afropolitan.

Paulina Alberto takes up these questions of narrative as analysis and creative power in the form of a seminar she offers on what she calls "racial storytelling," which uses recent historical fiction alongside foundational historical texts about race in Argentina. She operates from the premise that stories have disproportionate power to persuade, convey meaning, shape how we engage others, and linger as we navigate our quotidian lives. Students not only learn how such stories are constructed and marshaled but also how they can be transformed or countered. The experience and experiment with storytelling helps students engage with and begin to understand the challenge of antiracist work.

David Schoenbrun offers theorization and a sample of a new narrative that challenges understandings about Africa's distant past and how the concept of the Afropolitan might also inform that time and space. He calls for a "deeper history of the Afropolitan" to reach a new plateau of historical inquiry. His intervention searches for a history where absences and silences of the traditional archives are filled with what he calls the "unusual archives"—evidence found in a plethora of diverse sources within archeology, linguistics, art history, historical and climate ecology, landscape history, and geography. He proposes a creative nonfiction to demonstrate the mobility of Africans before the fifteenth century. In his wonderfully evocative essay about a fourteenth-century couple making their way in and around Great Zimbabwe with *vashambadzi* (travelers), he posits that ceramicists, weavers, healers, and others walked African coasts and interiors and "discovered" the African continent and shaped its histories.

Both Alberto and Schoenbrun are fundamentally concerned with the power of storytelling, albeit in different times and spaces in the history of Africa and the African diaspora. While several of our authors are interested in creating new narratives of African and African diaspora history through their analysis, Schoenbrun powerfully reminds us of some of the limits in extant historical methods, which can be especially acute for historians of Africa. The powerful narrative force and documentary evidence of the histories of slave trades and colonialism has meant that other continental histories of movement and mobility still remain to be written. Thus, both Alberto and Schoenbrun demonstrate how storytelling holds enormous potential for students and scholars to move past inadequate methodologies and to amplify silenced perspectives. Stories enable us to witness, draw multidirectional and multidimensional connections, and testify against racialist absurdities. Storytelling can impact how data is used and how meaning is inferred from archival records. Storytelling can uplift and mobilize; it is a practice central to apprehending Black subjectivities on the continent and in its diaspora, because stories can validate and restore.

Beyond the Intersectional Afropolitan

To tell the story of the Afropolitan, a shared, albeit constructed, racial identity might seem to be central. However, Mbembe and others have insisted on contrasting capacious and flexible categories of the Afropolitan with Pan-Africanism or, more specifically, Afrocentrism.[15] Viewing Africa, and especially South Africa, as a locus of Afropolitanism, Mbembe emphasizes that Africa is not bounded by race and that diverse people can (and have for centuries) claimed Africa as a home and marker of identity.[16] But the assumed and reductive opposition between Pan-African and Afropolitan models may foreclose analytical possibilities to center complex racialized identities. In her essay, Martins Marcos critiques this particular focus of Afropolitanism "beyond" race and proposes *quilombismo* (fugitivity or *marronage*, meaning escape from slavery) as a theory informed by praxis. It is significant that the term *quilombismo*—theorized as a verb, theory, and arts movement by Brazilian scholars—does not translate directly into English, where *maroon* is a noun or adjective. She suggests that creative attention to a broader formulation of fugitivity and diaspora could lend itself to what Mbembe calls for as a "planetary reading of [our] predicament" that does not resort to race or nation.[17]

At the same time, a fully realized Afropolitan should also engage critically with gender and sexuality, among other things.[18] While some scholars have shown how the central Black feminist theory of intersectionality is both marginalized and policed, scholars also still need to attend to intersectionality in their approach to transnationalism in gender and sexuality studies in the Global North.[19] For example, scholars of Africa have questioned whether intersectionality captures all of the forces at work in African contexts.[20] Also, the common narrative of the origins and theorization of intersectionality often ignores early and continued contributions from outside the United States. Martins Marcos notes the concept of *améfricani-dade*, developed by the Black Brazilian feminist Lélia Gonzalez in the 1980s to account for the particular global experience of Black and Indigenous people, especially women. Thus Martins Marcos frames a theory around these practical theories of race, gender, diaspora, and fugitivity precisely in an effort to transcend persistent "analytic traps."[21]

Similarly, Carcelén-Estrada analyzes art, the colonial archive, and orality as an "archive of memory" to work with Afropolitanism and critique it at the same time. Citing common portrayals of Afropolitanism as a "universalizing cosmopolitanism and privilege," she analyzes a deeply racialized and gendered sense of the Chocó (the Pacific coastal region spanning northern Colombia and Ecuador) defined by a critical Black feminist practice tied to the geography and a long history of struggle against colonial and neocolonial "extractivist" practices. Carcelén-Estrada's use of gender analysis is expansive as she uses the famous painting *Los dones de Esmeraldas* not only to reveal how Indigenous and Black women are excluded from official narratives but also to show how the Indigenous painter Gallque subtly challenged the Spanish crown he was serving by representing the maroon leader Arobe and his sons as well as his own masculine and autonomous self as an Indigenous man.

After exploring the gaps in the colonial archive and how women scholars, in particular, have challenged the omission of women of the African diaspora in a region known for its *palenques* (free Black communities) and African-descended communities, Carcelén-Estrada concludes with historical and contemporary examples of Chocoan women using orality in songs and community organizing as part of their own processes of self-fashioning. Deeply engaged with visual, textual, and oral archives alongside intersectionality as a decolonial approach, Carcelén-Estrada may push beyond some of the limits of intersectional praxis and her own critique of Afropolitan scholarship. In her discussion of the ways that charged debates over intersectionality have hamstrung Black feminist praxis, Jennifer Nash proposes a process of reclaiming a space of "radical freedom-dreaming and visionary world-making."[22] Indeed, Carcelén-Estrada intellectually embraces Chocoan expressions of a Blackness as defined by femininity, sexuality, and joy. At the same time, by recognizing Chocoan women's activism as both inherently local and yet potentially "translatable," Carcelén-Estrada ultimately provides another possible way to define Afropolitanism.

Given that one of the inescapable themes in writing on the Afropolitan is its association with rampant consumerism and commodification, it is worth examining this theme in light of intersectionality and calls to rethink approaches to it. Critics (and defenders) of this trope often point to ubiquitous African-themed merchandise as a problem or a promise. However, in the long history of merchandising Blackness in fashion, scholars such as Monica Miller and Tanisha Ford have shown that there are ways in which commercialization can be turned on its head not only for aesthetic purposes but also for political effect.[23] Here, this question is addressed in differing historical and contemporary contexts. For example, Fretwell and Ndubueze Mbah reveal how consumption of cloth and/or European forms of dress buttressed the status of elites in Dahomey and returned Liberated Africans in Old Calabar, often at the expense of the enslaved. Both authors point out the poignant and troubling relationship between African elite wealth and the vulnerability of others to enslavement.

For the contemporary period, Dawn Fulton argues that the Black women writers she samples purposefully create women characters who engage consciously with fashion in an effort to underscore Black (women's) life and joy as a direct counterpoint to Afro-pessimism. Perhaps the most obvious nod to the iconography of fashion and consumption is Mediavilla's discussion of FIMA. Yet Mediavilla notes that the founder and participants in this event see it as a pathway to promote and redefine development in West Africa through their own networks and exchange. FIMA seems to work within Western ideals of consumerism and development, and FIMA organizer, Sidahmed Seidnaly, who is now known as Alphadi, was able to acquire international partners for the event. However, the origins of FIMA in landlocked Niger initially worked outside of Western priorities and initiatives. In these ways, FIMA in Niger encompasses the multilayered meanings of the Afropolitan. Niger is a diverse, majority-Muslim African country that evokes a long, complex, and ongoing history of migration in central Africa, as old trans-Saharan routes are plied today by people seeking ways to manage the treacherous crossing of the Mediterranean to reach Europe.[24] Mbah's evocation of a discrepant cosmopolitanism that enjoins elite travel of people, products, violence, and inequality could not be more apt when contrasting that reality with the luminous and everyday images from FIMA. In the end, however, it is not simply a derivation of Western-style fashion or ideology on display during the festival. FIMA should be a reminder of how products and ideas can be vernacularized and transformed into something new, in this case, on the edge of the Sahara Desert.

Overview of Articles

We chose to begin the issue with two research articles that adroitly theorize the Afropolitan as a historical phenomenon in eighteenth- and nineteenth-century West Africa, before the formal onset of European colonial rule across the continent. But the push and pull of the transatlantic slave trade also shaped the different ways that Afropolitanism was manifest in the kingdoms of Dahomey and Old Calabar. In the first article, Elizabeth Fretwell analyzes how the elite sartorial culture of Dahomey was based in the circulation and adoption of cloth and styles of dress from African and European sources as a means of distinguishing elites from the general population and the enslaved who crossed the Atlantic or who labored in Dahomey itself. Crucial to Fretwell's argument is the fundamental history of exchange between Dahomey and neighboring communities and polities. She relates the threads of this integrated regional exchange to the woven cloth produced on different types of looms that allowed Dahomean weavers to produce quality cloth valued for its "composite parts." In fact, traders on the coast to the south of Dahomey exported "Allada" cloth, which had diverse regional origins, before Africans began importing myriad types of cloth, yarn, and clothing in exchange for captives. These origins of the aesthetic use of imported cloth partly fueled Dahomey's expansion and reputation as a military force in the region.

Perhaps no event better showed this connection between cloth and military power than the annual customs (*Hwetanu*) ceremony. While European travelers often highlighted the month-long event for the practice of ritualized human sacrifice, their descriptions and drawings depicting it also revealed how much the festival served as a means to collect, display, and distribute cloth. The celebration, which often drew African and European outsiders, also allowed the Dahomean leadership and other elite attendees to display their differences through particular types of dress, cloth as gifts, and even draped cloth as decoration. It is worth noting that woven Yoruba "Oyo" cloth remained a top choice as a gift despite a market flooded with imported cloth from Europe (often produced in South Asia).[25] The king and other elites would assemble that combination of clothing items from near and far to indicate the power and reach of the kingdom. Elite women and men would layer different types of pagne (cloth used to wrap the body) as well as hats, jewelry, and other accessories that contrasted with the more basic coverings that the majority of people wore. Fretwell interprets this difference as a way for elites to signify their "belonging" to a wider world. She thus raises the question of how different Africans may have seen themselves as part of or excluded from different worlds. However, she reminds us that broader, diverse African worlds that extended into the hinterland had preceded and continued with the incorporation of Africans into a wider Atlantic.

In contrast to Fretwell's focus on elite insiders, Ndubueze Mbah highlights the mobility and self-fashioning of "Liberated Africans," who returned to Old Calabar from Sierra Leone in the later nineteenth century as self-described "Black Englishmen." Mbah theorizes their Afropolitan identity, in terms of their dispersion as well as their attempts to immerse themselves back into Old Calabar society, to the consternation of British palm oil traders and local Old Calabar elites. Like Fretwell, Mbah exposes how the processes of the slave trade interacted with the activities of the Liberated Africans, who in this instance forged "freedom papers" to undermine local elites as well as to enrich themselves. Mbah analyzes the indeterminacy of the Liberated Africans' activities as an example of what James Clifford has described as "discrepant cosmopolitanism," a cosmopolitanism deeply tied to the violent forces and inequality that shaped people's movement.[26]

Mbah's article highlights the improbable journey of Liberated Africans, who had been intercepted by naval forces after the 1807 Act for the Abolition of the Slave Trade went into effect. People were "emancipated" in Sierra Leone, among other places, though their freedom was often circumscribed by apprenticeships, forced marriages, or forced relocation, making the story of these Liberated Africans that much more remarkable.[27] Almost one hundred thousand people landed in Sierra Leone; about one-third of them had been enslaved in the region of the Bight of Biafra, where Old Calabar was an important port city. After 1850, an untold number of Liberated Africans returned to Old Calabar. Rather than consider them disappeared, Mbah argues that Liberated Africans and what he calls their "Afropolitan freedom politics" emerge through their petitions, through complaints about them in British archives and from Old Calabar elites, and in the British attempts to ultimately deport them back to Sierra Leone. Liberated Africans frustrated African and European officials because of the way they tried to turn ideals about free trade (in palm oil) and free (slave) labor to their advantage. When Liberated Africans returned, they not only adopted an identity as "Black Englishmen" to counter their marginal outsider identity, but they also "embodied" emancipation in their status and used ideas such as freedom as a political right to undercut the Old Calabar social order. The returnees' use of petitions and "freedom papers" to redeem the enslaved also countered the protected status of Old Calabar elites, who could trade palm oil and retain enslaved people in an era when the Atlantic slave trade, but not slavery, was illegal. However, the Liberated Africans were using the redeemed slaves as domestic servants and trafficking them to other locations such as Fernando Po (Bioko), an island that is part of what is now Equatorial Guinea, as indentured labor, thereby evading the British law abolishing the slave trade. When the redemption practices of the Liberated Africans challenged the status quo too much, however, the British banned them to protect domestic slavery and the power of the Old Calabar elites.

Like Fretwell, Mbah uncovers the "underbelly" of an Afropolitanism that relied not only on African innovation but also on the exploitation of others within slavery and capitalism. While the personal histories and activities of the Liberated Africans of Old Calabar appeared contradictory, these Afropolitans also reflected their times and the possibilities and limits of radical anti-imperial politics. In telling their story, Mbah also highlights the work involved in reading against and along the grain of sources to reveal deeply "archived subalterns." Similarly, the reflective essays that follow use creative and thoughtful readings of archives, literature, monuments, and photographs to render visible other possibilities for Afropolitanism, despite the afterlives of slavery and empire.

In her essay, Antonia Carcelén-Estrada questions traditional archives for their systematic silence of Black women's voices in the history of the Esmeraldas in Ecuador. Instead, she favors "orature" (oral literature) produced by and for Black women in the Esmeraldas region of Ecuador to reconstruct a past that affirms their right to exist and live in a dignified community. She begins with the famous 1599 painting *Los dones de Esmeraldas* by Andrés Sánchez-Gallque to question the dominant narrative of the people in the Esmeraldas. Carcelén-Estrada observes how the painting creates "an image (and a gaze) that disregards power and gender relations in the production of historical sources, archives, and narratives by completely omitting African diaspora women from the historical imagination." This distortion evolves from colonial times to the present in the dominant historical narrative, assisted by the structural violence of the state and its neoliberal policies of development, which dispossess and displace Black women.

Against this structural violence, Black women in Esmeraldas are rewriting history and reimagining the past as a strategy that searches for a "memory in-place" to reject migration and dispossession. In this sense, these women cannot afford the idealized middle-class (or elite) mobility often associated with Afropolitanism; their lived experiences demand a different type of identification and activism. Instead, these women employ oral histories to identify "colonial differences and class privileges, and demand to be visible in the making of Esmeraldas's history while using that history to stop the migration to urban centers" and create sustainable economies at home. These women are building alternative archives, orature, to write a counter-narrative in which they are at the center of Esmeraldas as a territory and a Black community. Thus Carcelén-Estrada challenges linear ways to measure time by introducing the dominance of Black women behind the painting of *Los dones*. She triangulates this colonial history with contemporary Black women's activism to combat the "nostalgia" and "amnesia" of Ecuador mestizo elites, who fixate their gaze on the history of conquest. Instead, Carcelén-Estrada documents the decolonial knowledge that centers Black women's experiences of resilience, struggle, and rebellion.

Patrícia Martins Marcos offers the themes of *quilombismo* and diaspora to make Afropolitanism more inclusive and to engender a "dialectic" between the concepts. Martins Marcos evokes the long history of marronage in opposition to Western epistemologies in the Lusophone world that render Blackness "unthinkable" and "inherently foreign" and thus make Black people appear ineligible for citizenship. She draws on the idea of the *quilombo* as a historical place of refuge against slavery and *quilombismo* or fugitivity as a practice and an epistemology that challenges Lusophone myths of nation and empire.

To contextualize countervisual practices in contemporary Portugal, Martins Marcos documents how Black artists and activists like the Angolan Kiluanji Kia Henda or the Afro-Luso-Brazilian trio Aurora Negra (Black Dawn) employ visual *quilombismo* as a form of countervisuality—what Martins Marcos calls countervisual *quilombismo*—to establish the right to be and be seen in the national narrative. Using their physical presence to interrupt hyperwhite, sanitized spaces such as the Portuguese World Exhibition of 1940, Black artists create a maroon moment to insert themselves within national borders. Or, in the case of the Guinea-Bissau–born woman politician Joacine Katar Moreira, by staging an official photograph in front of colonial murals in the Parliament's "Noble Hall" to stare defiantly back at the viewer and represent her own "historicity and self-determination." Occupying monuments to conquerors is one strategy of countervisual *quilombismo* in which photographers capture for posterity a disruptive moment in which Black women, children, and men redefine the narrative of white conquest.

In her contribution, Dawn Fulton challenges the image of a white Paris and past images of Black Paris through her analysis and alternative reading of three contemporary Francophone African writers—Léonora Miano, Rokhaya Diallo, and Lauren Ekué—who write about the Afropolitan experiences of middle-class Black women in Paris in new ways. Fulton recasts the most common critiques of excessive consumerism and apoliticism in Afropolitanism. She notes how Miano and Diallo defy what Diallo calls the image of Paris as a "monochromatic city" beyond the common areas associated with Black activism in favor of a kind of "permeation, a claim to ubiquity that doesn't lose its hold on the particular, highly personalized definitions of home." The "staunchly bourgeois" protagonists in Miano's fiction and the stories and images in Diallo's book of portraits of Black women sporting their natural hair in Paris also challenge previous (often masculine) narratives of migrant misery and victimization by highlighting the music, film, and visual media that define the daily routines and livelihoods of Black women in twenty-first-century Paris.

Fulton particularly focuses on the characters in Lauren Ekué's writings to show the possibility of reconciling consumption with political consciousness by "affirming a fundamental historical awareness in the very act of dismissing it." A key example of this subtle "discursive maneuver" occurs when the protagonist of Ekué's *Icône urbaine*, Flora d'Almeida, subtly refers to her own lack of experience with the histories of "slavery, segregation, dictatorship, ethnic wars or apartheid" and pushes those histories aside as a "Pandora's box [that] will remain well sealed." Fulton also highlights Ekué's attention to the particular ways gender shapes the "intersection between capital and ethics." Ekué's protagonists are aware of the limits of self-empowerment through consumption: they "find their wallets 'mutilated' by these relentless beauty regimens." Ekué's uses of language and literary format also play with this Afropolitan practice of reconciling consumption with activism. She writes for people who are not "traditional" readers, a conscious decision that informs her informal style. "Beneath the apparent superficiality of Ekué's short sentences and abundant exclamation points," Fulton argues, "lies a determination to forge a studied sociological landscape while merging vectors of readership across class, race, and education." That a character as seemingly apolitical and "hyperconsumerist" as Flora can remark on the connections between slavery and the commodification of Black celebrity, or tease a potential future career using media to change the image of Black women, also reveals a tension between the individualist Afropolitan and the possibility of a more radical collective politics. Ekué thus transforms consumption into "symbolic capital" that has the potential to empower Black women and reaffirm their agency. Fulton's readings and reflection challenge understandings of Afropolitanism by expanding its definitions and potential strategies for political activism.

Opportunities to imagine new narratives for Afropolitanism are also highlighted by Paulina Alberto in her essay for our feature Teaching Radical History. Alberto presents powerful anti-racist pedagogies by examining racial ideologies as "stories" to understand "how these ideas circulate, persuade, shape behaviors, influence life chances, and persist in the Americas and beyond." She teaches students to identify, debunk, and deconstruct racial stories through the study of historical narratives, primary sources, and literature and guides them through the ways in which metanarratives of the modern states of Argentina and Brazil were created. She provides an example from her own research on the early twentieth-century rise and fall of Raúl Grigera, a Black Argentine performer who immediately evokes the image of the Afropolitan in yet another time and place. Alberto also tests her students' skills by asking them to extrapolate their analysis to the contemporary United States. Moreover, Alberto pushes her students beyond traditional analysis, asking them to critically and constructively write their own racial stories—"countermyths"—that oppose the stories they have studied in class. Alberto equips students with the categories of analysis that have been developed by Black scholars and critics of the past and present. Students remark that they feel "empowered" by the knowledge and skills, with perhaps one of the most powerful lessons being that "anti-racist work . . . is never stable and never done."

Shifting from the way students might imagine new narratives in the future, David Schoenbrun searches for the deeper roots of Afropolitan mobility in early African history in his Intervention in this issue. In an effort to write beyond Eurocentric paradigms about Africans, he suggests sampling early Afropolitan stories of "cultured mobility." Schoenbrun recognizes that more technical sources for the earlier period are less accessible, and he argues for combining the theory of Afropolitanism with creative nonfiction. Using the figure of the *vashambadzi*, the Shona word for a purposeful traveler, he describes African landscapes shaped by the "rhythmed mobility" and communal work of ordinary farmers, artisans, and healers.

In many ways, Schoenbrun's thoroughly innovative approach engages themes and concerns shared by his fellow contributors related to the archive and evidence as well as narrative, as discussed above. Schoenbrun is not only creative in how he deploys historical linguistics, archeology, and explanatory footnotes to give content and shape to his story; he is thoughtful about issues of affect and moral belonging that express the interiority of his characters through their skills and networking, personal relationships, and ultimate successes and/or failures. His main characters are a young couple, Mma and Tswan, who start their marriage on the road with *vashambadzi* artisans. Mma's skills as a weaver and the work of her husband, Tswan, as a hunter sends them through towns, a destructive fire, trial by ordeal, and interaction with long-distance ivory trade routes, with devastating consequences. Inspired by Hartman's call for "narrative restraint" and respect for gaps, "black noise," and unfinished business, Schoenbrun leaves threads of his narrative undone, respecting these past Afropolitans' "persistence of movement," as he tells the story of Mma, Tswan, and their fellow coast walkers. The article works as a profound intellectual intervention that deploys creative nonfiction as a novel form of historical analysis.

The issue ends with three photographic essays that embody, question, and reimagine the Afropolitan. The photographer Héctor Mediavilla attended the International Fashion Festival in Africa (FIMA) at the urging of the writer Lauren Ekué. The festival's founder, Sidahmed Seidnaly, now known as Alphadi, represents a spin on the classic story of an Afropolitan. He was born in Mali, raised in Niger, and trained in France and through global fashion networks, but he is based in Niamey, Niger, outside the typical "Afropolitan city." Alphadi established the festival in 1998 to create jobs, promote tourism, and foster peace in the region, though the subsequent rise of Islamism has led to protests against the images projected by FIMA. Despite interruptions and even the relocation of the event, Mediavilla was able to attend it in Niger in 2013 and 2016. Focusing his photographs on the preparations for the festival and the daily lives of some of the designers and models, he sought to show where "glamor coexists with precariousness." His approach is not unlike some of his photography on *sapeurs*—the famously well-dressed African trendsetters and self-described artists who Mediavilla photographed against Congolese rather than Parisian landscapes. For Mediavilla, the seeming contradictions in the festival and the images it produces fit well with an expansive view of the Afropolitan that Eze describes as "not half this or that . . . [but] this *and* that."[28]

Emeka Okereke, whose photography graces the cover and opens our introduction, contributes a collaborative essay with his colleague and friend Mathangi Krishnamurthy, a South Asian anthropologist. They discuss Afropolitanism in relation to the series of photographs he took during his project in Bangladesh. Having originally met in Chennai, India, Okereke and Krishnamurthy ruminate on their own Afropolitanism and "Asiapolitanism," remarking that despite how they seem to represent a quintessential cosmopolitanism, "Brownness, Blackness, and gender complicate everything." Indeed, Krishnamurthy describes Okereke as a "hiding presence" in his photographs because his subjects do not engage him or his camera. She suspects correctly that he took the photographs in this way because his presence would have otherwise caused a stir. Okereke agrees that the photographs reflect a non-encounter/encounter because our powerful, multilayered identities often make any border crossing a paradoxical moment. He concludes that the photographs thus represent a search for a "portal of transcendence" where all encounters are possible, where hybridity and intimate negotiations are commonplace. For him, that "needful utopia" is Afropolitanism.

In the Afterword, the visual artist Aniova Prandy describes how she has come to see her latest award-winning installation, *The Sugar Maafa*, as an Afropolitan practice after recently learning of the term. Using the Swahili word for disaster, *maafa*, her artwork effectively tells the story of the remaking of the Caribbean after the fifteenth century through the multivalent symbolism of sugar, silk cushions, and iron collars, representing the transatlantic trade, enslaved labor, capitalist profit, torture, and marronage. Prandy sees the term *Afropolitan* as decolonial because of the way it reimagines people, societies, and histories. She embraces the term and closes our collection by affirming the Afropolitan in all their possibilities.

Rosa Elena Carrasquillo is professor of Caribbean/Latin American history and Helen M. Whall Chair of Gender, Race, and Social Justice at the College of the Holy Cross, Worcester, Massachusetts. Her research interests include interdisciplinary education, gender and race relations in Latin America, Latinx history, and visual culture. Her latest book is *The People's Poet: Life and Myth of Ismael Rivera, An Afro-Caribbean Icon* (2014). Her current book project is on visual culture, colonialism, and race in Santo Domingo, Dominican Republic.

Melina Pappademos is the director of the Africana Studies Institute at the University of Connecticut. She researches and teaches widely on politics and culture in the Caribbean, Cuba, and the African diaspora. Supported by Harvard University, Ford Foundation, and Fulbright-Hays, her first book, *Black Political Activism and the Cuban Republic*, won the Southern Historical Association's Murdo J. Macleod Best Book Prize in 2012. Her current project examines Blackness and culture in twentieth-century Cuba.

Lorelle Semley is professor of history at College of the Holy Cross. Her books include *Mother Is Gold, Father Is Glass: Gender and Colonialism in a Yoruba Town* (2011), the award-winning *To Be Free and French: Citizenship in France's Atlantic Empire* (2017), and, most recently, with Roger Little, *Louis Joseph Janvier, Une chercheuse: Roman d'un Haïtien* (2021). She has published widely on gender, urban, and legal history in Africa and the African diaspora. Her current book project on Black Bordeaux has been supported by an ACLS Fellowship and NEH Fellowship.

Notes

1. The Invisible Borders Trans-African Project, https://invisible-borders.com/.
2. Participants: Borders Within—Bangladesh, https://bangladesh.borders-within.com/about -borders-within-bangladesh/participants/.
3. Ugwuede, "Let's Try On New Clothes."
4. Mbembe, "Afropolitanism," 27.

5.   Samatar, "Toward a Planetary History of Afrofuturism."

6.   Coetzee, *Afropolitanism*. The book reprints articles published in a special issue of the *Journal of African Cultural Studies* in 2016. Wawrzinek and Makokha, *Negotiating Afropolitanism*; Ede, "Afropolitan Genealogies." The scholarly references are too numerous to cite, as are popular culture references to the Afropolitan in fashion, music, and design, including the South African fashion magazine *The Afropolitan*.

7.   Selasi, "Bye Bye Barbar." The most commonly cited critiques of this vein of Afropolitanism are Emma Dabiri, "Why I Am (Still) Not an Afropolitan," and Grace Musila, "Part-Time Africans."

8.   Eze, "We, Afropolitans," 117.

9.   Black scholars writing on the African diaspora have been writing global histories well before the "transnational" turn in US history. Kelley, "'But a Local Phase of a World Problem.'" The common reference to a new cosmopolitanism is the work by Kwame Anthony Appiah. Appiah, *Cosmopolitanism*. For a more direct discussion of Kant and race that broaches new possibilities of the cosmopolitan, see Mills, "Black Radical Kantianism." For a literary discussion of Black cosmopolitanism, see Nwankwo, *Black Cosmopolitanism*.

10. Mirzoeff, *How to See the World*, 5.

11. Mirzoeff, *The Right to Look*, 25.

12. See an example of the arc of Hartman's work, from *Scenes of Subjection* to *Lose Your Mother* to *Wayward Lives, Beautiful Experiments*.

13. Hartman, "Venus in Two Acts," 11–12. Marisa Fuentes refers to the way enslaved women's lives appear or don't appear in the archives as a form of "mutilated historicity" (*Dispossessed Lives*, 6).

14. Hartman, "Venus in Two Acts," 12.

15. Balakrishnan, "Afropolitanism and the End of Black Nationalism"; Mbembe and Balakrishnan, "Pan-African Legacies."

16. Membe, "Afropolitanism," 28; Eze, "We, Afropolitan," 16.

17. Mbembe and Balakrishnan, "Pan-African Legacies," 31.

18. However, we recognize that neither heteronormative nor queer or transgender sexualities are addressed directly in this issue. On the questions of queer Afropolitan analysis, see Adjepong, *Afropolitan Projects*, and M'Baye, "Afropolitan Sexual and Gender Identities."

19. Nash, *Black Feminism Reimagined*.

20. Meer and Müller, "Considering Intersectionality in Africa."

21. Mohanty, "'Under Western Eyes' Revisited."

22. Nash, *Black Feminism Reimagined*, 130.

23. Miller, *Slaves to Fashion*; Ford, *Liberated Threads*. For a visual example of the aesthetics and politics of Black dress, see Ahmir "Questlove" Thompson's documentary of the 1969 Harlem Cultural Festival, *Summer of Soul (. . . Or, When the Revolution Could Not Be Televised)* (US, 2021).

24. Brachet, *Migrations transsahariennes*.

25. Kobayashi, *Indian Cotton Textiles in West Africa*.

26. Clifford, "Traveling Cultures," 108.

27. For a map of the expanse of locations where people were brought in Africa, the Americas, and Asia, see the overview map from the digital humanities project *Liberated Africans*, https://liberatedafricans.org/about.php.

28. Eze, "We, Afropolitans," 117.

References

Adjepong, Anima. *Afropolitan Projects: Redefining Blackness, Sexualities, and Culture from Houston to Accra*. Chapel Hill: University of North Carolina Press, 2021.

Appiah, Kwame Anthony. *Cosmopolitanism: Ethics in a World of Strangers*. New York: W. W. Norton, 2007.

Balakrishnan, Sarah. "Afropolitanism and the End of Black Nationalism." In *Routledge International Handbook of Cosmopolitanism Studies*, edited by Gerard Delanty, 575–85. 2nd ed. New York: Routledge, 2018.

Brachet, Julien. *Migrations transsahariennes: Vers un désert cosmopolite et morcelé, Niger*. Paris: Le Croquant, 2009.

Clifford, James. "Traveling Cultures." In *Cultural Studies*, edited by Lawrence Grossberg, Cary Nelson, and Paula A. Treichler, 96–116. London: Routledge, 1992.

Coetzee, Carli, ed. *Afropolitanism: Reboot*. New York: Routledge, 2019.

Dabiri, Emma. "Why I Am (Still) Not an Afropolitan." *Journal of African Cultural Studies* 28, no. 1 (2016): 104–8.

Ede, Amatoritsero. " Afropolitan Genealogies." *African Diaspora* 11, nos. 1–2 (2019): 35–52.

Eze, Chielozona. "We, Afropolitans." *Journal of African Cultural Studies* 28, no. 1 (2016): 114–19.

Ford, Tanisha C. *Liberated Threads: Black Women, Style, and the Global Politics of Soul*. Chapel Hill: University of North Carolina Press, 2015.

Fuentes, Marisa J. *Dispossessed Lives: Enslaved Women, Violence, and the Archive*. Philadelphia: University of Pennsylvania Press, 2016.

Hartman, Saidiya. *Lose Your Mother: A Journey Along the Atlantic Slave Route*. New York: Macmillan, 2008.

Hartman, Saidiya. *Scenes of Subjection: Terror, Slavery, and Self-Making in Nineteenth-Century America*. New York: Oxford University Press, 1997.

Hartman, Saidiya. "Venus in Two Acts." *Small Axe*, no. 26 (2008): 1–14.

Hartman, Saidiya. *Wayward Lives, Beautiful Experiments: Intimate Histories of Social Upheaval*. New York: W. W. Norton, 2019.

Kelley, Robin D. G. "'But a Local Phase of a World Problem': Black History's Global Vision, 1883–1950." *Journal of American History* 86, no. 3 (1999): 1045–77.

Kobayashi, Kazuo. *Indian Cotton Textiles in West Africa: African Agency, Consumer Demand, and the Making of a Global Economy, 1750–1850*. Cham, Switzerland: Palgrave Macmillan, 2019.

M'Baye, Babacar. "Afropolitan Sexual and Gender Identities in Colonial Senegal." *Humanities* 8, no. 4 (2019): 1–16. https://doi.org/10.3390/h8040166.

Mbembe, Achille. "Afropolitanism." In *Africa Remix: Contemporary Art of a Continent*, edited by Simon Njami, 26–29. Johannesburg: Johannesburg Art Gallery, 2007.

Mbembe, Achille, and Sarah Balakrishnan. "Pan-African Legacies, Afropolitan Futures: A Conversation with Achille Mbembe." *Transition*, no. 120 (2016): 28–37.

Meer, Talia, and Alex Müller. "Introduction: Considering Intersectionality in Africa." *Agenda* 31, no. 1 (2017): 3–4.

Miller, Monica L. *Slaves to Fashion: Black Dandyism and the Styling of Black Diasporic Identity*. Durham, NC: Duke University Press, 2009.

Mills, Charles W. "Black Radical Kantianism." *Res Philosophica* 95, no. 1 (2018): 1–33.

Mirzoeff, Nicholas. *How to See the World: An Introduction to Images, from Self-Portraits to Selfies, Maps to Movies, and More*. New York: Basic Books, 2016.

Mirzoeff, Nicholas. *The Right to Look: A Counterhistory of Visuality*. Durham, NC: Duke University Press, 2011.

Mohanty, Chandra Talpade. "'Under Western Eyes' Revisited: Feminist Solidarity through Anticapitalist Struggles." *Signs: Journal of Women in Culture and Society* 28, no. 2 (2003): 499–535.

Musila, Grace A. "Part-Time Africans, Europolitans, and 'Africa Lite.'" *Journal of African Cultural Studies* 28, no. 1 (2016): 109–113.

Nash, Jennifer C. *Black Feminism Reimagined: After Intersectionality*. Durham, NC: Duke University Press, 2019.

Nwankwo, Ifeoma Kiddoe. *Black Cosmopolitanism, Racial Consciousness, and Transnational Identity in the Nineteenth-Century Americas*. Philadelphia: University of Pennsylvania Press, 2014.

Samatar, Sofia. "Toward a Planetary History of Afrofuturism." *Research in African Literatures* 48, no. 4 (2017): 175–91.

Selasi, Taiye. "Bye-Bye Barbar." *Callaloo* 36, no. 3 (2013): 528–30. (Reprint of "Bye-Bye Babar," *LIP Magazine*, March 3, 2005.)

Ugwuede, Kay. "Let's Try On New Clothes." *Trans-Bangladeshi*, February 2020, 1, 3.

Wawrzinek, Jennifer, and J. K. S. Makokha, eds. *Negotiating Afropolitanism: Essays on Borders and Spaces in Contemporary African Literature and Folklore*. Amsterdam: Rodopi, 2011.

"Domesticating the Unfamiliar"

Afropolitan Dress in the West African Kingdom of Dahomey

Elizabeth Ann Fretwell

In an account of his 1727 encounter with King Agaja of Dahomey, a European slave trader described the monarch as dressed with "a Gown on, flowered with Gold, which reached as low as his Ancles; an *European* embroidered Hat on his Head; with Sandals on his Feet."[1] Elsewhere describing Agaja as "richly" dressed while lounging on a length of silk, the trader's descriptions emphasized the diverse origins of the clothing that covered the royal body.[2] Agaja's hat was European, while the "flowered" fabric of his gown could have been either locally woven and embellished or imported. Agaja also wore sandals, which royal shoemaker lineages recognize as arriving to the Fon-speaking kingdom via the migrations of consumers and captive craftspeople from the nearby Yoruba empire of Oyo.[3] During Agaja's reign (1718–40) and into the nineteenth century, elite Dahomean women also wore similar ensembles that combined Fon practices of wrapping and draping cloth with clothing and accessories imported through networks of exchange in the West African interior and the Atlantic. This article shows how the sartorial culture of elite Dahomeans was a materialization of what Achille Mbembe has called "worlds-in-movement" and represented an Afropolitan aesthetic of "itinerancy, mobility, and displacement."[4] In doing so, it demonstrates how the concept of Afropolitanism serves as a useful framework for examining globally facing societies in the precolonial African past

Radical History Review
Issue 144 (October 2022) DOI 10.1215/01636545-9847788
© 2022 by MARHO: The Radical Historians' Organization, Inc.

and how Dahomean Afropolitan dress practices were imbricated in the violence of Atlantic slaving and slavery.

Afropolitanism has been described in a myriad of ways: as a scholarly approach, a situational identity, an ethic, or an aesthetic practice. These different conceptualizations all share an emphasis on Africans as dynamic participants in African and global processes of migration and transcultural exchange. Some scholars have stressed the exciting "future" that Afropolitanism presents for countering characterizations of Africans as primitive, static, nativist, or perpetual victims; for transcending racial hierarchies; or for dismissing Afro-pessimism.[5] In contrast, critics argue that Afropolitanism's emphasis on domestication "throws Africans into a cultural abyss of culturelessness," or that it centers privileged elites.[6] In an attempt to extend the concept to marginalized groups, other scholars explore the commonalities of Afropolitanism among different strata of African societies and the new African diaspora.[7] Along this vein, this article traces the history of precolonial Dahomean dress, a story normally left out of larger considerations of Afropolitanism, to show the deep historical roots of Afropolitanism on the continent and how the domestication of global and African commodities has long distinguished African elites from the masses.[8] Other historians have likewise emphasized the "cosmopolitanism" of certain precolonial African societies, from Zanzibar to Kongo and Asante, during the eighteenth and nineteenth centuries.[9] Beginning in the mid-eighteenth century, Dahomey, too, had diverse cities and was well integrated into oceanic networks of exchange. The kingdom sent envoys as far afield as Europe and Brazil; after the opening of the Dahomean capital of Abomey to outsiders in the early 1700s, a number of Europeans came to visit the city, although entrance within its walls was regulated. Yet Dahomean elites, including royal families, state administrators, and traders, were more specifically "Afropolitan," underscoring mobility and exchange not just between Dahomey and the West but also with other continental African and diasporic communities, particularly those in Brazil.

The history of elite dress in Dahomey reveals how Afropolitanism can, like some iterations of cosmopolitanism, have a precarious ethical foundation.[10] For the Ghanaian philosopher Kwame Anthony Appiah, cosmopolitanism is an aspiration, as its "two ideals—universal concern and respect for legitimate difference—clash."[11] Cosmopolitans, past and present, might embrace and transcend difference, and even acknowledge their own privileged social positions, but the recognition of the humanity of others often proves harder to achieve. Furthermore, the wealth and privilege needed to travel or consume other cultures reflects an inequitable accumulation of resources that is perhaps particularly acute in African contexts. Dahomey's urban centers were pluralistic, where elites embraced "others," and notions of status and identity circulated and materialized on bodies. Elites acknowledged and celebrated difference by assembling textiles and accessories from local, regional, and Atlantic sources into a layered look that domesticated these materials into a unique style. This look, however, drew on forms acquired through the violent seizure of objects, markets, and craft knowledge, and was financed by the profits of slave trading and enslaved labor. Dahomey was a major participant in the Atlantic slave trade, and its primary port of Ouidah, which Dahomey captured in 1727, had the dubious distinction of exporting one of the highest numbers of captives by volume, or about 10 percent of all African captives transported across the Atlantic.[12] Dahomean elites likely drew much of their wealth either directly or indirectly from the slave trade, which Dahomean sources characterized as a "normal" and regular aspect of exchange.[13] By the mid-nineteenth century, a declining slave trade in coastal Africa triggered a late but relatively smooth transition to an economy organized around the production of palm products.[14] Yet the kingdom continued to rely on warfare and slaving, since enslaved labor cultivated export crops and transported them to the coast from state and private plantations.[15] Even as the crux of the Dahomean economy shifted from commerce to agriculture, wealth remained tied to the trade and labor of bonded Africans.

The sartorial culture of the Dahomean elite distinguished them as a privileged group within a local framework, while it also served as an expression of their inclusion within a larger Atlantic world in which outward appearance helped mediate the difference between enslaver and enslaved. Within Dahomey, the king was the highest power, and his influence and wardrobe only grew over time, from the kingdom's founding at the turn of the seventeenth century to the decades preceding French colonization in the 1890s. Dahomean kings controlled a significant portion of trade, and the palace also exerted a measure of direct rule over dress, religion, and artistic production.[16] Suzanne Preston Blier argues that Dahomean art was assemblage and that artists had "a propensity for the appropriation of forms and imagery from the outside" to create "new and often strikingly innovative Danhomè objects."[17] In a similar manner, elite (but not commoner) dress was a composite of styles and materials that, brought together and layered on a single body, referenced both real and imagined mobilities. But this aesthetic cannot be disassociated from the role of elite Dahomeans as slavers and slaveholders within a violent Atlantic-wide "slave war."[18] Warfare and slaving provided a means of acquiring currency, goods, markets, and craft knowledge and then funneled this wealth to the sartorial practices of free Dahomeans.[19] While Blackness was associated with enslavement in many Atlantic slave societies, dress also helped to delineate bondspeople from free.[20] As Simon Gikandi has shown, modern notions of aesthetics and taste developed out of the profits of slaving and as a contrast to "slavery and its ugliness."[21] Cécile Fromont notes that the "interrelated, global realms of luxury exchange and human trafficking" among Africans and early modern Europeans led to a shared "culture of collecting and networks of taste and design."[22] As part of this common system of material and aesthetic exchange, Dahomean elites advanced a "culture of taste" on the African side of the Atlantic, which, like that of slaveholding Euro-Americans, emerged as a counterpoint to enslavement.

Framing Dahomean elite sartorial assembling as an Afropolitan expression of "anti-victimhood," this article traces the complex connections between this culture of dress and the realities of the Atlantic slave trade. Through an analysis of oral sources, European travelers' accounts, slave narratives, and material and visual culture, this article begins with Dahomey's long-standing integration into African and Atlantic networks of sartorial exchange. In doing so, it reveals how Fon conceptions of self, constructions of Dahomean authority, and active participation in warfare drove and were driven by vestiary incorporation. The article then considers how Dahomeans in the capital of Abomey used cloth and clothing to connote difference in terms of political authority, gender, ethnicity, and race within their plural community, and how clothing, specifically the adoption of the clothing of the "other," played a role in constructing identity and upholding social and economic inequalities. The final section considers the sartorial layering of the elite as an Afropolitan practice of domestication that transcended various local identities to distinguish elites as citizens of Dahomey and as free people of the Atlantic world more generally.

Migration, Exchange, and War in the Making of Dahomey

Dahomean Afropolitanism grew out of the kingdom's long integration in regional trade and exchange, a stark contrast to Western colonial notions of a "traditional" or static African past. Furthermore, Fon speakers embraced their own alterity by emphasizing their history as a migrant people and the diverse origins of their composite textile culture. According to a spokesman for the Dakodonou lineage, the founders of the kingdom were migrants, first as Adja people from Tado, which is in present-day Togo, and then during a second migration from Allada, about sixty kilometers to the south of the Dahomean capital of Abomey. The story continues that, around the turn of the seventeenth century, the followers of Dakodonou, the first king of Dahomey, moved to the area around Abomey, where they encountered the region's original inhabitants, the Guedevi, and their leader, Dan. After killing Dan, Dakodonou built his palace on top of the entrails of his vanquished enemy. *Dahomey* translates to "in the belly of Dan."[23] Multiple scholars suggest that the foundation story is probably a myth created to legitimize the Dahomean Alladahonu (people of Allada) dynasty within the history of the older, and initially more powerful, kingdom of Allada. Instead, Dahomey, similar to other West African kingdoms founded in the seventeenth century, likely grew as a result of lineage alliances formed in response to pressures from the increasingly important Atlantic trade.[24] Although historical evidence is contradictory about the actual origins of the Dahomean kingdom, the foundation story, whether fact or myth, points to the central place of mobility in the political imagination of Fon speakers.

This self-conception as a migrant people is evident as well within the kingdom's textile culture. Dahomeans wove wrappers (pagne) using two different types

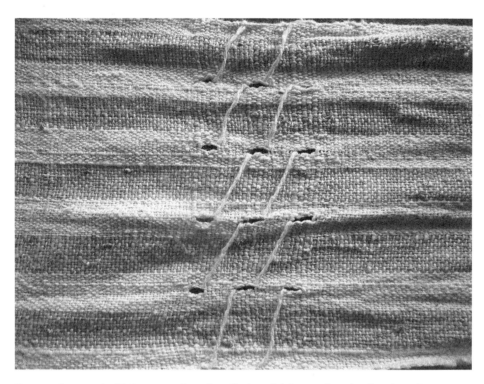

Figure 1. Cotton and raffia interweave from the collection of Alphonse Ahouado. Photo by author, Abomey, Benin, 2015.

of wooden looms—vertical looms like those found in the Yoruba kingdoms to the west, and horizontal looms similar to those used in the Asante empire to the east. Alphonse Ahouado, an Abomean weaver and the official spokesman for Beninois weavers, explained the diversity of weaving technologies through the Dahomean foundation story. According to him, the Guedevi, the early inhabitants of the region, used vertical looms like the various groups to the west. When the Gbe-speaking ancestors of the Fon arrived from the east, they brought the horizontal loom, a complex machine operated by foot and relying on a system of pulleys and counterweights to weave textiles.[25] European visitors to precolonial Dahomey dismissed the horizontal varieties as dubious tools, calling them "extremely rude," "artless," and, hyperbolically, "the most awkward machines imaginable."[26] Yet Dahomeans produced high-quality cloth on the looms, which Europeans purchased at "a high price" for "counterpanes."[27] Although weavers made both cotton cloth (*kanvo*) and raffia cloth (*dévo*), the most highly valued textiles were interweaves of cotton and raffia such as this more recent production from Ahouado's collection (fig. 1).[28] From production technology to finished product, Dahomean-produced textiles incorporated different elements, bringing them together in a product with a higher value than its composite parts.

A regional market system supplemented local textile production and predated the kingdom period, allowing for the importation and consumption of cloth and clothing goods from other areas of West Africa. Archeological sites in southern Benin suggest "the emergence of commodity production and both intra- and interregional exchange between the early fifteenth and late sixteenth centuries."[29] Individuals and households produced goods and then sold them on the market to purchase foodstuffs and "textiles, basketry, calabashes, and wooden and ceramic vessels."[30] As the kingdom's power and influence increased, so too did Dahomean access to African textiles, and European traveler's accounts are rife with descriptions of cloth identified as not associated with Fon speakers but originating from Oyo, "Nago," or even the Sahel. Dahomey's clear integration within the larger political and economic system of West Africa suggests that textiles imported from other African groups were probably familiar or even widespread from the earliest years of the kingdom.

After the early sixteenth century, this part of coastal West Africa integrated into Atlantic textile markets first as a textile exporter before importing cloth in exchange for captives. At the Alladan port of Offra, Portuguese, Dutch, and Swedish merchants purchased captives, ivory, and "Allada" or "Ardra" cloth to resell in the Gold Coast and São Tomé.[31] The historian Colleen Kriger suggests that the seventeenth-century European moniker "Allada cloth" included textiles woven on both vertical and horizontal looms from Edo and Yoruba sources, despite being sold by the kingdom of Allada.[32] While recorded differences among these textiles support the existence of a developed regional textile market within West Africa, European sources are much clearer about the origins and types of cloth sold along the coast. There, African traders acquired calicos, chintz, and "Guinea cloth" from India as well as linens, silesias, silks, and velvets from Europe.[33] There was also a robust coastal market in accessories and inputs such as hats, ribbons, and yarn as well as new and secondhand clothing items such as gowns, shirts, jackets, and, most commonly, "kerchiefs" or hemmed, usually small, square pieces of cloth that West Africans used as head coverings, neckerchiefs, or loincloths.[34] Importation from Atlantic trade supplemented local production and regional exchange to create a host of options for Dahomeans who had the means to dress well.

However, the violence of Atlantic slaving and slavery undergirded the development of these systems of sartorial exchange. In 1850, an elite brigade of women warriors (*ahosi*, "palace women," or *mino*, "our mothers," but called "Amazons" by Europeans), sang to King Ghezo (1818–58) about the relationship between warfare and dress: "War is our great friend; without it there is no cloth, no armlets, let us to war, and conquer or die."[35] The British had sent naval officer Frederick Forbes, the man who transcribed the song, to Dahomey to convince Ghezo to abandon its well-established participation in the transatlantic slave trade. As early as the sixteenth century, coastal areas of the Bight of Benin, which the British would come to call the "Slave Coast," were important ports of embarkation for captives. By the late seventeenth century, Dahomey had become an important supplier of captives to coastal polities that traded directly with Europeans. In the 1720s, Dahomey conquered the kingdoms of Allada and Hueda and the latter's port city of Ouidah, expanding the territory and grandeur of the kingdom, and giving Dahomey direct access to transatlantic trade. The era from Dahomey's coastal conquests in the 1720s to the nineteenth century, when the Amazons sang their song, was a period rife with the interrelated violence of warfare and enslavement, and, as suggested by the Amazons' song, their part in processes of sartorial incorporation.

Narratives of two men captured in the mid-nineteenth century perhaps best articulate the trauma and violence of enslavement in Dahomey. In the 1840s, Mahommah Gardo Baquaqua was captured near Djougou, north of Abomey, and endured long marches from his home to the capital, and eventually to the coast. During several weeks of captivity in Abomey, Baquaqua felt uneasy and fearful, thinking that he too would become a victim of human sacrifice, which was annually practiced in the capital.[36] As he was loaded onto the slave ship, Baquaqua again perceived his imminent death and "felt alarmed for [his] safety, and despondency had almost taken sole possession of [him]."[37] Another captive, Cudjoe Lewis, or Kossula, a man taken by Dahomean troops and transported to the US in 1861, tearfully described his seizure to Zora Neale Hurston in a series of 1927 interviews. Dahomean soldiers broke down the walls of his community after they refused to pay tribute to the king. Kossula described the horrors of the nighttime raid and beheadings of the community's leader and its elderly. He recalled how he begged and pleaded with the Dahomean troops to find his family, but concluded that "dey got no ears for cryin'. De king of Dahomey come to hunt slaves to sell."[38] Similar to Baquaqua, Kossula was imprisoned in Abomey and spent a few days in the king's palace, which he described as "made out of skull bones."[39] After a forced march to the coast and several weeks of waiting there, he boarded the slave ship *Clotilda*, where the crew stripped him and other African captives of his "country cloth," or dress, and forced him to make the Atlantic crossing nude.[40] Kossula recognized this intentional act of dehumanization for what it was and told Hurston, "We come in de 'Merica soil naked and de people say we naked savage. Dey say we doan wear no clothes. Dey doan know de Many-costs snatch our clothes 'way from us."[41] In their narratives, the two men revealed their fear of Dahomean and white traders alike and their experiences of containment and marching, including a literal disrobement, or the violent process of commodification.[42]

Dahomean traders trafficked captives, like Baquaqua and Kossula, exchanging them for mostly cowries and textiles along the coast. However, the women warriors may have been singing of a more direct relationship between warfare, cloth, and armlets, since wars and raids also led to the seizure of booty, markets, and textile-making artisans. Dahomean monarchs established the kingdom's periodic markets (*ahi*) after military conquests. By capturing the conquered enemies' *vodun* protector of a market, the king absorbed their commercial and religious power into the kingdom. For example, Guézo founded the primary Abomey *ahi* after his 1830–32 conquest of Mahi. The market was renamed Houndjro and remains the site where most fabric is traded in the former capital city.[43] Over the course of war, Dahomeans also captured craftspeople who made clothing and accessories. In 1727, a slave trader described Muslim dyers from deep in the interior who, although captive, were treated "kindly" by Agaja due to their "Art of dying Goat and Sheep-skins with divers Colours, which they made into Cartouch-boxes for the Soldiers."[44] Family traditions also root the lineages of royal shoemakers and some weavers in Yoruba-speaking areas of present-day Benin and Nigeria.[45] According to a master appliqué maker, the Yemandjè, a lineage of needleworkers who made Dahomean regalia and are closely associated with the kingdom's history and art production, were initially "made to come" to Abomey during the reign of King Agonglo.[46] These craftsmen sewed symbolic images of animals and inanimate objects on pagne, hats, parasols, and banners for royal households and *vodunsi* (adherents to a *vodun*). These sartorial producers, although initially forced into migrating and of bonded status, could gain a relatively exalted position within the court of Dahomey due to their individual talent and the appeal of their products, although they retained dependent status, becoming essentially an extension of the king.[47]

Dahomeans also captured men of European descent or formerly enslaved people from the Americas, further introducing clothing practices from beyond the continent to the kingdom. The English trader Bulfinch Lambe, himself a captive and the first European to record his observations of Abomey, described a tailor living in the palace in the 1720s during the reign of King Agaja: "An old mulatto Portuguese, which he [King Agaja] bought of the Popoe people . . . and though this white man is his slave, yet he keeps him like a great caboceroe [slave trader], and has given him two houses, and a heap of wives and servants . . . once in two or three months, he mends . . . some trifle or other for his majesty."[48] Lambe also suggested that "any sort of white man that is free" might also choose to emigrate to Dahomey, as "his majesty [is] paying every body extravagantly that works for him."[49] Lambe's description of the "mulatto Portuguese" tailor resembles accounts of captive Yoruba craftspeople found in oral tradition and scholarly accounts. Agaja showered this tailor in wealth and wives, and the craftsman had access to goods and people not afforded to rural enslaved people, although all of it was at the behest of Agaja. Clearly, Agaja and other Dahomean monarchs highly valued the skills and products of clothing producers, from Yoruba shoemakers to Hausa dyers and "Portuguese" tailors, and sought to domesticate their products into Dahomean material culture. Indeed, that textiles, secondhand clothing, and accessories ranked so high within the Atlantic trade for captive labor hints at their importance to Fon social and political life. However, Lambe's description also makes it clear that there was not much work for the palace tailor. Fon speakers in the early eighteenth century wore almost exclusively wrapped and draped cloth that required little stitching, although the prizes of warfare and the profits of slaving would contribute to increasingly more diverse sartorial culture over the next century and a half.

Dress and Difference in Precolonial Dahomey

The ritual display of textiles and their adornment on bodies were central to notions of distinction within a plural Dahomey, delineating power, status, and identity for subjects and outsiders alike. The fancy layered dress of the Afropolitan elite contrasted with that of the masses, as it incorporated materials associated with foreign and local identities. In the realm of formal politics, Dahomean kings materialized their authority by gifting, receiving, and displaying fabric during public ceremonies, most importantly at the yearly festival of Xwetanu, or Annual Customs. During this month-long ceremony, the monarch celebrated his ancestors and showcased Dahomean military, material, and royal might. Agaja first held Xwetanu around 1710, and the ceremony continued until French conquest in the 1890s.[50] Narratives of Xwetanu tended to focus on the festival's more gruesome aspects, such as the ritual deaths of dozens to thousands of men, women, and children and the display of the skulls of enemy combatants.[51] Yet the ceremonies also involved gift giving, meetings of high-ranking officials, marriages, and the distribution and display of cloth and performances of vestiary difference.

At Xwetanu, cloth flowed from subjects and outsiders to the monarch and from the king back to them, solidifying their relationships. The quality of this exchanged cloth reflected the rank of the person and their proximity to royal power, also helping demarcate Dahomeans from foreigners. In the slave trader Robert Norris's account of the 1772 ceremony, King Tegbesu (1740–74) demanded that the governors of the French, British, and Portuguese trading forts at Ouidah travel to the interior for the event. He required European attendees to "make a present on the occasion" to include "at least one piece of Indian damask, or some other handsome silk," while African merchants paid their tribute in cowries.[52] Other attendees included "the vice-roy [*sic*] of Whydah [Yovogan], and the governors of the different towns and provinces," and each of these local administrators came with presents and "an account of their conduct, and of every circumstance which the king wishes to be informed of."[53] Norris wrote that local administrators "who acquit[ted] themselves to [the king's] satisfaction, have the honor to receive some mark of his appropriation; which is generally a large cotton cloth, manufactured in the Eyo country, of excellent workmanship, which they afterwards wear for an upper garment."[54] The finely made cloth from Yorubaland signified the king's approval of the administrator, and when the administrator wrapped the Eyo fabric around his body, he made his royal endorsement public. The slave trader Archibald Dalzel noted that the Dahomean "Prime Minister" received the first choice of fabric "and

Figure 2. Francis Chesham, *Last Day of the Annual Customs for Watering the Graves of the King's Ancestors.* From Archibald Dalzel's *History of Dahomey* (1793).

the rest following his example, according to their rank."[55] Men of rank proclaimed their status through the types of gifts given to the king, while the king redistributed the textiles to reaffirm administrative and social categorizations.

The king also distributed cloth as part of "a profusion of presents" to ordinary people to show his authority over and benevolence to his subjects.[56] Francis Chesham's engraving *Last Day of the Annual Customs for Watering the Graves of the King's Ancestors* portrays royal gift giving and makes clear its relationship to monarchial authority (fig. 2).[57] In the far left of the engraving, a large pile of fabric sits on the platform (*attoh*) that holds the king, his entourage, and visiting dignitaries. A man underneath the platform seems to be inspecting a newly acquired pagne. In the right of the image a piece of cloth whizzes through the air from the platform toward the masses, who hold their hands up in anticipation. Although Chesham likely did not witness Xwetanu, his engraving reflected eighteenth-century descriptions. Norris described the platform as covered with "piled heaps of silesias, checks, callicoes, and a variety of other European and Indian goods; a great many fine cotton cloths that are manufactured in the Eyo country; and a prodigious quantity of cowries."[58] The king distributed these imported cloths and other goods, with first choice the Yoruba "Eyo [Oyo] cloth" or the rich silks transported from the coast.[59] While human sacrifice may have been important in instilling fear among Dahomean subjects, Europeans, and enemies in neighboring African communities, the gifting of cloth and other goods served to foster loyalty to the monarch.

Much of this cloth ended up as dress, yet it is important to note that lengths of fabric also played a role in the kingdom's social and political life as they were exchanged, stacked, and ritually displayed. Early colonial observers noted how the quality of exchanged cloth signified rights within marriage, and how the ongoing spiritual power of the deceased was embodied within funerary shrouds, practices likely established during the kingdom period.[60] In terms of formal politics, the king's subjects prostrated themselves on "crimson velvet cloth" before the king, while attendants held up fabric around the monarch to protect him from the popular gaze when he ate or drank.[61] Lengths of cloth held taut barricaded the king, who was located behind a "higher enclosure of finer cloth," while lesser-quality cloth created a barrier between other members of the court and the public.[62] In 1871, the British naturalist J. A. Skertchly observed a "gigantic" patchwork textile called the Nunupweto, which he translated as the "'omnipotent' cloth," at the center of a public ceremony. The quilt-like object was sewn of "samples of every kind of textile fabric that is imported into the kingdom," including various sized pieces of "denhams, chintzes, silks, vento-pullams, velvets, &c.," which had been assembled together in a random pattern to "an enormous length of four hundred yards and a breadth of about ten feet."[63] According to Skertchly, Ghezo commissioned the Nunupweto and Glele planned to wrap himself in the massive cloth after Dahomey emerged victorious in its war against Abeokuta (Glele's armies lost that war, however). Attendants hoisted the unwrapped cloth over the heads of a cheering crowd by attaching it to long poles, while Glele scolded "that the people ought to be ashamed to put him to so great an expense as was entailed by the constant additions to the Nunupweto cloth" to encourage them in their upcoming campaign against Abeokuta. Later, court servants piled other "native and European" textiles into great heaps "until the accumulation formed a wall of gorgeous-coloured fabrics nearly six feet high, the grandest silks being selected as the uppermost cloths," creating what Skertchly called "a most gaudy picture."[64] The sheer size of the Nunupweto and the abundance of fabric displayed by being pulled taut or stacked high shows how Fon valuations of fabric exceeded its practical use in dress, as lengths of cloth were deployed to intimidate, impress, and foster allegiances.

Wrapped and draped on bodies as dress, cloth helped to distinguish its wearers in terms of gender, ethnicity, and race. While Europeans conflated these forms of identity with bodies, Dahomeans both reified and transcended embodied identity through dress. Male and female soldiers alike dressed in "a tunic, short trowsers [*sic*] and skull-cap," collapsing the gendered distinction between the two groups even as regiments were formed around sexual difference.[65] The uniforms of the Amazons, along with their reported claims that "we are men," led Forbes to conclude that "they have changed their sex."[66] Other masculine women and feminine men likewise occupied politically important positions. A late nineteenth-century visitor noted that the palace recruited sons of prominent families and raised them as "women" to guard the palace and for other roles.[67] These feminine men, perhaps castrated as eunuchs, guarded the palace—a political domain of women—wearing women's clothing. The historian Edna Bay details how, in contrast, "women whose function was to oversee the male ministers of state wore *agbada*, men's gowns in Yoruba style," reinforcing their status as part of the "male" political world beyond the palace walls.[68] These sartorial inversions of gender reaffirmed politically substantive conceptions of different roles for men and women and gendered divisions of power, while disassociating them from sex.

Dahomeans also consciously used the careful manipulation of clothing and style to construct and upend differences between themselves and other groups of West Africans. Kings invited dignitaries from Asante and elsewhere to Xwetanu, and these foreigners were identified by their dress.[69] Muslim traders from the Sahel lived in the kingdom and, as early as 1727, a British trader noted "black Gentlemen" from "a Nation far inland" who wore sewn robes and "cloth wreathed about their Heads."[70] In the 1850 "Procession of the King's Wealth," Forbes described "16 malams (Mohomedan priests from Haussa)" dressed as such, although he argued, "I much doubt, except in dress and some outward show, that these priests are Mahomedans; the very fact of their prostrating to the king would go far to prove them not."[71] The sixteen men may or may not have been Muslim Hausa religious leaders, but by wearing their garb in a royal procession, they conveyed the monarch's alliances with the Muslim fringes of the kingdom at the same time that they linked Sahelian Islamic dress with a minority-Muslim Dahomean population. Another mid-nineteenth-century visitor claimed that Ghezo had people destined for sacrifice "made to personate in dress and avocation Oyos."[72] While perhaps not from Oyo, they were dressed like the kingdom's enemy before their ritual deaths. The association of specific forms of dress with religious or ethnic identities reinforced differences at the same time that it allowed the court to manipulate them for performances of power.

European accounts also recall men of African descent who adopted fitted styles and thus a European persona (*yovo*).[73] Dahomeans were aware of European styles not just from imported clothing but also through the clothed bodies of European visitors, traders, and captives and of diasporic returnees. By the nineteenth century, the coastal Aguda community of returnees from Brazil and their descendants also wore world fashions and adhered to other aspects of European town culture, including literacy.[74] At Xwetanu in 1850, Forbes saw fourteen "liberated 'Bahia' Africans, in the European costume," men formerly enslaved in Brazil and now living in Dahomey.[75] Elsewhere, Forbes claimed that "any native who leaves his country, even as a slave, and returns, if he wears the dress of a foreigner, is termed ee a voo [*yovo*], a white man."[76] As explored earlier, the gifting of cloth helped foster distinctions between European and African merchants through their different textile obligations to the monarch. But fully adopting the European costume of a three-piece suit might bestow "white" status. In his 1820 account, John M'Leod noted that "the king occasionally confers the title of white man on some of his subjects, which authorizes them to assume the European dress, to carry an English umbrella, wear shoes, and in short to play the parts of white men in all respects."[77] Yet Burton also recalled "two 'black white men,' natives of the country, dressed in trowsers [*sic*] and blouses, but shoeless, walking under ragged parasols."[78] This description reveals the limits and unevenness of these men's transformations; while identified as "black white men" they received a parasol, normally reserved for royalty, even if "ragged," but their lack of shoes marked them as "natives" constricted by sumptuary law that gave the king exclusive rights over footwear. Men of African descent, Fon speakers or not, who returned from abroad or who worked as secretaries and scribes, wore European ensembles, symbolizing their status as *yovo*.[79]

An image in the French magazine *Le petit journal* underscores how dress highlighted difference during the era of French conquest. King Béhanzin (1890–94) sent an envoy to Paris in 1893 in hopes of brokering a peace deal during the Second Franco-Dahomean War (1892–94). Although the French refused to meet with the men, the mission received some attention in the French press (fig. 3). The caption identified the man in the center as Chedingen, the "chief of mission," flanked by other high-ranking administrators within the Dahomean bureaucracy. The king's secretary Dosso stood behind, while the three men seated on the floor were identified as "slaves." The slaves each wore a single pagne, while the slave in the middle clutched a box used to transport the *recade* (ceremonial axe) held by Chedingen. In contrast, the secretary sported the three-piece suit of the *yovo*, a reference to the literacy necessary to his occupation, which exempted him from the sumptuary restrictions that applied to other Dahomeans. Chedingen and the other high-ranking men donned a layered look of different types of fabric, some sewn and others wrapped, and accessorized with hats, *recade*, and other adornments.

Afropolitan Aesthetics and Power

Elites, with the king foremost among them, began domesticating the styles associated with neighboring African groups into their own sartorial practice by at least the early eighteenth century and, during the next two centuries, further incorporated fabrics, accessories, and styles from Europe, Asia, and the Americas. The layered look of the elite was an Afropolitan materialization of "worlds-in-movement" that also served to delineate those elites who lived in *tò* (town) from the rural folk in

Figure 3. King Béhanzin's mission to Paris. *Supplément illustré du Le petit journal* (1893).

the *glètà* (country or bush).[80] While the "slaves" in the illustration from *La petit journal* wore wrappers, most men and women in Dahomey, who lived and labored in rural areas, wore a *gòdó*, or loincloth, a length of cotton or raffia cloth draped between the legs and attached at the waist with a belt or cord, as daily dress, similar to the men in the bottom right corner of Chesham's engraving (fig. 2). Textiles and accessories flowed from various global, regional, and local networks to the two anchors of Dahomean urban life—the market (*ahi*) and the palace—and the palace communicated style to the rest of society during public ceremonies and rituals like Xwetanu. The assembling or layering styles of the elite celebrated their place within Africa and the greater Atlantic world at the same time as they distinguished elite from the rural masses who, over the course of the nineteenth century, were increasingly captive outsiders.

European accounts of Dahomean kings, like the trader's report of Agaja in this article's opening vignette, described the king's public dress as including wrapped cloth of domestic and foreign origin as well as sewn clothing tailored locally or imported as ready-made from Europe. Elaborate accessorizing complemented textile-based clothing. During a Dutch trader's audience with Agaja in 1733, the king changed his outfit four times. At first "clad in a European red velvet dress-coat embroidered with golden galloons . . . wearing the most beautiful shoes and had a white cap on his head," Agaja returned wearing "a black dress-coat, also richly embroidered with gold," and even later "a long frock-coat of red velvet." The trader noted one final change when "the King disappeared again, and returned clad like a Negro in a great silver-embroidered cloth."[81] Other Europeans also described the king donning different clothes over a short period. The Briton Frederick Forbes described a number of different ensembles worn by Ghezo in 1851. Initially, Ghezo wore "a white silk flowing robe, flowered in blue, and a gold-laced hat" for the procession of the king's wealth, but "dressed in an old black waistcoat, a white night-cap, and a cloth round his loins" while seated on the royal platform where he witnessed offerings and distributed gifts.[82] At another point, Forbes recalled Ghezo as "plainly dressed, in a loose robe of yellow silk slashed with satin stars and half-moons, Mandingo sandals, and a Spanish hat trimmed with gold lace; the only ornament being a small gold chain of European manufacture."[83] According to local historian Bachrou Nondinonchao, Dahomean kings from at least Agaja to Béhanzin lacked any sort of official royal costume, although they held exclusive rights over certain clothing items and accessories.[84] Their outfits were an assemblage of items that hinted at the far reaches of the kingdom's influence and contacts.

Dahomeans' willingness and even preference to incorporate forms associated with outsiders into royal dress might be best explained through the story of Tegbesu's 1740 accession to the throne and his symbol, the tunic-wearing buffalo (fig. 4). According to oral tradition, King Agaja sent one of his young sons, Tegbesu, as tribute to Oyo, where he was raised as a ward of the court. Eventually Tegbesu returned to Dahomey and took the throne, but his years abroad had left him with a taste for Oyo style, including clothing, hats, and sandals. The official history of the kingdom explains Tegbesu's royal symbol, the tunic-wearing buffalo, as representative of his struggles to ascend the throne. After Agaja's death, political factions vied over who would become the new king. During this period, Tegbesu had to wear Agaja's tunic for a full day, but a plotter, a supporter of a different member of the

Figure 4. Bas-relief depiction of King Tegbesu on a compound wall in Abomey. Photo by author, June 2021.

royal family for king, filled the shirt with nettles. The tale emphasized Tegbesu's perseverance and strength, since he persisted in wearing the uncomfortable shift and eventually became king.[85] But the account also hinted at the role of clothing in forming ideas about who was fit to rule. Perhaps, returning from Oyo clad in Yoruba wear, the king had to prove his ability to lead Dahomey by literally donning the shirt of the previous king. But, once he was king, Tegbesu changed course and is remembered for his successful borrowing of Yoruba styles and transforming them into Dahomean sartorial culture.

At public festivals, kings from Agaja to Béhanzin conveyed to their subjects and others the desirability of specific types of clothing and accessories, although restrictions limited some patterns and styles to the royal body.[86] Xwetanu was one of the few times that people saw the body of the king and those of palace women (*kposi*). Skertchly described a part of the ceremony called "Avo-use-gbe" in which Glele, aided by palace women, changed into numerous different outfits, some of them forms associated with enemy kingdoms, neighboring communities, or Europeans. After each change of clothes, Glele danced before the crowds while servants held an umbrella over him. During the Avo-use-gbe, the Amazons sang, "Gelelé has changed his cloth for his father and has danced many times for Gézu; / Gézu will therefore remember his son and will prosper his arms against Abeokeuta."[87] The Amazons' song suggests that the ritual was done to ensure victory against the Yoruba polity and, although the ceremony was directed to the ancestors (Ghezo), it must have also made an impression on the living when they saw the king's sartorial wealth and thus learned what constituted valued cloth, clothing, and accessories as well as the identifiable dress of the enemy.

Dahomean elite men, such as state administrators, slave traders, and private merchants, wrapped cloth gifted from the king; they also undoubtedly purchased their own fabric in Dahomean markets or traded directly with other Africans and Europeans. Descriptions of these elite men reveal a complex system of distinction that relied on differences in color, fabric, and ornamentation, even as it combined different elements. A longer length of pagne indicated a higher-status man, with greater value placed on certain foreign fabrics such as Eyo cloth from Yorubaland or silks, velvets, and brocades imported from Europe. Dalzel described Dahomean men's dress:

The dress of the men, in *Dahomey*, consists of a pair of striped or white cotton drawers, of the manufactory of the country, over which they wear a large square cloth of the same, or of European manufacture. This cloath [*sic*] is about the size of a common counterpane, for the middling class; but much larger for the Grandees. It is wrapped about the loins, and tied on the left side by two of the corners, the others hanging down, and sometimes trailing on the ground. A piece of silk or velvet, of fifteen or eighteen yards, makes a cloth for a *Caboceer*. . . . The arms and upper part of the body remain naked, except when the party travels or performs some piece of work, when the large cloth is laid aside, and the body is covered with a sort of frock or tunic, without sleeves.[88]

While a wealthy "Caboceer" (slave trader) might wrap his torso in "silk" or "velvet" up to fifteen or eighteen yards (*grande pagne*), most men wore cloth that was "about three yards long."[89] These lengths of cloth wrapped or draped around one's body limited the movements of elite men, preventing them from making quick movements or engaging in strenuous labor. Dalzel also notes that occasionally men might remove their top wrappers to don a tunic made from a single piece of cloth folded once and sewn together on the sides with a neck hole at the fold.[90] A variation of this style of tunic was worn during Béhanzin's convoy to France nearly one hundred years later (fig. 3).

Underneath the wrapped pagne, elite men wore tailored items, and they completed the look with accessories. In an image from a French postcard (fig. 5), King Béhanzin, Dahomey's last independent monarch, and his family wear multiple lengths of different types of wrapped pagne. On both Béhanzin's upper and lower body, he wore West African woven cloth. The seams of the strip cloth are visible on

Figure 5. Béhanzin family, Abomey. 4FI-1393. Courtesy of Archives Nationales du Sénégal, Dakar.

the solid upper wrapper, while the under wrapper is striped, likely woven of white and indigo-dyed yarn, although the black-and-white image makes it impossible to tell. Underneath the pagne, elite men sported a pair of tailored baggy shorts (*tchanka*). Dalzel called them "a pair of striped or white cotton drawers of the manufactory of the country," while Norris characterized "country dress" as "a pair of wide drawers."[91] Local traditions in Abomey recognize this short pant with a panel in between the two legs as uniquely Fon, as opposed to almost all other types of tailored clothing and accessories, which are openly acknowledged as having origins in the Yoruba-speaking Oyo empire or in Europe. Other adornments complemented Fon *tchanka* and layered pagne. The king wore fancy European- and Yoruba-style hats and also held exclusive rights over footwear.[92] Local shoemakers produced sandals for the royal body during a secretive ritual, and they attributed the style to Tegbesu as one of his imports from Oyo.[93] Other elite men wore necklaces made of coral or other local and imported beads, and high-ranking men, as in the image from *Le petit journal*, carried *recade* (axes) and staffs, with the lower-ranking "Caboceers" carrying ornamental blunt sabers.[94] The use of these accessories was but one aspect of a complex culture of male adornment in which rank and status were materialized on the body, clearly delineating the wealthy from those who wore a single pagne or *gòdó* loincloth.

The pagne was also the basic unit of elite women's dress, and they too accessorized with imported items. The amount of fabric covering a woman's body was related to her wealth and age, with younger and poorer women wearing less fabric.

In 1724, Lambe, in a letter written while a captive of the court, described the "wives" of the king as wearing uniforms of wrapped pagne. Although the king had "at least 2,000 wives," "160 or 200 or them" would occasionally exit the palace together to collect water. Then they would "one day wear rich silk waist cloths, called **** [*sic*]; another day they all wear scarlet clothes, with three or four large strings of coral round their necks, and their leaders sometimes in crimson, sometimes in green, and sometimes blue velvet clothes, with silver gilt staffs in their hands, like golden canes."[95] These wrapped styles might be finished with "Country Jewels, which are a fort of Beads of divers Colours" imported from a "far inland Country."[96] Women wrapped their "rich silk waist cloths" differently than men and often "simply wound round their persons above the breasts" or waists.[97] Younger women of wealth might wear one wrap covering the waist to the floor or mid-calf, and a second from above the breasts to above the knee. Married women might cover these wrappers with a third pagne, wrapped about the waist and occasionally removed and retied to strap a baby on their backs, a style of wrapping that is evident among the women in the image of Béhanzin's family (fig. 5). Pins or other means did not fix wrapped cloth, and women moved their pagnes throughout the day, reattaching and shifting the fabric, which covered and revealed certain parts of their bodies.

The highest-ranking women in Dahomey (*kposi*) worked in political, military, or ritual functions and resided in the royal palace; they occasionally wore elaborate dresses imported from Europe. Chesham's engraving of the platform at Customs (fig. 2) portrays *kposi* wearing fancy fitted costumes of European origin. A Yoruba woman who served as a servant to one recalled how "on the day of the sacrifice, the wives of the king dressed in very fine clothes, because it was a celebration; and the servants in fine clothes."[98] While Chesham undoubtedly incorporated his own understanding of what entailed "fine clothes" in his depiction of Xwetanu, his rendering closely aligns with the accounts of later European observers such as Forbes, who characterized *kposi* gowns as in the style of "Charles II."[99] Forbes's 1851 reference to the English Restoration monarch of the mid-seventeenth century alluded to a style of women's dress characterized by voluminous skirts, low necklines, bright colors, and a general disheveled appearance. Two decades later, Skertchly recalled Glele's "leopardesses" [*kposi*] as being dressed *à la polonaise*, a style of European women's dress popular in late eighteenth-century Britain. He wrote, "The leopardesses were dressed in white waistcoats, bound with scarlet velvet, and a long petticoat of violet and green figured silk descended to the ankles. Above this a 'polonaise' of dark blue velvet reached half way down the petticoat."[100] Accessories designed specifically for European men such as "Charles II's hat" and "gilt helmets" completed the *kposi*'s ensembles.[101] Writing from a post-emancipation society, British observers such as Forbes and Skertchly referenced forms of dress from their own history to convey the excesses of the slave-trading Dahomean court to their readers. But some of the *kposi*'s dress came to Dahomey directly as secondhand from

Europe, traded along the coast for captives or the products of captive labor, revealing a shared system of clothing, slaving, and exchange among Dahomean and European elites.

Conclusion

Achille Mbembe has described Afropolitanism as the "future," and a way of understanding Africa that moves scholarship beyond the traditionalism of Afrocentrism or the racialism of Pan-Africanism. Afropolitanism refocuses the scholarly gaze on "the many ways in which Africans, or people of African origin, understand themselves as being part of the world."[102] He and others have celebrated the liberatory potential of this approach to understanding the continent and its new diaspora, and the possibilities that Afropolitanism offers for alternatively transcending racial hierarchies or pushing back against Afro-pessimism. Scholars including Mbembe have also pointed to the deep origins of Afropolitanism on the continent. Indeed, the dress of the Dahomean elite in the eighteenth and nineteenth centuries provides an illuminating historical example of how Africans rejected "nativism" and negotiated "tradition" by seeing themselves as part and parcel of the larger world. Members of the Dahomean royal family, state administrators, and traders assembled textiles and accessories associated with identifiable others into a layered look that celebrated mobility, exchange, and "being part of the world." But the case of Dahomean dress also provides a revealing historical example of how Afropolitanisms, like cosmopolitanisms, can lack an ethical foundation. Elite dress in Dahomey was imbricated in an Atlantic system of warfare and slaving. It also served as an expression of power over locally marginalized groups and of the common interests and experiences between Dahomean elites and other slavers and slaveholders within the Atlantic.

Elizabeth Ann Fretwell is assistant professor of African history at Old Dominion University in Norfolk, Virginia. She is currently writing a book on tailors and tailored dress in Benin from the era of the Dahomey kingdom to the recent past.

Notes

1. Snelgrave, *New Account*, 35.
2. Snelgrave, *New Account*, 60.
3. Dah Atchassou, interview with author, Ahouaja, Abomey, December 10, 2014.
4. Mbembe, "Afropolitanism," 26.
5. Mbembe and Balakrishnan, "Pan-African Legacies"; Gikandi, "Foreword," 9–11.
6. Moyo, *Decolonial Turn*, 96–97. This elite strain of Afropolitanism is best represented by Taiye Selasi's use of the term in "Bye-Bye Babar." Critiques of its consumerist and elitist foundations include Dabiri, "Why I Am (Still) Not an Afropolitan," and Eze, "We, Afropolitans," 117.
7. Lawrence, "Afropolitan Detroit," 21; Skinner, *Bamako Sounds*.
8. Mbembe calls for us to historicize the Afropolitan ("Afropolitanism," 27–28).

9. Prestholdt, *Domesticating the World*, 88; Getz, *Cosmopolitan Africa*.

10. A point well made by Eze, "We, Afropolitans," 117.

11. Appiah, *Cosmopolitanism*, xv.

12. Law, *Ouidah*, 2. See also slavevoyages.org.

13. Thornton, "Dahomey in the World," 452. Thornton importantly notes that "no national income accounting has ever been done to calculate how much of Dahomey's national wealth or royal revenues flowed directly from the slave trade" ("Dahomey in the World," 455).

14. Soumonni, "Compatibility of the Slave and Palm Oil Trades."

15. Manning estimates that "first- and second-generation slaves" likely made up one-fourth to one-third of Dahomey's population in the decades preceding French conquest in the 1890s. See Manning, *Slavery, Colonialism, and Economic Growth*, 192.

16. Green, "Sumptuary Laws"; Blier, "Europia Mania," 250.

17. Blier, "Art of Assemblage," 187–88. Royal and elite arts incorporated motifs and themes from outsiders, in contrast to commoner art forms, such as power objects (*bocio*), which remained "relatively uninfluenced" (Blier, "Europia Mania," 254).

18. Vincent Brown describes a "borderless slave war: war to enslave, war to expand slavery, and war against slaves, answered on the side of the enslaved by war against slaveholders, and also war among slaves themselves" (*Tacky's Revolt*, 7).

19. Blier, too, highlights the violence of Fon material forms, noting that assemblage follows processes of dis-assemblage (*lo*), or the Dahomean removal of people, goods, and gods from communities defeated through war ("Art of Assemblage," 201). Yet by focusing on this warfare as slave producing, we can also see how assemblage of luxury elements becomes essential for constructing identities as free people.

20. For example, in the French Caribbean, the Code Noir required masters to furnish slaves with clothing, and specific styles, colors, and fabrics were associated with bondage, even as enslaved people practiced forms of sartorial resistance. DuPlessis, *Material Atlantic*, 131. On Peru, see Walker, *Exquisite Slaves*, 18–19.

21. Gikandi, *Slavery and the Culture of Taste*, 34.

22. Fromont, "Taste of Others," 277.

23. Nestor Dako-Wegbe, interview with author, Houawe Zoungonsa (Bohicon), Benin, December 10, 2014.

24. Monroe, *Precolonial State*, 62–64.

25. Alphonse Ahouado, interview with author, Musée d'Abomey, Abomey, September 15, 2015.

26. Burton, *A Mission to Gelele*, 2:260; Skertchly, *Dahomey as It Is*, 495; Dalzel, *History of Dahomey*, xxiv–xxv.

27. Dalzel, *History of Dahomey*, xxiv–xxv.

28. Alphonse Ahouado, interview with author, Musée d'Abomey, Abomey, September 15, 2015.

29. Monroe, *Precolonial State*, 41.

30. Monroe, *Precolonial State*, 39.

31. Green, *Fistful of Shells*, 174.

32. Kriger, "Mapping the History," 102–3.

33. Alpern, "What Africans Got," 6–10.

34. On secondhand in coastal trade, see Alpern, "What Africans Got," 10. On the European merchants, see Morton-Williams, "A Yoruba Woman," 105. On accessories and inputs, see Skertchly, *Dahomey as It Is*, 58.

35. Forbes, *Dahomey and the Dahomans*, 2:108.

36. Law and Lovejoy, *Biography of Mahommah Gardo Baquaqua*, 142.

37. Law and Lovejoy, *Biography of Mahommah Gardo Baquaqua*, 151.

38. Hurston, *Barracoon*, 46–49.

39. Hurston, *Barracoon*, 52.

40. Hurston, *Barracoon*, 54.

41. Hurston, *Barracoon*, 55. Hurston identified the "Many-costs" as Kru boatsmen. According to Fuglestad, canoemen in Ouidah were Ga or Fante (*Slave Traders by Invitation*, 6).

42. Scholars have noted the high death tolls of captives during marches to the coast and as they awaited European purchase. See Fuglestad, *Slave Traders by Invitation*, 13.

43. Ahoyo, "Les marchés d'Abomey et de Bohicon," 165–66. The local historian Bachrou Nondinonchao also attributes a similar origin to Abomey's Gbèdagba market after a conquest of Soclogbo (interview with author, Abomey, June 6, 2021).

44. Snelgrave, *New Account*, 80.

45. Dah Atchassou, interview with author, Ahouaja, Abomey, December 10, 2014.

46. Ernest Fiogbe, interview with author, Abomey, Benin, September 4, 2015.

47. Bay describes artisan incorporation into the palace as taking place through the idiom of marriage, as *ahosi*, or "wives of the king" (*Wives of the Leopard*, 20).

48. Lambe, "From the Great King Trudo," 184–85.

49. Lambe, "From the Great King Trudo," 184–85.

50. Coquery-Vidrovitch, "La fête des coutumes," 696–716.

51. It is important to distinguish "Annual Customs" from "Grand Customs" (*Ahosutanu*), or the weeks-long ceremony that took place two years after the death of a king. Coquery-Vidrovitch argues that only in Grand Customs did human sacrifices exceed five hundred people, while about one-tenth the number might be sacrificed on an annual basis ("La fête des coutumes," 703). Robin Law has argued that the characterizations of Dahomey as a "militaristic and despotic state" in European narratives largely replicated the Dahomean regime's own self-representations ("Slave-Trader as Historian," 220).

52. Norris, *Memoirs of Bossa Ahádee*, 87.

53. Norris, *Memoirs of Bossa Ahádee*, 87.

54. Norris, *Memoirs of Bossa Ahádee*, 87.

55. Dalzel, *History of Dahomey*, xxiii–xxiv.

56. Norris, *Memoirs of Bossa Ahádee*, 125.

57. Dalzel, *History of Dahomey*.

58. Norris, *Memoirs of the Reign of Bossa Ahádee*, 125.

59. Norris, *Memoirs of the Reign of Bossa Ahádee*, 112.

60. Le Hérissé, *L'ancien royaume*, 265.

61. Forbes, *Dahomey and the Dahomans*, 2:75.

62. Forbes, *Dahomey and the Dahomans*, 2:40; Skertchly, *Dahomey as It Is*, 205; Norris, *Memoirs of Bossa Ahádee*, 110.

63. Skertchly, *Dahomey as It Is*, 215–17.

64. Skertchly, *Dahomey as It Is*, 217–18.

65. Forbes, *Dahomey and the Dahomans*, 1:27.

66. Forbes, *Dahomey and the Dahomans*, 1:23.

67. Flueriot de Langle, "Croisières à la côte d'Afrique," 241–81.

68. Bay, *Wives of the Leopard*, 11.

69. Blier, "Art of Assemblage," 202.

70. Snelgrave, *New Account*, 79–80. See also Norris, *Memoirs of Bossa Ahádee*, 102–3.

71. Forbes, *Dahomey and the Dahomans*, 2:214.

72. Burton, *A Mission to Gelele*, 1:199.

73. *Yovo* is sometimes translated as "foreigner," and while this is true, it is largely associated with white foreigners. For example, the kingdom's position of Yovogan managed coastal trade with Europeans. Today, light-skinned Beninois are often jokingly referred to as *yovo*, while dark-skinned foreigners (usually from the West, not other parts of Africa) might be called *yovo* as well.

74. The Brazilians are also Fon speakers, although they retained a unique position socially and economically.

75. Forbes, *Dahomey and the Dahomans*, 2:214.

76. Forbes, *Dahomey and the Dahomans*, 1:33, 1:219.

77. M'Leod, *Voyage to Africa*, 106.

78. Burton, *Mission to Gelele*, 2:52–53.

79. Green writes, "Those who knew how to write and read in European languages were called *yovo*, and were often either of mixed African-European descent, or occasionally of Fon background themselves" (*Fistful of Shells*, 308).

80. Law argues that in Dahomey, "urbanity was defined not (or not only) by size and concentration of population, but by political autonomy and the role of the town as the seat of administration" (*Ouidah*, 81). I would add that material culture also defined "urbanity."

81. "Diary Elet," in Van Dantzig, *The Dutch and the Guinea Coast*, 295–97.

82. Forbes, *Dahomey and the Dahomans*, 1:36, 1:45.

83. Forbes, *Dahomey and the Dahomans*, 1:77.

84. Bachrou Nondinonchao, interview with author, Abomey, June 6, 2021.

85. Dah Atchassou, interview with author, Ahouaja, Abomey, December 10, 2014.

86. Skertchly, *Dahomey as It Is*, 495.

87. Skertchly, *Dahomey as It Is*, 218–221.

88. Dalzel, *History of Dahomey*, xvi.

89. Norris, *Memoirs of Bossa Ahádee*, ix.

90. Alphonse Ahouado, interview with author, Abomey, September 15, 2015.

91. Dalzel, *History of Dahomey*, xvi; Norris, *Memoirs of Bossa Ahádee*, ix.

92. The king permitted foreigners to wear shoes while in the kingdom. Dalzel, *History of Dahomey*, xvi.

93. Dah Atchassou, interview with author, Abomey, December 10, 2014.

94. Forbes, *Dahomey and the Dahomans*, 2:25–26. In Abomey, these axes remain an important display of male authority into the present.

95. Lambe, "From the Great King Trudo," 190–91.

96. Snelgrave, *New Account*, 35.

97. Skertchly, *Dahomey as It Is*, 487–88.

98. Morton-Williams, "A Yoruba Woman," 108.

99. Forbes, *Dahomey and the Dahomans*, 2:64.

100. Skertchly, *Dahomey as It Is*, 204.

101. Forbes, *Dahomey and the Dahomans*, 2:238.

102. Mbembe and Balakrishnan, "Pan-African Legacies."

References

Ahoyo, Jean-Roger. "Les marchés d'Abomey et de Bohicon." *Les Cahiers d'Outre-Mer* 28, no. 110 (1975): 162–84.

Alpern, Stanley B. "What Africans Got for Their Slaves: A Master List of European Trade Goods." *History in Africa* 22 (1995): 5–43.

Appiah, Kwame Anthony. *Cosmopolitanism: Ethics in a World of Strangers.* New York: W. W. Norton, 2006.

Bay, Edna. *Wives of the Leopard: Gender, Politics, and Culture in the Kingdom of Dahomey.* Charlottesville: University of Virginia Press, 1998.

Blier, Suzanne Preston. "The Art of Assemblage: Aesthetic Expression and Social Experience in Danhomè." *RES: Anthropology and Aesthetics* 45 (2004): 186–210.

Blier, Suzanne Preston. "Europia Mania: Contextualizing the European Other in Eighteenth- and Nineteenth-Century Dahomean Art." In *Europe Observed: Multiple Gazes in Early Modern Encounters*, edited by Kumkum Chatterjee and Clement Hawes, 237–70. Lewisburg, PA: Bucknell University Press, 2008.

Brown, Vincent. *Tacky's Revolt: The Story of an Atlantic Slave War.* Cambridge, MA: Harvard University Press, 2020.

Burton, Richard F. *A Mission to Gelele, King of Dahomey.* London: Tinsley Brothers, 1864.

Coquery-Vidrovitch, Catherine. "La fête des coutumes au Dahomey: Historique et essai d'interprétation." *Annales. Histoire, Sciences Sociales* 19, no. 4 (1964): 696–716.

Dabiri, Emma. "Why I Am (Still) Not an Afropolitan." *Journal of African Cultural Studies* 28, no. 1 (2016): 104–8.

Dalzel, Archibald. *The History of Dahomey, an Inland Kingdom of Africa.* 1793; repr., London: Cass, 1967.

DuPlessis, Robert S. *The Material Atlantic: Clothing, Commerce, and Colonization in the Atlantic World.* Cambridge: Cambridge University Press, 2016.

Eze, Chielozona. "We, Afropolitans." *Journal of African Cultural Studies* 28, no. 1 (2016): 114–19.

Flueriot de Langle. "Croisières à la côte d'Afrique (1868)." In *Le tour du monde*, 241–304. Paris, 1876.

Forbes, Frederick E. *Dahomey and the Dahomans, Being the Journals of Two Missions to the King of Dahomey, and Residence at His Capital in the Years 1849 and 1850.* 2 vols. London, 1851.

Fromont, Cécile. "The Taste of Others: Finery, the Slave Trade, and Africa's Place in the Traffic of Early Modern Things." In *Early Modern Things: Objects and Their Histories, 1500–1800*, edited by Paula Findlen, 273–94. London: Routledge, 2021.

Fuglestad, Finn. *Slave Traders by Invitation: West Africa's Slave Coast in the Precolonial Era.* New York: Oxford University Press, 2018.

Getz, Trevor R. *Cosmopolitan Africa, c. 1700–1875.* New York: Oxford University Press, 2013.

Gikandi, Simon. "Foreword: On Afropolitanism." In *Negotiating Afropolitanism: Essays on Borders and Spaces in Contemporary African Literature and Folklore*, edited by Jennifer Wawrzinek and J. K. S. Makokha, 9–12. Leiden: Brill, 2011.

Gikandi, Simon. *Slavery and the Culture of Taste.* Princeton, NJ: Princeton University Press, 2011.

Green, Toby. *A Fistful of Shells: West Africa from the Rise of the Slave Trade to the Age of Revolution.* Chicago: University of Chicago Press, 2019.

Green, Toby. "Sumptuary Laws in Precolonial West Africa: The Examples of Benin and Dahomey." In *The Right to Dress: Sumptuary Laws in a Global Perspective, c. 1200–1800*, edited by Giorgio Riello and Ulinka Rublack, 461–78. Cambridge: Cambridge University Press, 2019.

Herskovits, Melville J. *Dahomey: An Ancient West African Kingdom.* 1938; repr., Evanston, IL: Northwestern University Press, 1967.

Hurston, Zora Neale. *Barracoon: The Story of the Last "Black Cargo."* New York: HarperCollins, 2018.

Kriger, Colleen. "Mapping the History of Cotton Textile Production in Precolonial West Africa." *African Economic History*, no. 33 (2005): 87–116.

Lambe, Bulfinche. Letter "From the Great King Trudo Audati's Palace of Abomey, in the Kingdom of Dahomey," November 27, 1724. In Forbes, *Dahomey and the Dahomans*, 181–95.

Law, Robin. *Ouidah: The Social History of a West African Slaving Port, 1727–1892.* Athens: Ohio University Press, 2005.

Law, Robin. "The Slave-Trader as Historian: Robert Norris and the History of Dahomey." *History in Africa* 16 (1989): 219–35.

Law, Robin, and Paul Lovejoy, eds. *The Biography of Mahommah Gardo Baquaqua: His Passage from Slavery to Freedom in Africa and America.* Princeton, NJ: Markus Wiener, 2007.

Lawrence, Sidra. "Afropolitan Detroit: Counterpublics, Sound, and the African City." *Africa Today* 65, no. 4 (2019): 19–37.

Le Hérissé, Auguste. *L'ancien royaume du Dahomey: Mœurs, religion, histoire.* Paris: Emile Larose, 1911.

Manning, Patrick. *Slavery, Colonialism, and Economic Growth in Dahomey, 1640–1960.* Cambridge: Cambridge University Press, 1982.

Mbembe, Achille. "Afropolitanism." In *Africa Remix: Contemporary Art of a Continent*, edited by Lucy Durán, 26–30. Johannesburg: Jaana Media, 2007.

Mbembe, Achille, and Sarah Balakrishnan. "Pan-African Legacies, Afropolitan Futures." *Transition*, no. 120 (2016): 28–37.

M'Leod, John. *A Voyage to Africa with Some Account of the Manners and Customs of the Dahomian People.* London: John Murray, 1820.

Monroe, J. Cameron. *The Precolonial State in West Africa: Building Power in Dahomey.* New York: Cambridge University Press, 2014.

Morton-Williams, Peter. "A Yoruba Woman Remembers Servitude in a Palace of Dahomey, in the Reigns of Kings Gelele and Behanzin." *Africa: Journal of the International African Institute* 63, no. 1 (1993): 102–17.

Moyo, Last. *The Decolonial Turn in Media Studies in Africa and the Global South.* Cham, Switzerland: Palgrave Macmillan, 2020.

Norris, Robert. *Memoirs of the Reign of Bossa Ahádee, King of Dahomy, an Inland Country of Guiney* [. . .]. 1789; repr., London: Cass, 1968.

Prestholdt, Jeremy. *Domesticating the World: African Consumerism and the Genealogies of Globalization.* Berkeley: University of California Press, 2008.

Selasi, Taiye. "Bye-Bye Babar." *LIP Magazine*, March 3, 2005.

Skertchly, J. A. *Dahomey as It Is; Being a Narrative of Eight Months Residence in the Country.* London, 1874.

Skinner, Ryan Thomas. *Bamako Sounds: The Afropolitan Ethics of Malian Music.* Minneapolis: University of Minnesota Press, 2015.

Snelgrave, William. *A New Account of Some Parts of Guinea and the Slave-Trade.* London, 1732.

Soumonni, Elisée. "The Compatibility of the Slave and Palm Oil Trades in Dahomey, 1818–1858." In *From Slave Trade to "Legitimate" Commerce: The Commercial Transition in Nineteenth-Century West Africa*, edited by Robin Law, 78–92. New York: Cambridge University Press, 2002.

Supplément illustré du Le petit journal. "Au Dahomey (Les fétiches de Kana.—Le dieu de la guerre)." November 26, 1892.

Thornton, John. "Dahomey in the World: Dahomean Rulers and European Demands, 1726–1894." In *Africa's Development in Historical Perspective*, edited by Emmanuel Kwaku Akyeampong, Robert H. Bates, Nathan Nunn, and James A. Robinson, 447–59. New York: Cambridge University Press, 2014.

Van Dantzig, A. *The Dutch and the Guinea Coast, 1674–1742.* Accra, Ghana: GAAS, 1978.

Walker, Tamara J. *Exquisite Slaves: Race, Clothing, and Status in Colonial Lima.* New York: Cambridge University Press, 2017.

The Black Englishmen of Old Calabar

Freedom and Mobility in the Age of Abolition in West Africa

Ndubueze L. Mbah

Achille Mbembe calls for detailed histories that show how Afropolitan practices have characterized diverse intra-African mobilities. Afropolitanism evokes a geography of circulation and hypermobility, of flows and networks, and not of territoriality. Afropolitan histories show how Africans traversed boundaries. As an epistemology, Afropolitanism is a critical reflection on the ways in which Africans of multiple origins define themselves as African, as part of the world, and as agents in the making of the modern world order, including by domesticating the unfamiliar or repurposing colonial languages in new ways. Sociologically, it has meant that Africans fashioned a dynamic modus vivendi with colonialism. Mbembe states, "If we define Afropolitanism the way I have done—in terms of movement, mobility, circulation—and if we study popular forms of everyday life [which] are the richest archives of Afropolitan practices," it becomes evident that survival "is to a large extent dependent on the capacity to move and to move constantly; on the capacity to recycle all kinds of things, to put them to uses they were not originally intended for."[1] It is the "intense traffic of objects and of worldviews," the everyday work of turning one thing into another, "the process of conversion," that one might call forgery, which constitutes an Afropolitan way of embracing the world.[2] I argue that Afropolitanism could transcend survival, as it enabled Africans to define freedom as mobility and to generate rebellion, self-fashioning, and anti-imperial ideologies

Radical History Review

Issue 144 (October 2022)   DOI 10.1215/01636545-9847802

© 2022 by MARHO: The Radical Historians' Organization, Inc.

of belonging. Being Afropolitan meant African imperial subjects subsumed European and African identity logics unpredictably.

Afropolitanism affords a critical perspective for recovering the agencies and consciousnesses of Liberated Africans—African captives rescued from Atlantic slave ships and emancipated and resettled in Freetown, Sierra Leone, in the first half of the nineteenth century. When some of the Liberated Africans left Freetown in the second half of the nineteenth century to return to Old Calabar in Nigeria, their original homeland, and claim it as part of their world, they were marginalized as "natives of Sierra Leone," accused of selling slaves, and forced into exile as Black Englishmen and British subjects. As returnees from Freetown to Old Calabar, the Liberated Africans used intra-African migration, engaged in disruptive transatlantic small-scale trading in palm oil, and practiced slave emancipation to advance their social mobility and freedom politics. They also used petitions to the British consular government of the Bight of Biafra to claim protection as "British subjects" who advanced "free trade" and emancipation. I argue that their mobilities, petitions, and tactics of free trading and slave "redemption" constituted a "discrepant cosmopolitanism."[3] Their practices of British subjecthood were nonconformist and troubling to imperial notions of Anglo-cosmopolitanism. Returnees developed ideas of British subjecthood beyond the colony of Sierra Leone in ways that were incongruent with British policy and challenged European monopolies. They articulated ambivalent ideas of freedom and created unfree labor practices that led antislavery British consuls to protect domestic slavery. Their agencies reveal how marginal Africans refashioned abolitionist ideals beyond the initiatives of Europeans and African elites and generated and embodied "critical cosmopolitanism."[4]

As a result of British antislavery and slave-trade interdiction between 1808 and 1863, 99,752 African captives were rescued from Atlantic slave ships and emancipated in Freetown by the British Vice-Admiralty Court and Courts of Mixed Commission. Styled as "Liberated Africans," these recaptives became "freedom's debtors," their labor bound to the British Empire.[5] About 72,284 resettled in the Sierra Leone colony; the rest were forcibly relocated to fulfill the labor and defense needs of Britain's Atlantic empire.[6] Roughly 32 percent (31,471) of the 99,725 Liberated Africans who were landed and emancipated at Freetown originally embarked from the Bight of Biafra.[7] During the 1850s, an unknown number of these Liberated Africans returned to Old Calabar, motivated by commercial opportunism, kinship reckoning, desire for a homeland, encouragement by Christian missionaries, and a quest to evade precarious living and the violent British colonial system of military and labor recruitment.[8] The Liberated African Registers and the Trans-Atlantic Slave Trade Voyages Database provide approximate information about the African names, sex, age, and bodily features of the Liberated Africans. They survive in missionary and colonial records as objects of European mediation, and their experiences are buried in illegible archives, characterized by looming silences, unarticulated motives, and partial representation. But the Liberated Africans did speak, if one reads against the grain of British consular officials' reports and correspondences. We encounter Old Calabar Liberated Africans in the British archives through their petitions protesting unlawful seizure of their palm oil by European merchants despite their status as British subjects; denunciations of Liberated Africans by Old Calabar elites for "stealing away" domestic slaves with promises of "freedom papers"; and British consuls' efforts to deport returnees from Old Calabar to Sierra Leone. Both the existence and implications of Liberated Africans' voices, especially their writings, claims, and discourses of freedom and rights as British subjects beyond Sierra Leone, have received limited attention in scholarship, which has emphasized European abolitionist, imperial, and social policies toward them.[9]

Represented as beneficiaries of liberation, Liberated Africans faced a future of forced migration and liminal freedom. In 1859, the British consul Thomas Hutchinson deported three Liberated African returnees (William Isam Hazeley, Thomas Feury, and Mr. Matthews) for endangering British capital through illegal transatlantic palm oil trading that threatened the Liverpool monopoly, and for stealing away domestic slaves from local elites to sell them in Fernando Po and Sierra Leone.[10] In so doing, the consul mobilized an imperial notion of Anglo-cosmopolitanism against the returnees' Afropolitan freedom politics. In the view of British consuls, Liberated Africans could only enjoy the right of British protection as subjects in the Sierra Leone colony, where their labor serviced British imperial military and infrastructure needs; to be a "Liberated African" entailed limited freedom.[11] Thus, Liberated African rights of British subjecthood did not extend to territories such as Old Calabar, which Britain aspired to convert into a protectorate.[12] But, as I demonstrate, returnees defined "liberation" as rights to mobility and economic autonomy. They understood their rights as British subjects to have transcended Sierra Leone, entitled them to unfettered participation in free trade, and justified their emancipation of domestic slaves. In effect, they appropriated abolition principles, at least as Thomas Fowell Buxton had popularly defined them in 1840: free trade and free labor.[13] I extricate the agencies, discourses, and worldviews of Liberated Africans from a deluge of European voices contained in Foreign Office, British consular, and Presbyterian missionary records. I have endeavored to discover and project the voices and consciousness of Liberated African returnees, through a process that entailed sifting through hundreds of pages of European and elite African discourses to find the occasional moments when "Liberated" and other subaltern Africans *spoke*. The majority of archival sources examined here were handwritten manuscripts. Hence, I have also tried to be attentive to writing as a performative mode of African literary cosmopolitanism.

Returnees as "African White Men": Atlantic Cosmopolitanism in Old Calabar

The systems of slavery, dependency, and economic control maintained by Old Calabar rulers and local merchants left Liberated African returnees with limited options of social integration and economic uplift, such that most returnees saw

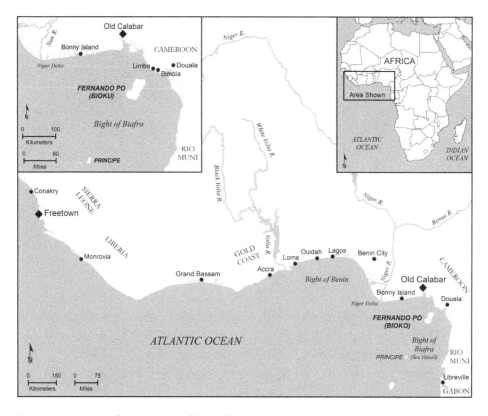

Figure 1. Late nineteenth-century map of West Africa showing Atlantic coastal Old Calabar (Nigeria), Freetown (Sierra Leone), and Fernando Po (now known as Bioko, Equatorial Guinea). Map by Brian Edward Balsley, Certified Geographic Information Systems Professional (GISP).

social identification as Englishmen a necessary condition of their existence in Old Calabar, as well as a survival tactic.

Until the mid-eighteenth century, when the Port of Bonny superseded it, Old Calabar was the principal port of the Bight of Biafra's Atlantic slave trade, and remained critical to British slave trade until abolition forced local merchants to reorient their networks from slave supply to palm oil supply in the nineteenth century.[14] In analyzing the mutual impact of British-Calabar relations between the seventeenth and twentieth centuries, David Imbua argues Old Calabar mediated the Biafra region's integration into the Atlantic political economy by globalizing the local and localizing the global, integrating strangers, and adapting local institutions to international economic systems, thereby embodying early Atlantic cosmopolitanism in West Africa.[15]

Old Calabar merchants functioned as "trust" middlemen between European traders on the coast and Biafran hinterland suppliers and networks over a three-hundred-year period. Leveraging the Atlantic slave trade economy, the "elite of freemen" integrated vast numbers of captives into society as slaves and dependents and asserted autochthonous and ancestral right to political rulership and social mastery over the enslaved majority population. Within Old Calabar, slaves were defined as "outsiders" and property of the ruling elite and lacked "economic, social, or political rights."[16] To maintain control over slaves and dependents, the elite developed a political system known as house rule (*ufok*), whereby the polity was divided into houses or wards, each under a "duke-patriarch."[17] The "political strength" of a ward became measured in the number of its slaves.[18] The most powerful wards dominated coastal trade first in slaves and then, after 1807, in palm oil; they also exercised control over the towns.[19] The elite maintained slavery and dependency as the basis of political administration, agriculture, and trade.[20] Their capacity to spread debt, create dependents, and expand slavery enabled them to consolidate wealth and power.[21] Much of the expansion of the population between 1805 and 1846 was due to the settlement of large numbers of slaves in rural agricultural estates to produce palm oil and food, and provide vigilante forces for elites.[22] Slaveholding quadrupled in the nineteenth century, attended by a wider social gulf between the town-dwelling free population and rural-dwelling slaves, the expansion of plantations, and an increase in the abuse of slaves.[23]

Slavery facilitated elite cosmopolitanism. Since the mid-eighteenth century, elite traders cultivated a transatlantic cosmopolitan habitus as "civilized gentlemen," investing in English literacy, conspicuous consumption, and mastering the cultural conventions of European merchants. They sent their sons to be educated in Bristol, Liverpool, and London and domesticated English architecture, dining rituals, and leisure and sartorial practices, which enabled them to provide hospitality to European traders and increase their trading prospects.[24] This history of elite cosmopolitanism explains why Old Calabar leaders would see Liberated Africans who asserted Anglo-cosmopolitan rights to free trade and emancipation of domestic slaves as unwelcome interlopers and outsiders who were neither citizens nor dependents.[25]

Autonomy was circumscribed to the elite class of merchants, who weaponized the multigrade institution of *ekpe* (male secret society) to make and enforce laws, settle inter-ward disputes, impose boycotts and fines, and arrest and punish offenders.[26] As "the actual executive government" of Old Calabar, ekpe enabled the elite to control dependents and slaves and define citizenship.[27] A few "trading slaves" gained membership and "act[ed] the role of freemen," but ekpe functioned to subjugate slaves, women, and strangers, although European merchants purchased membership as a mechanism of recovering their "trust" debts.[28] The polity's enslaved population made substantial efforts, including the use of popular protests, to ameliorate their condition, but they never demanded freedom in terms of autonomy from their masters. They demanded rights of greater social inclusion as protected members of society. They sought freedom from arbitrary acts of murder at the hands of masters. But rather than attempt to overthrow the ruling elite, they allied with their ward leaders in internal politics.[29]

In the second half of the nineteenth century, when Liberated Africans returned to Old Calabar, slavery and dependency remained foundational to the society's political and economic systems. Emancipation, as Liberated Africans embodied it, did not exist in Old Calabar as tacit knowledge. Emancipation turned a slave "adrift a poor, houseless, defenseless thing," without the protection of a patron and without belonging in a ward.[30] The type of freedom as a political right and autonomous social reproduction that Liberated Africans sought were alien in Old Calabar. Liberated Africans would be deemed dangerous because they modeled a radical notion of freedom for slaves in Old Calabar, who began to seek similar freedoms of trading and belonging. Encouraged by consuls like Hutchinson, local elites would weaponize the ekpe society to ostracize Liberated Africans, deeming them to be the same as foreign white men.[31]

Liberated Africans entered Old Calabar as rebellious migrants in two respects. First, they tried to extend their rights of being British subjects beyond Sierra Leone into a non-British territory, despite the lack of British metropolitan official support and mounting British consular and mercantile opposition. Second, being neither local slaveholding freemen nor dependent domestic slaves, they existed in Old Calabar as foreigners who violated local conventions of belonging. These dual sources of marginalization made economic survival difficult for Liberated Africans and explain why they embraced the liminal social identity of Black Englishmen.

In 1853, "100 Liberated Africans of the Ibo tribe" petitioned that they wanted to emulate the Yoruba example in 1839 and be sent as "missionaries" to "their [own] country."[32] Officials in Freetown determined that "Ibo country" was "Calabar," specifically Creek Town, and secured the agreement of Creek Town's king Eyo Honesty II as well as leaders of Duke Town, who promised to welcome, provide land, and "look upon [the returnees] as white men, because they [had] learnt white-man fashion."[33] In 1854, the first Liberated African emigrants returned to Old Calabar and began participating in a lucrative palm oil trade.[34] However, rather than settling as arranged and expected in Creek Town, some Efik-speaking emigrants chose to settle in Duke Town, where they "originally belonged."[35] In Creek Town, viewed as predominantly Igbo, returnees rented houses and hired out their artisan and literary services to local elites. In Duke Town, Efik returnees settled in the Presbyterian station and an adjoining area that became known as the "Sierra Leone people's settlements."[36] These resettlement patterns reflected the ethnic demography of Old Calabar, which comprised principally Igbo and Efik peoples.

The returnees embraced European and African Presbyterian missionaries as patrons. Established between 1841 and 1844, the mission opposed slavery, witchcraft trials, and poison oaths and increasingly generated a community of outcasts,

Table 1. "Names of Ten Persons Connected with Duke Town Mission House, Being Natives of Old Calabar or Neighboring Countries Redeemed from Slavery." Enclosure 3, in Dispatch 11, Fernando Po, January 31, 1856, FO 84/1001, BNA.

English name	Native name	Born in or brought from	Age
Mary Taylor Anderson	Asuna	Egbo Shary	About 20 Years
Sarah Anderson	Iqua Esian	Efik	About 18 Years
Agnes Tod	Mbodio	Ibo	About 10 Years
Andrew Somerville	Eni	Efik	About 6 Years
John Gray	Ered	Efik	About 3 Years
Thomas Hogan	Efiong	Efik	About 2 Years
Joseph Jameson	Ekpe	Mburikam	About 15 Years
Isabella Elliot	Inyang	Egbo Shary	About 12 Years
Janet Anderson	Angwa Okun	Egbo Shary	About 18 Years
Anna Miller Anderson	Iqua	Efik	About 9 Months

refugees, and emancipated slaves, variously gifted to them, purchased by them, and rescued by them.[37] Local people viewed the refugees (table 1), for whom missionaries secured consular "manumission papers," as both "slaves of the house or ward ruled by the missionaries" and "whitemen's slaves."[38] To meet missionaries' incessant requests for manumission papers, Hutchinson created one that became formulaic (fig. 2). Missionaries extended their governing authority beyond the redeemed natives to include Liberated Africans.[39] Mission residence afforded returnees a refuge to pursue free trade, and some would imitate missionaries' "redemption" practices, transforming them into mechanisms to acquire domestic servants for themselves and traffic redeemed slaves as indentured servants. Overall, the mission station constituted a marginal community. Missionaries were the only class of Europeans allowed to reside within Old Calabar. Until 1891, several hundred European traders, so-called supercargoes (captains of trading vessels) acting as agents of Liverpool financiers, lived on their ships with their mixed European and African crews, paid *comey* (custom dues) to Old Calabar rulers, and stored their wares in rented onshore houses.[40]

Associated with missionaries, Liberated Africans were viewed as Europeans and outsiders by the local population within Old Calabar. In 1855, one missionary remarked that as "well-behaved British subjects of the darkest complexion," the Liberated Africans in Old Calabar were "considered white people and treated as such."[41] Those who had recently arrived "from Sierra Leone, and who are British Subjects" were "viewed by the laws of Calabar as white people, and not amenable to [*ekpe*] law."[42] Liberated Africans were distinguished by their English literacy, Christian religion, and Anglo-cosmopolitan sartorial habits. The translation of returnees' Anglo-cosmopolitanism as whiteness did not seem to have occurred with the "Saro" returnees in Lagos and Port Harcourt, by comparison.[43] The closest

Figure 2a–b. Old Calabar Freedom Paper. Enclosure 4, in Dispatch 11, Fernando Po, January 31, 1856, FO 84/1001, BNA. The text reads: "To all Whom these Presents Come, Greeting: Know ye that Mary Taylor Anderson, aged about Twenty years, whose country name is Asuna and who was born at Egbo Shary has been this day declared before me to have been originally a slave but to be now manumitted. This is therefore to declare that fact to all whom it may concern and to forbid any one into whose hands she may come, from again making her a slave under the pain of incurring the displeasure of Her Britannic Majesty's Government and of suffering such penalty as the government may attach to such a step. Given under my hand at Duke Town, River Old Calabar, this Twenty Second day of January One Thousand Eight Hundred and Fifty-Six. Thomas Hutchinson. Her Britannic Majesty's Consul for the Bight of Biafra and the Island of Fernando Po."

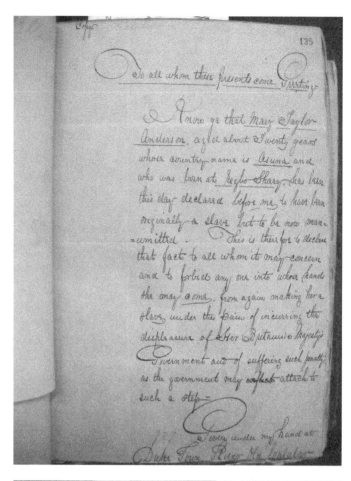

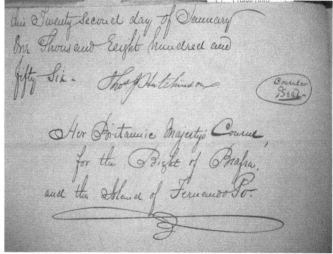

approximation would be in Liberia, where African American settlers were locally seen as "black-white people" and white men.[44]

To maintain the informal status of "British subjects" in Old Calabar, returnees had to be "well-behaved" or, in British consul Hutchinson's words, exemplify "good character." Hutchinson believed "Christianity and Civilization are cause and effect in raising up Africa from her present condition of helpless infancy to the health and vigor of manhood."[45] British metropolitan officials warned that Liberated Africans in Old Calabar should be careful not to offend British traders in the area, even though the British government, as their protector, had taken "a warm interest" in their "safety and welfare."[46] Imperial discourses, combined with missionary governance of returnees' domesticity, framed Anglo-cosmopolitan masculinity in terms of literacy, character, and access to metropolitan authorities. Consequently, returnees embraced the everyday performance of Anglo-cosmopolitan masculinity as freed, civilized, literate, and rights-bearing British subjects, as a survival mechanism. Many of them went to Old Calabar bearing "letters of introduction" attesting to "an excellent Christian character" from Freetown missionaries, "certificate of Christian character & conduct" from the Mixed Commission Court, and "testimonials" of good character to secure consular protection.[47]

"Market Is for All Men": Returnees' Afropolitan Petitions and Free Trading

Liberated Africans in Old Calabar couched their claims to British subjecthood within petitions asserting their right to free trade. Their petition discourses reveal the ways in which their Afropolitanism entailed claiming multiple and sometimes conflicting identities as natives of Old Calabar, natives of Sierra Leone, and British subjects who sought British protection while also questioning the governing power of British consuls. Thus, the returnee Peter Nicholls wrote to a Liverpool ship captain in 1855: "I have to request that you will replace my 16 puncheons of palm oil without delay. . . . I am as much a British Subject as you are, and have all the same right to trade in any part of the world. . . . I protest against your procedure as being at once a breach of all the laws of Commercial honor and honesty, and a violation of my privileges as a subject of the Queen of England."[48] Nicholls had left Sierra Leone for Old Calabar in October 1854 to trade in palm oil but by November 1855 had taken up the occupation in Fernando Po when his goods were seized by the Liverpool ship captain "in the assumption" that Nicholls owed debts to the British traders as an African resident of Creek Town of Old Calabar. Nicholls insisted, "[I] beg explicitly to state that I am no native of Old Calabar: for less do I comprehend what is meant by my property having been seized to pay another's debts."[49] In a bid to monopolize Old Calabar's palm produce trade in the 1850s, British merchants had given out enormous quantities of trade goods as "trust" to local elite merchants, and then resorted to *panyarring* (seizure of natives and trade goods) as a means of recovering their credit, a practice that originated from the polity's Atlantic slave trade.[50] By 1855, consuls had come to the conclusion that panyarring was the only means of recovering British capital.[51] Nicholls was the first returnee to suffer pan-yarring.[52] His cargo was seized against debts owed by none other than his friend King Eyo II.[53] But Nicholls had his own vision of what Liberated Africans expected their British subject rights to look like.

Nicholls had been born in Old Calabar around 1804 and enslaved by 1820. The British Navy seized the ship taking him across the Atlantic and emancipated him in Freetown, where he went to school and worked as a house servant before enlisting as a soldier in the British Royal African Corps. In 1829, he was promoted to the rank of sergeant for being an "intelligent African." Between 1832 and 1840, he converted to Wesleyan Christianity, married his first wife, and served in Guinea (Isle de Los) and the Gambia as a color sergeant earning £42 a year. In 1840, the Royal African Corps was reorganized as the Third West India Regiment. To avoid posting to Jamaica in 1841, Nicholls purchased a discharge. With £407 saved up, he began trading in Freetown and, like other recaptives, amassed several hundred pounds and property.[54] He returned to Old Calabar in 1854 and a year later was elected an elder of the Duke Town Church.[55] He was influential among the returnee community and well-known in both Freetown and Old Calabar as a "native of Egbo Shary." Egbo Shary was considered to be "the mother country" of Efik people; Nicholls spoke the Efik language well and could communicate with many Old Calabar people who did not know English.[56] This made him a highly successful trader.

In his October 1855 journal, the consul at Fernando Po wrote that King Eyo II was using Nicholls to sell his palm oil in England in "mail packets" rather than paying his trust debts to British vessels. When confronted, King Eyo II responded that "he had received cloth, guns, brass rods, etc. from Mr. Nicholls, that Mr. Nicholls had also paid Duke [Eyamba II of Duke Town] himself *comey* [custom dues] the same as the [European] vessels."[57] Thus, while British merchants viewed Nicholls as an African ward of local elites, King Eyo II viewed him as equivalent to a white trader who paid *comey*. Although born in Old Calabar, Nicholls earned the privilege of a "British Subject" through emancipation and military service. Hence, he emphasized that he was not a "native of Old Calabar" but rather a Sierra Leonean "British Subject." Nicholls denied Old Calabar citizenship when that identity threatened his right to free trade. He rather asserted Sierra Leone citizenship and British subjecthood. Negotiating rights as British subjects beyond Sierra Leone required Liberated Africans to fashion dynamic identities, as well as to understand and exploit the tenuous and complex administrative network of British consular government in West Africa. Nicholls would travel from Old Calabar to Fernando Po to swear an affidavit to the consul in order to have his oil returned to him as a "lawful purchase."[58] But the British trader refused, leading Nicholls to petition the new consul Hutchinson in January 1856 "to adopt such measures as shall cause my property to be returned and to *secure my rights as a British subject*."[59] At the same time, he also petitioned the governor of Sierra Leone "to enforce the restitution of my property."[60] These petitions forced the British ship captain to return Nicholls's property, although he threatened future violence against Nicholls.[61] As consuls "lacked the legal power to oblige the British supercargoes stationed in the rivers of the Bight of Biafra to adopt or obey any particular code of regulations," returnees used petitions to force consuls to protect them as "British subjects by all lawful means."[62] Nicholls's discrepant Anglo-cosmopolitanism forced Hutchinson to require British merchants to stop panyarring as a means of debt recovery.[63]

Yet, following Nicholls's case, European ship captains expanded "trust" credit to local elites in order to purchase the palm oil supply of Old Calabar "2½ years in advance."[64] They supplied goods on credit "recklessly" and used panyarring to recover supplies.[65] Another Liverpool ship captain, Davies, seized "six puncheons of palm oil" belonging to returnee Daniel Hedd.[66] Hedd's petition asserted, "I am a native of Sierra Leone and a British Subject." He wrote that Davies seized his property and threatened to imprison him.[67] Consul Hutchinson "did not deem it [his] duty" to ensure the restoration of Hedd's property. He argued that Hedd was neither a legitimate native trader nor a European merchant. Hedd was not a dependent of a native elite, had not paid custom duties like European traders, and resided on the mission premises. In the consul's logic, missionaries were obliged to avoid trading and focus on preaching.[68] Hedd therefore petitioned the metropolitan British foreign secretary, who reprimanded the consul for not protecting "the victim of injustice" from the "arbitrary and illegal" acts of a British merchant. The secretary ruled that residence on mission premises should not prevent free trade.[69]

At this point, British merchants at Old Calabar tried a different strategy. Under the pretext of abolishing panyarring, they initiated "a code of bye laws, and the formation of an Equity Court," in September 1856.[70] Ironically, Article 18 of the bylaws authorized supercargoes to imprison African debtors, and Article 12 stipulated that any "legitimate trader" at Old Calabar must "pay through the Court" a custom duty "of Twenty Thousand Coppers per annum" or "be liable to have their oil seized as smuggled produce" by British merchants.[71] As if the implications were not clear, the consul emphasized, "The twelfth Article has been inserted—chiefly to prevent the Sierra Leone men resident on the Mission premises from shipping oil to England, as they sometimes do, and which oil is <u>virtually</u> the property of the British supercargoes—who bring out vessels and cargoes at great expense."[72]

Citing the bylaws, Captain Davies refused to return Hedd's oil, arguing Liberated Africans came to Old Calabar as "paupers and penniless" rogues, but by promising "extravagant" profits to local elites "stole" palm oil supplies already purchased "by English capital."[73] When confronted by British merchants, local elites reported they already sold their supplies to the "Sierra Leone men."[74] As chairman of the Equity Court, captain Davies took time to explain that each British ship had on average a crew of forty men, costing £400 a month, as well as an annual custom duty valued at £200. The longer British ships waited to receive palm oil, the higher their operating cost. Liberated Africans, however, shipped small quantities on steamers regularly, ensuring quick profit turnover to local suppliers, and extending the wait period of British ships.[75]

Davies's complaint reveals how returnees' Afropolitanism or their aberrant assertion of British subjecthood legitimized their trading practices that challenged monopolies.[76] All European merchants at Old Calabar supported Davies in his refusal to restore Hedd's oil. Hutchinson explained, "It had lately become customary with certain persons in London to employ these Sierra Leone people on the Mission premises to act as foils for the shipping home of oil, which . . . was *bona fide* the property of the supercargoes."[77] In effect, liberated Africans mediated a capitalist struggle between established Liverpool companies and nascent London merchants. Missionary Edgerly, who supported Hedd, denounced the British Court of Equity proceeding as a "gross robbery."[78]

Subsequently, Hedd led eight other Liberated Africans in a petition that began, "We who are . . . British subjects" allege that "Davies Supercargo on board the ship *Calabar*" had "enticed the chief of the country" to "drive away all of the Sierra Leone people" at the "Mission Hill" to prevent them from bringing war, killing the natives, and taking possession of the country. "Since we come into this town," they wrote, "we reside with the mission, we never disturb any of the Calabar man neither violating their law, neither disturb any of those Captain in these River. Since we come from civilized country, we show Honor to them as our Superiors [but] we thinketh within ourselves that Market is for all men. From since Captain Davies entice the king to drive us, there is no peace amongst we and the country people."[79] Missionary Anderson also wrote to the consul in support of the Liberated Africans' petition, affirming that returnees' palm oil trade "offended the supercargoes," who then convinced Eyamba II and other elites "that large numbers of [Liberated Africans] from Sierra Leone" will come and "take possession of the country of Old Calabar." Eyamba II therefore "order[ed] all the Sierra Leone people out of the country," claiming they "had been located [in Duke Town] without his knowledge or consent."[80] The consul justified the eviction order. In his view, "Duke Town authorities will not recognize [Liberated Africans] as freemen because they know that formerly they were slaves." Thus justified, elites used ekpe society "to keep" the Liberated Africans confined "within their dwellings." The consul requested the foreign office to determine whether the Liberated Africans should be allowed to "remain at Duke Town," and "be subject to the existing laws of Old Calabar, or to the protection of British subjects."[81]

Secretary Clarendon offered a familiar British foreign office doublespeak: "In the absence of any special legislation," Liberated Africans "cannot of course be entitled to expect as a matter of Right that they shall be treated as British Subjects when they voluntarily return to, and become residents in, the territory of the native chief whose subjects they were by birth."[82] However, because the British government "have accordingly learnt with much gratification that the men referred to . . . are engaging in lawful and profitable pursuits," he continued, "the Africans in question are entitled to the sympathy and good offices of the British government, who will not tolerate the persecution with which those persons appear to be threatened, and will not fail to resent as an insult to this country any ill usage to which they may be exposed." Clarendon instructed the consul to conclude a treaty with Old Calabar chiefs "by which, for the satisfaction and security of the Liberated Africans, their Right to enjoy British protection shall be duly recognized." He asked the consul to abolish ekpe and "report in detail" any "illegal or arbitrary acts which may be committed by the supercargoes against the [Liberated] Africans."[83]

A June 1856 foreign office memo suggests that Liberated Africans' petitions for British subject rights in Old Calabar had an important impact. Clarendon observed that although returnees had taken the trade out of the hands of the "great Liverpool Houses" that had monopolized it, "both on commercial grounds and also with the view to the extinction of the slave trade, it would be good policy to encourage as much as possible the independent class of traders just springing into existence, for in proportion as these *natives* get interested in the palm oil trade, so they will become enemies to the slave trade." He concluded, "As regards . . . whether the Sierra Leone men (liberated slaves) are entitled to British protection . . . it would be politic to protect them wherever and whenever they are in reach of British protection."[84]

However, returnees' free trading and petitions had also encouraged redeemed natives to undertake free trading, thereby increasing the losses suffered by British merchants and leading them to violence. In an October 1856 letter styled in Rev. Anderson's handwriting, one such redeemed native, Etan Effiong, informed Hutchinson that Davies had seized his puncheon of oil, refused to restore it, dared him to seek the assistance of Anderson to petition the consul, and later threatened to take him on board his ship and put a rope around his neck. Effiong pleaded that as the consul "no will let black man do bad for white man; I look to you for protection & redress."[85] British captains resorted to violence to recover their credit. They went "into the natives' houses beating people with their sticks, & [went] out in their boats on the river at night to plunder canoes by seizing oil & men."[86] African retaliation included physical assault against British captains like Cuthbertson, as well as looting gunpowder and other trade goods from the onshore rental houses of captains like Davies and Sterne of the *Endragt*.[87] British captains later violently confronted Old Calabar elites and demanded they take responsibility for the British losses and injuries.[88] British consuls blamed the returnees for these conflicts.[89] And British captains blamed missionaries and returnees for the "manifest injustice" they "suffer as victims of swindling by the natives."[90]

These disputes culminated in the "*Olinda* incident," which Kenneth Dike described as the "biggest effort ever made by the African community to break the

Liverpool monopoly."[91] In August 1857, with the collaboration of Liberated Africans, King Eyo II loaded the independently contracted brig *Olinda* with oil "for his own personal benefit," despite owing debts valued at four hundred tons or £18,000 to British traders. Returnees saw the *Olinda* as an opportunity to expand their free trading. Duke Town slaves Bassey Henshaw, Yellow Duke, Egbo Tom, and Black Davis testified that the Liberated African William Isam Hazeley had promised them "big pay pass any white Captain" and consequently defrauded them of several puncheons of oil and ebony wood that he loaded on the *Olinda* at Creek Town. Captain Lewis of the *Olinda* affirmed this.[92] Consequently, several British captains assaulted Hazeley, causing him to petition the consul and demand the "justice to which all Her Britannic Majesty's subjects are justly entitled."[93] This incident led the consul to charge Hazeley and other returnees with lawlessness, resulting in the 1859 deportations that I referenced in the introduction of this article. Ironically, in justifying their power to exile Liberated African returnees, consuls defined them as British subjects.[94]

"Redemption": The Afropolitanism of Returnees' Emancipation Practices

This article began with the order to deport Hazeley in 1859, along with Feury and Matthews, who were engaging in a different activity—what the consul called "slave dealing" but the returnees defined as liberation or redemption. The criminal charges against Feury and Matthews are among the earliest records of Liberated Africans engaging in redemption in Old Calabar. Their cases reveal that Liberated Africans emulated the missionaries by first redeeming slaves or helping them to escape slavery, and afterward seeking British recognition of their emancipation. Feury allegedly tried to steal four of King Eyo II's slaves to sell them in Sierra Leone.[95] In a clandestine letter to his partner in Freetown, Feury warned of "the great mess" he would face if the king or other Old Calabar elites learned of the scheme.[96] Feury's choice of Freetown seemed strategic, because between the 1820s and 1850s, slaves continually fled adjacent territories to seek freedom within the Freetown colony and effectively obtained British protection.[97] In his defense, Feury claimed the enslaved boys would have been executed "according to country fashion" when the king died.[98] This argument was similar to claims made by other missionaries and British officials engaged in the same practices of redemption. But the consul dismissed Feury's defense because the king's successor, Young Eyo III, had vowed not to enact the ritual of killing slaves at his father's death, thereby ensuring enslaved peoples' safety.[99]

As for Matthews, Young Eyo III accused him of stealing "five of his domestic servants" and conniving to resettle and liberate these slaves in Sierra Leone.[100] Young Eyo sought to show that Matthews was not an emancipator but a slave dealer. He stated that Matthews arrived at Old Calabar in June 1858, visited Young Eyo's home, and presented him a "bag with money," requesting to buy a boy. Eyo refused, stating that he had promised the Church not to sell people. Matthews then informed Eyo that he had lived in England for seven years, and that nobody lived according to the minister's "talk." When Eyo still declined to sell, Matthews approached Young Eyo's father, King Eyo II, who also refused. On July 5, Matthews "took away 5 of [Young Eyo's] people." Young Eyo claimed that Matthews intentionally encouraged his slaves to run away. Young Eyo requested the consul to return his slaves, so that his other slaves would not emulate "these 5" and also "try to run away."[101] But when another vice-consul at Fernando Po interviewed Matthews about stealing Eyo's five slaves, Matthews admitted to attempting to purchase a boy slave at Old Calabar with the intention of taking him to Fernando Po "to act as a domestic servant" and to "give him his freedom" within a short time.[102] The vice-consul wrote that this practice led to slaves' becoming "respectable and honorable members of society."[103] But Matthews denied the charge of slave stealing and claimed they stowed away; the vice-consul supported this idea that Matthews merely facilitated the redemption of the slaves.[104]

Yet Consul Hutchinson exiled Matthews, alongside Feury and Hazeley, due to local elite pressure. In addition to Young Eyo III's outrage, King Ephraim of Duke Town complained to the consul, "A number of Sierra Leone men and others have come to reside in my town. Now these men say they are English man and British subjects and are not amenable to any law of mine. I do not understand when man do bad thing and keep no law, he say he be English man."[105] Ephraim denounced returnees' interference with domestic slavery. He was particularly incensed that his domestic slave Egbo Bassey had escaped to the mission station and obtained "British protection."[106] Emulating returnees, Bassey built a house in the Sierra Leone people's settlement, married a wife, embraced transatlantic palm oil trading, became baptized, and purchased slaves for whom he also secured consular manumission papers.[107] Missionaries prevented Ephraim's attempt to repossess Bassey and his twelve redeemed slaves in 1857, and helped them relocate to Fernando Po.[108] Subsequently, Old Calabar elites complained about the distribution of freedom papers to domestic slaves and saw Liberated Africans, especially, as exemplars of emancipation that led "to slaves being removed from Efik control."[109]

Thus the exile of Feury and Matthews was linked to antagonism between returnees and local elites over domestic slavery. Old Calabar slave-owning elites saw the Liberated Africans as opportunistic immigrants who used claims of emancipation and being British subjects to steal slaves to own or traffic as indentured domestic servants. Although missionaries and British officials also redeemed slaves, local elites blamed Liberated Africans.[110] In the view of local elites, missionaries and British officials acquired slaves by lawful purchase or as gifts, but Liberated Africans used dubious means to steal slaves. The different cases of Feury and Matthews suggest that returnees participated in redemption secretly and opportunistically, and their involvement only became apparent when they were caught. They also suggest that domestic slaves saw redemption as an opportunity to achieve a new type of freedom that was radical in Old Calabar—escaping slavery and dependency to live as recognized freedmen beyond the reach of their masters. These combined to create a perception of Liberated Africans as people who "steal away" slaves, and helps to explain the "excitement" among some Old Calabar elites to deport them. Otherwise, the elites feared, they "will lose all [their slaves] without cause."[111]

Redemption enabled Liberated Africans to acquire Old Calabar slaves as domestic servants and traffic them as indentured laborers without violating slave-trade abolition. Earlier, in 1855, a European missionary complained that Fernandinos (Liberated Africans on Fernando Po) came to Old Calabar "at various times" and "purchased slaves."[112] The consul acknowledged that he was aware of the "fact" that male and female slaves were purchased at Old Calabar and sold on Fernando Po Island as domestic servants. But he argued that "Fernando Po has always been <u>a refuge from slavery</u>," and Old Calabar slaves welcomed the opportunity of freedom on Fernando Po.[113] He expressed his "surprise" at the missionaries' complaint because "on many occasions they themselves have sent slaves to [Fernando Po] who were in danger in Old Calabar, but who immediately on arrival were at perfect liberty to do as they pleased." Most of the domestic servants sent from Old Calabar to Fernando Po were "boys & girls from 7 to 10 years of age." When these "liberated slaves" wished to marry, "a piece of land is granted them to erect a house on. They have no taxes whatsoever with the solitary exception of 5 percent on imports and 2½ percent on exports. They are in a word perfectly free and untrammeled. This is infinitely superior to a state of slavery in Old Calabar." He added that British officials like Admiral Bruce and Beecroft also sent redeemed slaves to the island.[114] But what the consul's report overlooked was that these so-called domestic servants promised land inheritance were soon converted into "quasi-slaves" serving "five-years apprenticeships" by the Spanish colonial governor.[115]

The above suggests that for a brief period, European administrators justified Liberated Africans' trafficking of redeemed slaves as a sort of liberation. In their antislavery logic, it was similar to how Old Calabar missionaries exploited the practice of redemption as a means of acquiring domestic servants. In June 1856, Consul Hutchinson reported the "applications" he received from European missionaries and settlers at Old Calabar for "manumission papers for the[ir] slaves." Hutchinson gave them a certificate that had been approved by an official in London.[116] One missionary provided the names of six "domestics of my household, who have been manumitted by me by purchase and who are unconditionally free, requiring only your consular certificate & to award them all the privileges of freedom." Another wrote, "I have redeemed some of the natives of this country, which I request you to give me a paper for each and you will very thankfully oblige." A third wrote that he had "redeemed the girl called 'Agnes Caldwell' and that she is free, no person having any claim of property in her."[117] These applications suggest that certain Europeans in Old Calabar could purchase or redeem a domestic slave and subsequently seek formal consular emancipation.

However, Liberated Africans at Old Calabar would stretch the limits of what redemption meant, and what privileges British subjecthood allowed, beyond local elites' tolerance and British consuls' countenance. As the global palm oil market crashed in the early 1860s, putting local elites under immense pressure to meet their palm oil quotas, several Afro-Brazilian returnees from the Gold Coast (called *tabom*) and Lagos (called *aguda*) joined a growing number of Sierra Leone Liberated African returnees at Old Calabar. These African British subjects caused "considerable trouble by trading, owning slaves, and playing the chiefs, missionaries, and agents off against one another."[118] As a result, the 1860s and 1870s were marked by elite opposition to the presence of Black Englishmen. In his petition to the Court of Equity, the then king of Duke Town Archibong III declared, "I will in no wise have any African born British subjects in my country who will not abide by the law of my country. . . . I therefore implore the court to inform the said British subjects dwelling in Old Calabar Towns under my control that those who will not abide by my country law must leave my country entirely." The king meant that the returnees violated local conventions by buying palm oil directly from the hinterland, instead of from coastal elite middlemen, and by duplicating freedom papers and using them to steal slaves.[119] Elites resorted to violence against returnees. Several Liberated Africans petitioned the consul, chronicling the "daily cruelties" of Archibong III, who arbitrarily seized, flogged, and imprisoned Liberated Africans like James Croker.[120] To escape persecution, some Liberated Africans left Old Calabar, and those that remained expanded demands for British protection.[121]

On their part, British consuls considered returnees to be a nuisance, such that when in 1878, the king began expelling returnees from Duke Town, the consul dismissed them as "the most meddlesome and dangerous people on the Coast."[122] In addition to the complaints of local elites, consuls had become alarmed by the audacious manner in which returnees, including at this period emancipated Africans from the West Indies, used fake freedom papers to acquire and sell domestic slaves. Returnees, including Hazeley, who defiantly returned to Old Calabar after his deportation, had come to depend on the labor of redeemed slaves to conduct petty trading in Old Calabar.[123] Consul White reported in 1885 that the redeeming of slaves had become "a most profitable trade amongst the natives of Sierra Leone settled in Old Calabar. They have found it to be a cheap way of procuring servants or of living on the proceeds of the labor of the negroes they have redeemed." Returnees sought to enlist British consuls in recovering their runaway redeemed slaves and domestic servants. The consul thought this "amount[ed] to legalizing slavery . . . under cover of the British flag." He further reported that "a British Sierra Leone woman had been trading on young girls" and that he had stopped a West Indian British subject from "taking away with him a young negro" from Old Calabar.

He concluded, "This so-called redeeming of slaves by Sierra Leonians is not popular with the natives of Old Calabar and they look with mistrust in such dealings."[124] The consul exiled many returnees charged with "revolting acts of barbarity" in order to reassure the elites of Old Calabar "who are law abiding and loyal" that their interests were secure under British protection.[125] Subsequently, he issued a "notice" prohibiting redemption and declared that Liberated Africans redeeming slaves "will be accused of slave dealing" and punished according to British law.[126] He warned that several condemned Liberated Africans were already "expiating their crimes in the jail at Freetown."[127]

After the deportations, the consul accounted for a remaining "48-colored British subjects at Old Calabar, viz: 13 from Accra, 7 from Lagos, 4 from the West Indies, 24 from Sierra Leone. Of these, 5 own 10 redeemed slaves to my knowledge. Their names are: Mrs. Brooks—2 slaves, Mrs. Pratt—2 slaves, Francis Phillip—3 slaves, P. B. Emmanuel—1 slave."[128]

Previous consuls had accommodated redemption, but the imperative of establishing British rule in the 1880s led officials to criminalize redemption and protect domestic slavery.[129] Old Calabar elites acceded to making Old Calabar a British protectorate on the condition that domestic slavery would be protected.[130] Unlike domestic slavery, however, redemption entailed forms of "slave dealing" and trafficking that flagrantly violated abolition. Throughout the 1880s, consuls weaponized the "discretion" of "magisterial authority" to deal with returnees who engaged in redemption, which had by then been deemed untenable.[131]

Conclusion

I have historicized Liberated Africans' Afropolitanism by examining their survival strategies or freedom politics after they had been "freed" in Sierra Leone and relocated to Old Calabar, where they could not belong because they were not slaves or dependents, freeborn slave-owning elites, or European merchants and missionaries. Their marginality made them vulnerable to dispossession, violence, and exile. But it also enabled them to imagine an expansive geography of economic migration and social mobility that included Freetown, Old Calabar, and Fernando Po. It led them to claim British subjecthood and forge rebellious economies of transatlantic free trading that challenged the Liverpool monopoly. And it enabled them to put redemption to different uses, namely as "a cheap way of procuring servants or of living on the proceeds of the labor of the negroes they have redeemed"—which Old Calabar elites viewed as dispossessive slave owning or what one might call "false emancipatory slave ownership." This expansion of the unfree labor economy was one of the most notable contradictory agencies of the Liberated Africans, because they had been so-called beneficiaries of emancipation from slavery and products of international abolitionism. Returnees articulated Afropolitan identity and belonging through contradictory strategies, by asserting freedom as rights-bearing British subjects while facilitating partial emancipation and reenslavement. Hence, I have tried to show that returnees embodied ambiguous ideas of freedom.

Moreover, it is by studying how African migrants dealt with forms of alienation or the "disembedding" of individuals from communities that we can comprehend their identity politics and unique philosophy of freedom in the age of abolition.[132] Returning to Old Calabar, from which many of them had been enslaved or embarked, Liberated Africans stood out as a living contradiction to domestic slavery and as exemplars of radical freedom to domestic slaves. This was why Old Calabar elites singled out returnees as dangerous. By asserting Anglo-cosmopolitan identity through residence on the mission station, dressing European, speaking English, and, especially, writing petitions, they induced Old Calabar people to view them as both African and white men. Indeed, returnees articulated multiple identities, depending on whether they were petitioning to be allowed to return to Old Calabar as their native country or original homeland, or were distinguishing themselves as natives of Sierra Leone to assert British subjects' rights to free trade, or were participating in redemption and self-fashioning themselves into fake emancipators. After all, it was the same class of Africans whose free trading the British foreign secretary deemed critical to "the extinction of the slave trade" that Consul White later criminalized for "slave dealing." These fluid identity configurations were instrumental responses to deracination, precarity, and marginalization and enabled the returnees to adapt, assert British subjecthood, and conduct free trade, and to emancipate, own, and traffic domestic slaves.

Returnees' Afropolitanism required the mobilization of different kinds of knowledge, including identifying and accessing different West African coastal spaces where economic opportunities existed, forging alliances with missionaries, making use of technologies of exchange such as the West African mail steamboats, and leveraging networks of Liberated Africans, sympathetic missionaries, and European captains in Old Calabar, Fernando Po, and Sierra Leone to relocate redeemed domestic slaves. It required knowledge of the authority limits of proximate British consuls, imaginative access to London metropolitan authorities, and deployment of effective discourses to gain the sympathy and support of British officials. Finally, returnees' cosmopolitanism was nonconformist because, in extending African British subject rights beyond the British colonial possession of Sierra Leone to Old Calabar, they also challenged European notions of subject territories, fixity of colonized subjects, and control over African mobility. As scholars have shown, such dissident norms of mobility of African subjects were strategic means of contesting control over spaces, access to resources, and identity.[133]

Mbembe, in answering the question, "Who is African and who is not?," defined "African citizenship" or Afropolitanism as a rights claim made by people despite race and birthplace, including people who have settled in Africa or created culture and knowledge in and of Africa through "their ways of being and doing," even if they also belong somewhere else. Second, he identifies the "dispersal" and "diasporas" of African people and "traces of Africa" in the world. These two realities characterize Afropolitanism as a product of "worlds-in-movement," including intra-African "itinerancy, mobility and displacement." Colonialism sought to "freeze" the African culture of mobility "through the modern institution of borders." Therefore, Afropolitan scholarship requires "recalling the history of itinerancy and mobility" and "talking about mixing, blending and superimposing," in opposition to fundamentalist notions of "custom" and "autochthony." It requires attention to "vernacularisation" and decolonial practices of African modernity to reveal the "history of the rest of the world" in Africa, the belonging of Africans to the world, the incoherent domestication of the unfamiliar, and the refusal of victim identity.[134] However, rather than Mbembe's cogent emphasis on mobility, contemporary scholars have focused on his reference to "a culture of consumerism that partakes directly of the flows of globalization."[135]

My understanding of Afropolitanism returns to Mbembe's emphasis on mobility. Returnees in Old Calabar articulated a shared *mentalité* of being Africans on the move, embodying multiple legacies of captivity and slavery, colonial resettlement, ethnogenesis, racialization, and imperial modernity. Their sense of being Africans accentuated multiple belonging. They claimed both Old Calabar and Sierra Leone as home, despite European efforts to create colonial borders beyond which imperial subjects' freedom rights were not guaranteed. They retained African languages and enacted reunions with lost kin, but they also used English language, Christian identity, European dress, and transatlantic freedom discourses to cultivate mobility and economic uplift. Beyond autochthony and authenticity, they focus our attention on utilitarian and fluid performances of whiteness as well as claims of nativeness. Critics have observed that Afropolitanism is limited in the way it illuminates elite consumerism and mobility.[136] This challenge is real for historians because of the difficulties in enabling archived subalterns to speak. Liberated Africans were not an elite class in Old Calabar, where local slaveholding merchants and European traders and consuls held sway. Theirs was a subaltern politics of survival, rebellious mobility, monopoly subversion, and anti-imperial performances of freedom. But returnees' Afropolitanism equally reified the centrality of capitalism and European consumption of African resources in identity making in nineteenth-century West Africa. Returnees negotiated mobility and socioeconomic uplift by inserting themselves within imperial networks of transatlantic exchanges. And they exploited a category of less privileged Africans, domestic slaves, as labor to secure their own fragile freedoms. Like nineteenth-century liberalism, Afropolitanism did not birth freedom and the end of slavery. Rather, it reflected how radical and anti-imperial African reinterpretations of freedom were only possible when categories of African peoples denied freedom to others within imperial contexts.

Ndubueze L. Mbah is associate professor in the Department of History and the Department of Global Gender and Sexuality Studies at the State University of New York at Buffalo. He is a historian of West Africa in the Atlantic world and the author of the award-winning monograph *Emergent Masculinities: Gendered Power and Social Change in the Biafran Atlantic Age* (2019). This article is drawn from research completed for his ongoing second book project, sponsored by the American Council of Learned Societies and entitled "African Rebellious Migrants: The Forgery of Abolition and the Quest for Freedom."

Notes

1. Mbembe and Balakrishnan, "Pan-African Legacies," 35.
2. Mbembe and Balakrishnan, "Pan-African Legacies," 36–37.
3. Clifford, "Traveling Cultures," 96–116.
4. Walkowitz, *Cosmopolitan Style*.
5. Scanlan, *Freedom's Debtors*, 3–4.
6. Anderson, *Abolition in Sierra Leone*, 1.
7. Anderson, *Abolition in Sierra Leone*, 33; Lovejoy, "Departures from Calabar."
8. Anderson, "The Diaspora."
9. Anderson and Lovejoy, *Liberated Africans*.
10. Hutchinson to Malmesbury, Fernando Po, February 28, 1859, "Transmitting Information Concerning Two Sierra Leone Men Sent Back to Their Native Country from Old Kalabar," Slave Trade Dispatch 4, 3 Enclosures, 96–100, Slave Trade Bight of Biafra 1859, FO 84/1087, British National Archives, Kew (hereafter BNA).
11. Anderson, "The Diaspora"; Fyfe, "Four Sierra Leone Recaptives"; Ryan, "A Moral Millstone?"; Misevich, "On the Frontier of 'Freedom,'" 220, 224; Schwarz, "Impact"; Lovejoy and Anderson, "Introduction," 3; Prochnow, "'Perpetual Expatriation,'" 362; Schwarz, "Reconstructing the Life," 179, 183, 205; Cole, *The Krio*, 3–7, 126; Sundiata, *From Slavery to Neoslavery*, 21–37, 56–69, 119–26; Northrup, "Becoming African," 3; Adderley, *New Negroes*, 25–26; Roldán de Montaud, "Misfortune"; Castilho, "Abolition."
12. For the territorial limits of Liberated Africans' rights as British subjects, see Misevich, *Abolition*; Crooks, *A History*, 189; "A Bill Intituled 'An Act to Remove Doubts as to the Rights of the Liberated Africans in Sierra Leone' Brought from the House of Lords 11 August 1853," Parliamentary Archives: GB-06. https://archives.parliament.uk/collections /getrecord/GB61_HL_PO_PU_1_1853_16and17V1n320 (full text also here: https://www .pdavis.nl/Legis_53.htm); Macdonald to Earl Grey, November 27, 1851, 332–33, *British Parliamentary Papers: Slave Trade, Vol. 90* (Irish University Press, 1968). Old Calabar elites signed a treaty of abolition with Britain in 1842, but Old Calabar remained independent until 1884, when it became a protectorate. For the 1842 treaty, see McFarlan, *Calabar*, 8–9; Waddell, *Twenty-Nine Years*, 663–64. For the 1884 treaty, see International Court of Justice, "Case Concerning the Land and Maritime Boundary between Cameroon and Nigeria, Counter-Memorial of the Federal Republic of Nigeria," 90–97, 109, May 1999, https://www.icj-cij.org/public/files/case-related/94/8602.pdf; "Treaty between Great Britain and Old Calabar, with the accession of Tom Shot, Efut, and Idömmbi (West Africa), signed on board Her Britannic Majesty's ship 'Flirt', anchored in Old Calabar River, 10 September 1884," Oxford Historical Treaties, 163 CTS 182, https://opil .ouplaw.com/view/10.1093/law:oht/law-oht-163-CTS-182.regGroup.1/law-oht-163-CTS -182?rskey=KEFjsY&result=18&prd=OHT.
13. Buxton, *Remedy*, 159–74.

14. Mbah, *Emergent Masculinities*, 108.

15. Imbua, *Intercourse and Crosscurrents*.

16. Latham, *Old Calabar*, 32.

17. Latham, *Old Calabar*, 33.

18. Latham, *Old Calabar*, 32–33.

19. Aye, *Old Calabar*, 31–41.

20. McFarlan, *Calabar*, 14–30; Aye, "Foundations of Presbyterianism," 16.

21. Simmons, "An Ethnographic Sketch," 3–4; Lovejoy and Richardson, "Trust, Pawnship," 350.

22. Latham, *Old Calabar*, 91–95; Jones, "Political Organization," 134–35; Nair, *Politics and Society*, 54–57.

23. Jones, "Political Organization," 118, 154–57; Duke, "Diary," 46; Waddell, *Twenty-Nine Years*, 336–37, 476–79, 642–44, 651–52; Marwick, *William and Louisa Anderson*, 341.

24. Behrendt, Latham, and Northrup, *Diary of Antera Duke*, 57; Nair, *Politics and Society*, 66; Sparks, *Two Princes*, 11, 24, 46; Northrup, *Trade without Rulers*, 22–25; Lovejoy and Richardson, "Trust, Pawnship," 341–42; Crow, *Memoirs*, 7–10; Adams, *Remarks*, 144; Robertson, *Notes on Africa*, 1313.

25. Marwick, *William and Louisa Anderson*, 325–27, 346; Nair, *Politics and Society*, 98; Latham, *Old Calabar*, 29.

26. Latham, *Old Calabar*, 37–38.

27. Simmons, "An Ethnographic Sketch," 16; Consul Hutchinson's Letter to Clarendon, Clarence, Fernando Po, February 20, 1857, "Giving Relation of an Incipient Civil War in Old Calabar," Slave Trade No. 8, 127, FO 84/1030, BNA. Hutchinson wrote, "Despotic power" was the "main prop of the Egbo institution" and was used "to make the [slaves] feel that domestic slavery is still maintained" for their own well-being.

28. For the "trading slaves," see Marwick, *William and Louisa Anderson*, 326; Latham, *Old Calabar*, 96–101. For European ekpe membership, see Lovejoy and Richardson, "Trust, Pawnship," 349; Holman, *Travels*, 392–93; Hart, *Report of the Enquiry*, 167. For European reliance on ekpe to settle disputes in the 1850s and 1860s, see Hutchinson to Clarendon, Fernando Po, November 1, 1856, "Detailing Circumstances of a Complaint against Captain Davies for Refusing to Return to the Man Who Claimed It a Cask of Palm Oil Picked Up by His Krumen," Dispatch 128, 527–28, FO 84/1001, BNA.

29. Latham, *Old Calabar*, 95.

30. Marwick, *William and Louisa Anderson*, 325–27, 346.

31. For the use of ekpe against Liberated Africans, see Marwick, *William and Louisa Anderson*, 341–46; Anderson to Hutchinson, Duke Town Old Calabar, May 30, 1856, "Complaint against the King of Duke Town," Enclosure 1, Dispatch 71, 262–65, FO 84/1001, BNA. For corroboration, see Edgerly to Hutchinson, Duke Town Old Calabar May 30, 1856, "Complaint against King Duke Ephraim," Enclosure 2, Dispatch 71, 266–67, FO 84/1001, BNA; Hutchinson to Duke Ephraim, Fernando Po, June 4, 1856, "Letter to the King of Duke Town," Enclosure 4, Dispatch 71, 271–72, FO 84/1001, BNA; and Goldie, *Calabar and Its Mission*, 188–89.

32. *Church Missionary Intelligencer*, 253.

33. *Church Missionary Intelligencer*, 253–59.

34. Dike, *Trade and Politics*, 114, 117; Dike, "John Beecroft," 7, 12; Nwokeji, *Slave Trade and Culture*, 180; Oriji, *Political Organization*, 140–41. Lynn, "From Sail to Steam." In 1855, the British consul Lynslager estimated "the oil produced in [Old] Calabar in one

year" to be 4,000–5,000 tons. See Journal of Proceeding of Acting Consul J. B. Lynslager in the River Old Calabar, October 1855, No. 14 of October 31, 1855, p. 172, FO 84/975, BNA.

35. Anderson to Hutchinson, Duke Town Old Calabar, June 17, 1856, Dispatch 76, 322–24, FO 84/1001, BNA.

36. Marwick, *William and Louisa Anderson*, 350; Anderson to Hutchinson, Duke Town Old Calabar, June 17, 1856, Dispatch 76, 322–24, FO 84/1001, BNA.

37. For missionaries securing consular manumission papers for redeemed slaves, see Anderson to Hutchinson, Duke Town Mission House, Old Calabar, January 21, 1856, Enclosure 5, in Dispatch No. 11, Fernando Po, January 31, 1856, FO 84/1001, BNA; Hutchinson to Anderson, H.M.S.V. "Bloodhound," River Old Calabar, January 18, 1856, Enclosure 2, Dispatch 11, 132–33, FO 84/1001, BNA; List of Persons Names Who Received Manumission Papers, Enclosure 3, in Dispatch 11, Fernando Po, January 31, 1856, FO 84/1001, BNA. For foundation of the mission, see Aye, "Foundations of Presbyterianism"; McFarlan, *Calabar*, 8–12; "Copy of Documents Read by Rev. Waddell to Prove the Right of the Missionaries to the Ground Held by Them in Old Calabar," Fernando Po, June 24, 1856, Enclosure 6, Dispatch 71, 275–81, FO 84/1001, BNA.

38. Latham, *Old Calabar*, 103.

39. For the Liberated Africans Thomas Paul and Robert Boyle, whom Rev. Anderson fined for beating their wives, see Anderson to Hutchinson, Duke Town Mission House, Old Calabar, January 18, 1855, in Dispatch 11, 130–31, "Slave Trade, West Coast of Africa, Bight of Biafra, 1856," FO 84/1001, BNA; Hutchinson to Clarendon, Fernando Po, January 31, 1856, "Enclosing Copy of Mr. Anderson's Letter & Reply Thereto, Copy of Manumission Papers with List of Names, Copies of Two Addresses and Replies," Dispatch 11, 128–29, FO 84/1001, BNA.

40. Latham, *Old Calabar*, 109–11; Crow, *Memoirs*, 285.

41. Marwick, *William and Louisa Anderson*, 326.

42. Marwick, *William and Louisa Anderson*, 326.

43. Fyle, "The Saro," 125–38.

44. Murray, *Atlantic Passages*, 2–3.

45. Hutchinson to the Agents of the United Presbyterian Church Mission in Old Calabar, January 22, 1856, 144–45, FO 84/1001, BNA.

46. Clarendon to Hutchinson, Foreign Office, October 19, 1856, Slave Trade No. 29, 68–71, FO 84/1001, BNA.

47. Waddell to Hutchinson, Creek Town Old Calabar, May 8, 1858, "Rev. Mr. Waddell's Defense to the Charges Made against Him," Enclosure 10 in Slave Trade 22, 195–200, FO 84/1061, BNA; William Isam Hazeley to Hutchinson, Creek Town Old Calabar River, March 5, 1858, "Counter Charge Made by William Isam Hazeley against Mr. Michael Hearn," Enclosure 3, in Slave Trade 22, 178–80, FO 84/1061, BNA.

48. Nicholls to Cuthbertson, Duke Town Old Calabar, October 31, 1855, Enclosure 5, Dispatch 23, 163, FO 84/1001, BNA.

49. Nicholls to Lynslager, Fernando Po, November 2, 1855, Enclosure 4, Dispatch 23, 165, FO 84/1001, BNA.

50. Nicholls to Lynslager, Fernando Po, November 2, 1855, Enclosure 4, Dispatch 23, 165, FO 84/1001, BNA.

51. King Eyo to Lynslager, Creek Town, Old Calabar, January 19, 1855, "King Eyo's Declaration of the Only Mode for Recovering Debts in Old Calabar," Enclosure 2, in

Dispatch 14, 300, FO 84/1001, BNA; Journal of Proceeding of Acting Consul J. B. Lynslager in the River Old Calabar, October 1855, 175; Hutchinson to Captain Davies and the Supercargoes of Old Calabar River, and King Eyo Honesty of Creek Town, June 17, 1856, Enclosure 3, Dispatch 14, 302, FO 84/1001, BNA; Hutchinson to Clarendon, Fernando Po, March 12, 1856, Enclosure 23, Dispatch 12, 156–57, FO 84/1001, BNA.

52. Hutchinson to Clarendon, Fernando Po, March 12, 1856, "Enclosing Papers Relative to the Seizure of R. Nicoll's Oil in Old Calabar by Capt. Cuthbertson," Enclosure 23, Dispatch 12, 156–57, FO 84/1001, BNA.

53. Hutchinson to Clarendon, Fernando Po, March 12, 1856, Dispatch 23, 156–57, FO 84/1001, BNA.

54. Fyfe, "Peter Nicholls."

55. Marwick, *William and Louisa Anderson*, 334.

56. Marwick, *William and Louisa Anderson*, 334, 572–73. Nicholls deemed Old Calabar his homeland, and when he died in Freetown in 1880, he bequeathed £50 to the Duke Town mission.

57. Journal of Proceeding of Acting Consul J. B. Lynslager in the River Old Calabar, October 1855, 171.

58. Lynslager to Cuthbertson, Fernando Po, November 5, 1855, Enclosoure 5, Dispatch 23, 167–68, FO 84/1001, BNA.

59. Nicholls to Hutchinson, Freetown Sierra Leone, January 7, 1856, Enclosure 6, Dispatch 23, 169, FO 84/1001, BNA.

60. Nicholls to Smyth, Freetown, Sierra Leone, January 7, 1856, Enclosure 2, Dispatch 23, 161–62, FO 84/1001, BNA; Hill to Hutchinson, Government House Sierra Leone, January 12, 1856, Enclosure 1, Dispatch 23, 159–60, FO 84/1001, BNA; Hutchinson to Governor Hill, Cameroons River, February 6, 1856, Enclosure 9, Dispatch 23, FO 84/1001, BNA.

61. Hutchinson to Clarendon, Fernando Po, March 12, 1856, Dispatch 23, 156–57, FO 84/1001, BNA; Cuthbertson to Hutchinson, *Africa*, Old Calabar, February 5, 1856, Enclosure 8, Dispatch 23, 173, FO 84/1001, BNA; Hill to Consul Hutchinson, Government House Sierra Leone, January 12, 1856, Enclosure 1, Dispatch 23, 159–60, FO 84/1001, BNA; Hutchinson to Hill, Cameroons River, February 6, 1856, Enclosure 9, Dispatch 23, FO 84/1001, BNA; Hutchinson to Cuthbertson, Fernando Po, February 2, 1856, Enclosure 7, Dispatch 23, 71–72, FO 84/1001, BNA.

62. Hutchinson to Clarendon, Fernando Po, September 23, 1856, Dispatch 115, 425, FO 84/1001.

63. "Hutchinson Reply to the Calabar Supercargoes Request for Him to Proceed in a Man-of-War up the Cross River," Enclosure 2, Dispatch 93, 367–68, FO 84/1001, BNA.

64. Davies to Hutchinson, Ship *Calabar*, Old Calabar, October 13, 1856, "Detailing His Reasons for His Refusal for Returning Hedd's Oil," Enclosure 4, Dispatch 126, 512–53, FO 84/1001, BNA; Hutchinson to Clarendon, Clarence Fernando Po, September 29, 1856, Slave Trade 24, 416 [415–17], FO 84/1001, BNA; Dike, *Trade and Politics*, 118–19.

65. Hutchinson to Clarendon, Fernando Po, June 24, 1856, "Enquiries on the Subject of the Complaint Made by Messrs. Stuart and Douglass," Dispatch 74, 1856, 295, FO 84/1001, BNA.

66. Hutchinson to Clarendon, Fernando Po, June 24, 1856, "Transmitting a Complaint by a Sierra Leone Man against a Liverpool Supercargo for Having Forcibly Taken His Oil in Old Calabar," Dispatch 75, 304, FO 84/1001, BNA.

67. Hedd to Hutchinson, Mission Hill, Duke Town, May 21, 1856, Dispatch 75, 306, FO 84/1001, BNA.

68. Hutchinson to Clarendon, Fernando Po, November 1, 1856, "Giving Account of Further Proceedings for the Recovery of Daniel Hedd's Oil," Dispatch 126, 502–5, FO 84/1001, BNA.

69. Clarendon to Hutchinson, "Case of Daniel Hedd," Dispatch 75, 309–10, FO 84/1001, BNA. Also, see Hutchinson to Clarendon, September 29, 1856, Slave Trade 24, 415–17, FO 84/1001, BNA; Hutchinson to Davies, Fernando Po, October 8, 1856, "Requesting the Return of Daniel Hedd's Oil," Enclosure 2, Dispatch 126, 508, FO 84/1001, BNA.

70. Hutchinson to Clarendon, Fernando Po, September 23, 1856, "Containing the Results of Investigation into an Assault Committed on a British Supercargo by Some of the Natives at Old Calabar," Dispatch 115, 428–29, FO 84/1001, BNA; Hutchinson to Clarendon, Fernando Po, September 24, 1856, "Transmitting Code of Bye-Laws Sanctioned for the Better Regulation of Trade between the British and Native Traders at Old Calabar, with Grant of a Price of Ground from the King and a Letter from the Supercargoes," Dispatch 116, 457–60, FO 84/1001, BNA.

71. "Code of Bye-Laws for the Regulation of Trade in Old Calabar," Enclosure 1, Dispatch 116, 461–68, FO 84/1001, BNA.

72. Hutchinson to Clarendon, September 24, 1856, "Transmitting Code of Bye-Laws," Dispatch 116, 458–59, FO 84/1001, BNA. Consul Richard Burton later led the revision of these bylaws in 1862. See "Agreement between the British and Other Supercargoes and the Native Traders of Old Calabar," Old Calabar River, May 5, 1862, *British and Foreign State Papers, 1864–1865*, vol. 55 (London, 1870), 186–89. Burton also reported that the circumstances leading to the "re-establishment of the Court of Equity" were complaints from the "senior supercargoes" and complaints from "the Sierra Leone emigrants" against "the natives." See Burton to Earl Russell, Fernando Po, May 22, 1862 (received July 12), *British and Foreign State Papers, 1862–1863*, vol. 53 (London, 1868), 1288–1292.

73. Davies to Hutchinson, *Calabar*, Old Calabar, October 13, 1856, Enclosure 4, Dispatch 126, 512–13, FO 84/1001, BNA.

74. Hutchinson to Clarendon, Fernando Po, November 1, 1856, Dispatch 126, 504, FO 84/1001.

75. Hutchinson to Clarendon, Fernando Po, November 1, 1856, Dispatch 126, 504, FO 84/1001.

76. For a perspective of subaltern profiteering, see Olwell, "'Loose, Idle, and Disorderly.'"

77. Hutchinson to Clarendon, Fernando Po, November 1, 1856, Dispatch 126, 502–5, FO 84/1001.

78. Hutchinson to Clarendon, Fernando Po, November 1, 1856, Dispatch 126, 504, FO 84/1001.

79. Complaint of the Sierra Leone Residents at Old Calabar, May 30, 1856, Enclosure 1, Dispatch 76, 315, FO 84/1001, BNA.

80. Anderson to Hutchinson, Duke Town Old Calabar, June 17, 1856, Dispatch 76, 324–25, FO 84/1001, BNA.

81. Hutchinson to Clarendon, Clarence Fernando Po, June 24, 1856, Dispatch 76, 312–13, FO 84/1001.

82. Clarendon to Hutchinson, Foreign Office, October 19, 1856, Slave Trade 29, 68–69, FO 84/1001, BNA.

83. Clarendon to Hutchinson, Foreign Office, October 19, 1856, Slave Trade 29, 69–71, FO 84/1001, BNA; Hutchinson to Clarendon, Fernando Po, November 26, 1856, "Acknowledging the Receipt of Despatch Slave Trade 29 on the Subject of the Liberated Africans Resident at Old Calabar," Slave Trade 32, 563, FO 84/1001, BNA.

84. Memo on Hutchinson's No. 76 of June 24, 1856, Foreign Office, August 20, 1856, 326–31, FO 84/1001. For the consul's acknowledgment, see Hutchinson to Clarendon, Clarence, Fernando Po, September 29, 1856, Slave Trade No. 25, 419–20, FO 84/1001, BNA.

85. Effiong to Hutchinson, Duke Town, Old Calabar, October 25, 1856, "Statement of Etan Effiong's Claim on Capt. Davies for a Puncheon of Palm Oil," Enclosure in Dispatch 128, 529, FO 84/1001.

86. Waddell to Hutchinson, Creek Town Old Calabar, May 8, 1858, Enclosure 10, Dispatch 22, 195–200, FO 84/1061, BNA; Ephraim to Hutchinson, September 15, 1856, "King Duke's Application to Bind Over Capt. Cuthbertson to Keep the Peace," Enclosure 8, Dispatch 115, 451, FO 84/1001, BNA.

87. For an account of twenty men who attacked Cuthbertson, "knocked him down, split his head in three places," and struck him on the abdomen and testicles, see "Complaint of Supercargoes at Old Calabar," Old Calabar River, August 25, 1856, Enclosure 1, Dispatch 112, 406–7, FO 84/1001, BNA; "Copy of the Supercargoes Application to the Consul," Enclosure 1, Dispatch 115, 430–32, FO 84/1001, BNA; Hutchinson to Commander Robeck, H.M.S.S. Myrmidon, Old Calabar, September 15, 1856, Enclosure 7, Dispatch 115, FO 84/1001, BNA; Rev. Messrs. Anderson, Edgerly, and Baillie's Defense of Henshaw Duke, Enclosure 6, Dispatch 115, 445–47, FO 84/1001, BNA. For looting of the cask houses, see Hutchinson to Clarendon, Fernando Po, November 1, 1856, Dispatch 129, 531–32, FO 84/1001, BNA.

88. Duke Ephraim to Hutchinson, October 28, 1856, "Complaining of Captain Sterne's Having Abused Him," Enclosure 2, Dispatch 129, 535, FO 84/1001, BNA.

89. Hutchinson to Clarendon, Fernando Po, January 2, 1857, 88–89, FO 84/1030, BNA; Foreign Office Memo, Consul Hutchinson's No. 47 of August 20, 1857, 381–83, FO 84/1030, BNA.

90. Supercargoes to Hutchinson, Old Calabar River, July 25, 1857, Enclosure 2, Dispatch 50, 417–19, FO 84/1030, BNA.

91. Dike, *Trade and Politics*, 122.

92. "Copy of Letter from Bassey Henshaw Duke of Old Kalabar Charging a Sierra Leone Man Named 'William Hazeley' of Having Defrauded Him of Six Puncheons of Oil," March 1858, Enclosure 1, Dispatch 23, 222, FO 84/1061, BNA; "Copy of Letter from Yellow Duke of Old Kalabar Charging the Said 'William Hazeley' with Having Taken Palm Oil and Ebony from Him without Paying for It," May 8, 1858, Enclosure 2, Dispatch 23, 224, FO 84/1061, BNA; "Copy of Letter from Consul Hutchinson to Mr. Lewis of the Brig 'Olinda' on Board Whose Ship Bassey Henshaw Duke's Palm Oil Was Taken," May 8, 1858, Enclosure 3, Dispatch 23, 226, FO 84/1061, BNA; "Copy of Mr. Lewis' Reply Stating That He Paid the Man Hazeley for the Oil in Question," May 10, 1858, Enclosure 4, Dispatch 23, 228, FO 84/1061, BNA; Hutchinson to Malmesbury, Fernando Po, May 25, 1858, Dispatch 23, 220–21, FO 84/1061, BNA. For the identities of these "Duke-ward slaves," see Latham, *Old Calabar*, 99.

93. Hazeley to Hutchinson, Creek Town, Old Calabar, March 5, 1858, Enclosure 3, Dispatch 22, 178–80, FO 84/1061, BNA; Waddell to Hutchinson, Creek Town Old Calabar, May 8, 1858, Enclosure 10, Dispatch 22, 195–200, FO 84/1061, BNA.

94. Hutchinson to Governor Hill, Fernando Po, February 24, 1859, "Copy of Consul Hutchinson's Despatch to Governor Hill Explaining the Crimes Committed by the Sierra Leone Men in Old Kalabar," Enclosure 1, Dispatch 4, 102–7, FO 84/1087, BNA; See Enclosure 14 of Dispatch 22 in FO 84/1061, BNA; and Enclosure 1–6 of Dispatch 23, FO 84/1061, BNA.

95. Hutchinson to Hill, Fernando Po, February 28, 1859, Enclosure 1, Dispatch 4, 105 [102–7], FO 84/1087, BNA.

96. Hutchinson to Governor Hill, Fernando Po, February 28, 1859, 108.

97. Misevich, "On the Frontier of 'Freedom,'" 207–13.

98. Hutchinson to Governor Hill, Fernando Po, February 28, 1859, 105. Rev. Waddell's account of Eyo II's death fits with Feury's defense. See Waddell, *Twenty-Nine Years*, 642–44.

99. Hutchinson to Governor Hill, Fernando Po, February 28, 1859, 105–6.

100. Hutchinson to Governor Hill, Fernando Po, February 28, 1859, 106.

101. "Copy of Young Eyo's Complaint against a Resident of Fernando Po for Taking Away Five of His Slaves," Enclosure 3, Slave Trade No. 4, 110–11, FO 84/1087, BNA.

102. Lynslager to Malmesbury, August 31, 1858, Clarence, Fernando Po, "Transmitting Letter from King Eyo Honesty of Old Calabar Making a Complaint against Mr. Matthews of Fernando Po Taking Five of His Son's Slaves Away," Dispatch 3, 345–47, FO 84/1061, BNA.

103. Lynslager to Malmesbury, August 31, 1858, Dispatch 3, 345–47, FO 84/1061, BNA.

104. Lynslager to Malmesbury, August 31, 1858, Dispatch 3, 345–47, FO 84/1061, BNA.

105. King Duke Ephraim to Hutchinson, Duke Town Old Calabar, May 6, 1858, "Copy of Letter from King Duke Ephraim Requesting the Sierra Leone Men to Leave His Territory," Enclosure 5, Dispatch 23, 230, FO 84/1061, BNA.

106. Marwick, *William and Louisa Anderson*, 336.

107. Latham, *Old Calabar*, 104; Marwick, *William and Louisa Anderson*, 531.

108. Nair, *Politics and Society*, 165.

109. Latham, *Old Calabar*, 109.

110. For Consul Hutchinson's manumission of a slave girl "Fanny" and others, see Hutchinson to Malmesbury, Clarence, Fernando Po, May 25, 1858, "Transmitting List of the Names of Slaves to Whom Papers of Emancipation Have Been Granted," Dispatch 27, 268–70, FO 84/1061, BNA.

111. King Eyo to Lynslager, Creek Town, Old Calabar, August 25, 1858, Enclosure in Dispatch 3, 348, FO 84/1061, BNA.

112. Edgerly to Lynslager, Old Calabar, October 11, 1855, Enclosure 1, Dispatch 16, 213, "Slave Trade Bight of Biafra, 1855," FO 84/975, BNA.

113. Lynslager to Edgerly, Old Calabar, October 12, 1855, Enclosure 2, Dispatch 16, 215, FO 84/975, BNA.

114. Lynslager to Clarendon, October 31, 1855, Dispatch 16, 201–11, FO 84/975, BNA.

115. Martino, "Touts and Despots," 35.

116. Hutchinson to Clarendon, Clarence Fernando Po, June 24, 1856, "Transmitting List of Manumitted Slaves," Enclosure 77, Dispatch 13, 332, FO 84/1001, BNA.

117. "List of Manumitted Slaves," Enclosure 1, 2, and 3, Dispatch 77, FO 84/1001, BNA.

118. Latham, *Old Calabar*, 107.

119. Archibong III to Court of Equity, October 10, 1876, Calprof. 3/2, Nigerian National Archives Ibadan, cited in Nair, *Politics and Society*, 165–66. Also, Latham, *Old Calabar*, 108.

120. Commodore William Hewett to Consul McKellar, September 13, 1876, Calprof. 4/1, vol. 5, and Encl. James Africans Croker to Commodore William Hewett, July 20, 1876, cited in Nair, *Politics and Society*, 165.
121. Latham, *Old Calabar*, 108.
122. Hopkins to Foreign Secretary, August 28, 1878, No. 29, FO 84/1508, cited in Latham, *Old Calabar*, 108.
123. Hazeley to Consul Burton, Duke Town, Old Calabar, May 6, 1862, *British and Foreign State Papers, 1862–1863*, vol. 53 (London, 1868), 1295; Hutchinson to Russell, Fernando Po, February 28, 1860, "Acknowledging the Receipt of Slave Trade No. 23 Jan 23rd Containing Copy of Complaint Made against Me by a Man Named Hazeley at Sierra Leone," Dispatch 12, 126–30, FO84/1117, BNA; Dike, *Trade and Politics*, 124.
124. White to Earl Granville, Old Calabar, February 1, 1885, "Redeeming Slaves—Objections To," Dispatch 8, 1 Enclosure, 149–53, Africa (Slave Trade), West Coast, Consuls at Old Calabar, Hewett, White, 1885, FO 84/1701, BNA.
125. White to Granville, Old Calabar, February 1, 1885, "Redeeming Slaves—Objections To."
126. "Redeeming Slaves," Enclosure in Acting Consul White's Dispatch, February 1/85, "Africa (Slave Trade), West Coast, Consuls at Old Calabar, Hewett, White, 1885," FO 84/1701, BNA.
127. White to Granville, Old Calabar, February 1, 1885, Africa Dispatch 8, 149–53, FO 84/1701, BNA.
128. Vice Consul White to Earl Granville, Old Calabar, February 9, 1885, Africa Dispatch 13, received March 23, 1885, p. 166, "Africa (Slave Trade), West Coast, Consuls at Old Calabar, Hewett, White, 1885," FO 84/1701, BNA.
129. See minutes in White to Granville, Old Calabar, February 1, 1885, Africa Dispatch 8, 149–53, FO 84/1701, BNA.
130. Major MacDonald to Marquis of Salisbury (received June 12, 1889), Dispatch 11, Enclosures 5, 7, and 11, pp. 159–61, FO84/1940, BNA.
131. For the case of Theophilus Phillips, a "Sierra Leone man" against whom Consul Edward Hewett exercised such a "discretion" in prosecuting him for having "bought and sold a native girl" at Bonny, see Hewett to Granville, Bonny, December 23, 1884, Dispatch 43, 340–41, Slave Trade, Africa (West Coast), 1884, FO 84/1660, BNA; "Statements of Several Persons Respecting a Case of Slave Trading by Theophilus Phillips a British Subject," 342–54, No. 43, Enclosure 1, Slave Trade, Africa (West Coast), 1884, FO 84/1660, BNA.
132. Sidbury and Cañizares-Esguerra, "Mapping Ethnogenesis"; Blackburn, *Making of New World Slavery*, 5.
133. Frost, *Work and Community*; Rockel, *Carriers of Culture*; Lydon, *On Trans-Saharan Trails*; Lentz, *Land, Mobility, and Belonging*.
134. Mbembe, "Afropolitanism," 26–27.
135. Mbembe, "Afropolitanism," 29.
136. Dabiri, "Why I'm Not an Afropolitan."

References

Adams, John. *Remarks on the Country Extending from Cape Palmas to the River Congo: Including Observations on the Manners and Customs of the Inhabitants, with an Appendix Containing an Account of the European Trade with the West Coast of Africa*. London: G. & W. B. Whittaker, 1823.

Adderley, Rosanne Marion. *"New Negroes from Africa": Slave Trade Abolition and Free African Settlement in the Nineteenth-Century Caribbean*. Bloomington: Indiana University Press, 2006.

Anderson, Richard Peter. *Abolition in Sierra Leone: Re-building Lives and Identities in Nineteenth-Century West Africa*. Cambridge, UK: Cambridge University Press, 2020.

Anderson, Richard P. "The Diaspora of Sierra Leone's Liberated Africans: Enlistment, Forced Migration, and 'Liberation' at Freetown, 1808–1863." *African Economic History* 41 (2013): 101–38.

Anderson, Richard, and Henry B. Lovejoy, eds. *Liberated Africans and the Abolition of the Slave Trade, 1807–1896*. Rochester: University of Rochester Press, 2020.

Aye, Efiong U. *The Efik People*. Calabar, Nigeria: Association for the Promotion of Efik Language, Literature, and Culture, 2000.

Aye, Efiong U. "The Foundations of Presbyterianism among the Calabar Clans: Qua, Efik, Efut." In *A Century and Half of Presbyterian Witness in Nigeria, 1846–1996*, edited by Ogbu Kalu, 1–27. Enugu, Nigeria: Ida-Ivory Press, 1996.

Aye, Efiong U. *Old Calabar through the Centuries*. Calabar, Nigeria: Hope Waddell Press, 1967.

Behrendt, D. Stephen, A. J. H. Latham, and David Northrup. *The Diary of Antera Duke, an Eighteenth-Century African Slave Trader*. New York: Oxford University Press, 2010.

Blackburn, Robin. *The Making of New World Slavery: From the Baroque to the Modern, 1492–1800*. 2nd ed. London: Verso, 2010.

Buxton, Thomas Fowell. *The Remedy, Being a Sequel to the African Slave Trade*. London, 1840.

Castilho, Celso Thomas. "Abolition and Its Aftermath in Brazil." In *AD 1804–AD 2016*, vol. 4 of *The Cambridge World History of Slavery*, edited by David Eltis, Stanley Engerman, Seymour Drescher, and David Richardson, 486–510. Cambridge, UK: Cambridge University Press, 2017. https://doi.org.10.1017/9781139046176.022.

Church Missionary Intelligencer: A Monthly Journal of Missionary Information, vol. 4. London, 1853.

Clifford, James. "Traveling Cultures." In *Cultural Studies*, edited by Lawrence Grossberg, Cary Nelson, and Paula A. Treichler, 96–116. New York: Routledge, 1992.

Cole, Gibril. *The Krio of West Africa: Islam, Culture, Creolization, and Colonialism in the Nineteenth Century*. Athens: Ohio University Press, 2013.

Crooks, J. J. *A History of the Colony of Sierra Leone, West Africa*. London: Dublin, Browne and Nolan, 1903.

Crow, Hugh. *Memoirs of the Late Captain Hugh Crow, of Liverpool*. London: Longman, Rees, Orme, Brown, and Green, and G and J. Robinson, Liverpool, 1830.

Dabiri, Emma. "Why I'm Not an Afropolitan." *Africa Is a Country* (blog), January 21, 2014. https://africasacountry.com/2014/01/why-im-not-an-afropolitan.

Dike, Kenneth. "John Beecroft, 1790–1854: Her Britannic Majesty's Consul to the Bights of Benin and Biafra 1849–1854." *Journal of the Historical Society of Nigeria* 1, no. 1 (1956): 5–14.

Dike, Kenneth. *Trade and Politics in the Niger Delta, 1830–1885*. Oxford: Clarendon Press, 1956.

Dixon-Fyle, Mac. *A Saro Community in the Niger-Delta, 1912–1984*. Rochester: University of Rochester Press, 1999.

Duke, Antera. "The Diary (1785–8) of Antera Duke in a Modern English Version." In *Efik Traders of Old Calabar*, edited by Daryll Forde. London: Oxford University Press, 1956.

Frost, Diane. *Work and Community among West African Migrant Workers since the Nineteenth Century*. Liverpool: Liverpool University Press, 1999.

Fyfe, Christopher. "Four Sierra Leone Recaptives." *Journal of African History* 2, no. 1 (1961): 77–85.

Fyfe, Christopher. "Peter Nicholls: Old Calabar and Freetown." *Journal of the Historical Society of Nigeria* 2, no. 1 (1960): 105–114.

Goldie, Hugh. *Calabar and Its Mission.* Edinburgh: Morrison and Gibb, 1890.

Hart, A. Kalada. *Report of the Enquiry into the Dispute over the Obongship of Calabar.* Enugu, Nigeria: Government Printer, 1964.

Holman, James. *Travels in Madeira, Sierra Leone, Teneriffe, St. Jago, Cape Coast, Fernando Po, Princes Island, Etc. Etc.* 2nd ed. London, 1840.

Imbua, David Lishilinimle. *Intercourse and Crosscurrents in the Atlantic World: Calabar-British Experience, 17th–20th Centuries.* Durham, NC: Carolina Academic Press, 2012.

Jones, G. I. "The Political Organization of Old Calabar." In *Efik Traders of Old Calabar*, edited by Daryll Forde, 116–60. London: Oxford University Press, 1956.

Latham, A. J. H. *Old Calabar, 1600–1891: The Impact of the International Economy upon a Traditional Society.* London: Clarendon Press, 1973.

Lentz, Carola. *Land, Mobility, and Belonging in West Africa.* Bloomington: Indiana University Press, 2013.

Lovejoy, B. Henry, and Richard P. Anderson. "Introduction: Liberated Africans and Early International Court of Humanitarian Effort." In Anderson and Lovejoy, *Liberated Africans*, 1–22.

Lovejoy, Paul. "Departures from Calabar during the Slave Trade." In *Calabar on the Cross River: Historical and Cultural Studies*, edited by David Imbua, Paul Lovejoy, and I. L. Miller, 23–49. Trenton, NJ: Africa World Press, 2017.

Lovejoy, Paul, and David Richardson. "Trust, Pawnship, and Atlantic History: The Institutional Foundations of the Old Calabar Slave Trade." *American Historical Review* 104, no. 2 (1999): 333–55.

Lydon, Ghislaine Lydon. *On Trans-Saharan Trails: Islamic Law, Trade Networks, and Cross-Cultural Exchange in Nineteenth-Century Western Africa.* New York: Cambridge University Press, 2009.

Lynn, Martin. "From Sail to Steam: The Impact of the Steamship Services on the British Palm Oil Trade with West Africa, 1850–1890." *Journal of African History* 30, no. 2 (1989): 227–45.

Martino, Enrique. "Touts and Despots: Recruiting Assemblages of Contract Labour in Fernando Pó and the Gulf of Guinea, 1858–1979." PhD diss., Humboldt-Universitat zu Berlin, 2016.

Marwick, William. *William and Louisa Anderson: A Record of Their Life and Work in Jamaica and Old Calabar.* Edinburgh, 1897.

Mbah, Ndubueze L. *Emergent Masculinities: Gendered Power and Social Change in the Biafran Atlantic Age.* Athens: Ohio University Press, 2019.

Mbembe, Achille. "Afropolitanism," translated from the French by Laurent Chauvet. In *Africa Remix: Contemporary Art of a Continent*, edited by Simon Njami, 26–27. Johannesburg, South Africa: Jacana Media, 2007.

Mbembe, Achille, and Balakrishnan, Sarah. "Pan-African Legacies, Afropolitan Futures: A Conversation with Achille Mbembe." *Transition*, no. 120 (2016): 28–37.

McFarlan, Donald. *Calabar: The Church of Scotland Mission, 1846–1946.* London: Thomas Nelson and Sons, 1946.

Misevich, Philip. *Abolition and the Transformation of Atlantic Commerce in Southern Sierra Leone.* Trenton, NJ: Africa World Press, 2019.

Misevich, Philip. "On the Frontier of 'Freedom': Abolition and the Transformation of Atlantic Commerce in Southern Sierra Leone, 1790s to 1860s." PhD diss., Emory University, 2009.

Murray, Robert. *Atlantic Passages: Race, Mobility, and Liberian Colonization.* Gainesville: University Press of Florida, 2021.

Nair, K. Kannan. *Politics and Society in South-Eastern Nigeria, 1841–1906: A Study of Power, Diplomacy, and Commerce in Old Calabar.* London: Frank Cass, 1972.

Northrup, David. "Becoming African: Identity Formation among Liberated Slaves in Nineteenth-Century Sierra Leone." *Slavery and Abolition* 27, no. 1 (2006): 1–21.

Northrup, David. *Trade without Rulers: Pre-colonial Economic Development in South-Eastern Nigeria.* Oxford: Clarendon, 1978.

Nwokeji, Ugo. *The Slave Trade and Culture in the Bight of Biafra: An African Society in the Atlantic World.* New York: Cambridge University Press, 2010.

Olwell, Robert. "'Loose, Idle, and Disorderly': Slave Women in the Eighteenth-Century Charleston Marketplace." In *More Than Chattel: Black Women and Slavery in the Americas*, edited by David Gasper and Darlene Hine, 97–110. Bloomington: Indiana University Press, 1996.

Oriji, John N. *Political Organization in Nigeria since the Late Stone Age: A History of the Igbo People.* New York: Palgrave Macmillan, 2011.

Prochnow, Kyle. "'Perpetual Expatriation': Forced Migration and Liberated African Apprenticeship in the Gambia." In Anderson and Lovejoy, *Liberated Africans*, 347–64.

Robertson, G. A. *Notes on Africa; Particularly Those Parts which are Situated between Cape Verde and the River Congo.* London, 1819.

Rockel, Stephen J. *Carriers of Culture: Labor on the Road in Nineteenth-Century East Africa.* Portsmouth, NH: Heinemann, 2006.

Roldán de Montaud, Inés. "The Misfortune of Liberated Africans in Colonial Cuba, 1824–76." In Anderson and Lovejoy, *Liberated Africans*, 153–73.

Ryan, Maeve. "'A Moral Millstone'? British Humanitarian Governance and the Policy of Liberated African Apprenticeship, 1808–1848." *Slavery and Abolition* 37, no. 2 (2016): 399–422.

Scanlan, Padraic X. *Freedom's Debtors: British Antislavery in Sierra Leone in the Age of Revolution.* New Haven: Yale University Press, 2017.

Schwarz, Suzanne. "The Impact of Liberated African 'Disposal' Policies in Early Nineteenth-Century Sierra Leone." In Anderson and Lovejoy, *Liberated Africans*, 45–65.

Schwarz, Suzanne. "Reconstructing the Life Histories of Liberated Africans: Sierra Leone in the Early Nineteenth Century." *History in Africa* 39 (2012): 175–207.

Sidbury, James, and Jorge Cañizares-Esguerra. "Mapping Ethnogenesis in the Early Modern Atlantic." *William and Mary Quarterly* 68, no. 2 (2011): 181–208.

Simmons, Donald. "An Ethnographic Sketch of the Efik People." In *Efik Traders of Old Calabar*, edited by Daryll Forde. London: Oxford University Press, 1956.

Sparks, Randy J. *The Two Princes of Calabar: An Eighteenth-Century Atlantic Odyssey.* Cambridge, MA: Harvard University Press, 2004.

Sundiata, Ibrahim. *From Slavery to Neoslavery: The Bight of Biafra and Fernando Po in the Era of Abolition, 1827–1930.* Madison: University of Wisconsin Press, 1996.

Waddell, Hope Masterton. *Twenty-Nine Years in the West Indies and Central Africa: A Review of Missionary Work and Adventure, 1829–1858.* London, 1863.

Walkowitz, R. L. *Cosmopolitan Style: Modernism beyond the Nation.* New York: Columbia University Press, 2006.

Oral Histories in the Black Pacific

Women, Memory, and the Defense of the Territory

Antonia Carcelén-Estrada

I first saw the portrait *Los dones de Esmeraldas* (1599) by Andrés Sánchez-Gallque in Madrid in 2009, where the weary eye of the guard over my shoulder and the multitude of tourists prevented me from taking pictures of decent quality. I took the tourist photograph and moved on. The second time I encountered the painting was in 2019, after it had crossed the Atlantic Ocean for the first time since 1599 and was exhibited at Ecuador's National Museum (MUNA). I should note that though in Spain I am a colonial subject, in Ecuador I belong to Quito's cultural white-mestizo elite.[1] *Mestizo* refers to a person of mixed lineage, European and Indigenous, and the term is often used to whiten the postcolonial population of Ecuador and erase colonial difference. This racial ideology of whitening promotes mixing with lighter-skinned people to create a population that appears more European and modern with little reference to the colonial past. The myth of *mestizaje* (mixing up) was heavily promoted through literature and popular culture since the beginning of the twentieth century, when the concept of Latin America sought to reinscribe the definition of the continent as no longer a Spanish colony but still a European-like land and peoples. In a tripartite colonial racial grammar, the Ecuadorian white-mestizo elite (purportedly without race) have access to capital and property and stand above the racialized Indigenous and Afro-descendant populations, who are impoverished, unattended, and unheard.

I was allowed to spend time alone with the painting. This time the guard acted as a lone audience member to the story of Esmeraldas's incommensurate history. My

Radical History Review

Issue 144 (October 2022)   DOI 10.1215/01636545-9847816

© 2022 by MARHO: The Radical Historians' Organization, Inc.

Figure 1. Author with
painting by MUNA, digital
photograph by Titi
Carcelén, 2018.

Figure 2. Portrait of *Los dones de Esmeraldas* (1599), by Andrés Sánchez Gallque, digital photograph by Titi Carcelén, 2018.

sister Titi, a professional photographer, was also there and snapped the details I was looking for: hats, signature, text, eyes, and strokes. This, the most famous portrait in colonial Spanish America, captures the distortion of Esmeraldas's past and present through the dissemination of an image (and a gaze) that disregards power and gender relations in the production of historical sources, archives, and narratives by completely omitting women of the African diaspora from the historical imagination.

The portrait's unveiling at MUNA on May 18, 2019 was an event for Quito's white-mestizo elite. It came accompanied by the art historian Andrés Gutiérrez Usillos's radiographic and sociohistorical study of *Los mulatos de Esmeraldas*, as the painting is known in the Spanish museums that commissioned the study.[2] In EFE's reporting of the unveiling, the Spanish news agency's journalist got the painter's name wrong, referring to him as Gualque, while art historians who were interviewed referred to the men in the painting as *mulatos*, taking the Spanish nomenclature as opposed to the painter's, who had called them *dones* in the portrait itself.[3] The Indigenous painter had chosen not a racial term but an honorific. At MUNA, four white-mestizo men wearing lab coats skillfully hung the painting on the dark, grey wall. The museum's director, Ivette Celi, nostalgically proclaimed, "It is like receiving a piece of one's own history that proves we are a diverse and complex territory."[4] Yet, of the story of the Arobe family featured in the painting, of Esmeraldas's Indigenous and African diasporic coastal nations—*nada*. Not a peep from Celi to historicize this complexity. Cast in this way, what happened in Esmeraldas was irrelevant historiographic material because what mattered was that MUNA had collaborated with El Prado, Spain's flagship museum, and that the painting had returned "home." This event legitimized MUNA's rebranding from an old-fashioned archive that for decades had piled up archeological remains and melted them for gold.

Although the new museum hoped to be "intercultural," the white-mestizo gaze was too deeply racist to be inclusive of other people's narratives. The new professional team working under the Ministry of Culture now had a clear national narrative of Ecuador's past, but it inevitably remained a white-mestizo history, one that clung to a relationship with Spain and its viceregal past. EFE's news clip ends with a panning shot of MUNA's entrance, where, as part of the museum rebranding, now sits a colorful sculpture of an Afro-Ecuadorian woman carrying baskets with both arms and a heavy load on her head.

The painting did not return "home" on its visit to Ecuador. Even though MUNA had just rebranded its Esmeraldas branch, now that the coastal museum exhibited selected archeological remains that highlighted a narrative of a foregone pre-Columbian past, its narrative of Esmeraldas suggests historical stasis, as if nothing had happened there since its conquest in 1599. There is no mention of anticolonial wars in the past centuries nor of Black women's activism in the present. Ironically, in Quito no Afro-Ecuadorian artists, activists, or plain citizens were invited to participate in such a monumental moment for history, which passed unnoticed, as many events of this historical magnitude do because of structurally racist narratives of Ecuador's past and present. Even if Afro-Ecuadorian women had been at the unveiling, they would have been policed because "they don't belong" there, according to a genocidal logic that denies the presence of Black women, in particular, in every space, except in exploited roles in service or entertainment, as the sculpture at the MUNA entrance crystallizes.[5]

In *Silencing the Past* (1995), Michel-Rolph Trouillot argued that colonial power relations erase facts, trivialize the historical events of the colonies, and privilege a Eurocentric notion of a fixed past, all complicit with the silencing of Haitian history.[6] This positivist narrative conceives slave revolution as "unthinkable"; the inconceivable Haitian Revolution fits in the narrative as distorting metaphor.[7] He concludes that "effective silencing does not require a conspiracy, not even a political consensus. Its roots are structural."[8] As in Haiti, the historical events of Esmeraldas are trivialized, and it has been impossible to conceive of this land as free, much less as anti-colonial and anti-patriarchal. The crafting of national memory at MUNA is just one example of the structural silencing of Esmeraldas's history and the role of Black women in it.

Xenophobia, though discursively rooted in narratives of hierarchy and othering, is different from racism in that the racialized experiences of marked ethnic groups shift through migration, while colonial racism on a body that is racialized as Black or Indigenous operates similarly across colonial borders, which is why Trouillot's analysis is relevant to Esmeraldas decolonial historiography. Eurocentric versions of public history can affect the ways in which historians approach the documents available to them. A Eurocentric obsession with the history of conquest in Esmeraldas has shaped the narrow narratives that historians have written on the region. Contemporary racialized territories remain trapped in that single moment in the past, a "chronotope" that functions as source of nostalgia and producer of national amnesia.[9] In the case of Esmeraldas, that fixed point in time-space is its conquest by Spain rather than its role in Ecuador's revolutions, which remain unthinkable despite Esmeraldas's *afroecuatoriano* population having fought in all major revolutions, most significantly as protagonists in the Liberal Revolution (1895–1925), particularly the Guerra de Concha (1913–16), the longest civil war in Ecuadorian history. Rather than stories of participation in the Shell Revolution, textbooks emphasize Ecuador's railroad system and cocoa and coffee export to sum up the liberal success. The same way that Trouillot obscures the roles of women in the Haitian Revolution, so does the history of Esmeraldas as portrayed in this painting. A Eurocentric, patriarchal historiography perpetuates conquest and war, and so does its counternarratives complicitly trapped "in a cage of melancholy."[10]

The Afropolitan turn brings new perspectives on history that avoid this temporal cage. Yet, as Janice Ho argues, the class binaries that structure critiques of Afropolitanism—mobile versus static, elite versus impoverished, bourgeois versus proletarian, diasporic versus continental Africans—do not fully capture the range, flux, and complexity of social class as lived experience and aspirational identity under globalization.[11] Thus, even as the Afropolitan turn reconsiders liberation struggles, displaces Afrocentrism, and sees a multiracial African modernity for the diaspora, I can't help but notice that this new "philosophy of history"[12] and "global entanglement"[13] in the experience of being African is a universalizing story of cosmopolitanism and privilege that disregards the race, gender, and class structures that make mobility (im)possible.

For women of the African diaspora in Spanish America, there is no escaping the gendered, racialized experience of past and present intercultural relations. Even at home, families still see each other in terms of "colorism," a by-product of mestizaje, which is an aspirational post-racial identity that, like Afropolitanism, hopes to overcome coloniality and achieve a global citizenship in parity with the cosmopolitan Global North. Women in Esmeraldas, on the contrary, demand a history that calls out colonial differences and class privilege, and they demand their own visibility in the making of Esmeraldas history while using that history to slow down migration to urban centers by creating new economies at home.

What does an intersectional approach to Esmeraldas's past look like when Black women are absent from the portrait, the exhibit, narrative, and memory itself? Organized women in the Black Pacific are not waiting for historians to lead the way. Using oral history and the repertoire of Chocó's diasporic memory, they have produced narratives of joy and happiness to counter the heavy narrative of suffering and victimhood seen in archival documents and historical narratives alike.[14] In this they agree with another tenet of the Afropolitan, by which Simon Gikandi urges scholars to find a language outside the trope of crisis to "overcome the malady of Afropessimism."[15] Therefore, Afropolitanism may seem to be an elitist framework, but it can be useful for inserting the history of Esmeraldas in a global context, though it cannot represent the whole experience of being African in the diaspora.

Women defend the South American Pacific with a grounded memory that rejects migration and dispossession as a reality. Their efforts to write their history then challenge a celebration of globalization or a multiracial experience with its cosmopolitan "liquidation of space" that undermines the territory as a political category.[16] The experience of women on the ground greatly differs from the international jet set in London, Paris, Boston, or New York, and may offer a different conceptualization of what Afropolitanism could entail. In this article, I explore the Black Pacific's gendered conceptions of territory and its impact on the legacy of Afro-Pacific women, their political organization, and epistemic contributions in the Chocó, a mangrove territory dominated by African diasporic communities that covers coastal territories from Northern Colombia to Ecuador, including Esmeraldas, and which figures at the heart of the Black Pacific.

To do this, I first look at how women are erased from the colonial archive, as evidenced in the documents at the Archivo General de Indias, Seville, that narrate the conquest of Esmeraldas from the point of view of Christian men at holy war, although portrayed differently in Sánchez-Gallque's painting. I then contrast the gendered and patriarchal representations of colonialism in Esmeraldas, the Ecuadorian Chocó, with women's histories that emerge from the paper trail left at colonial courts, where, with only their word (all they had was a court statement),

Figure 3. Map of the Chocó region on the Ecuadorian and Colombian Pacific.

enslaved women consistently fought for freedom through the eighteen century until the end of Spanish colonialism in South America. This legacy of liberation exposed by Afro-Latina scholars such as Aurora Vergara-Figueroa, Carmen Cosme, and Castriela Hernández finds echoes in today's autonomous resistance in *palenques*, the free territories in the Pacific founded by the African diaspora facing the threat of a neoliberal colonialism. These territories are defended by Black women who hold their ground and use oral history and critical feminist geography to produce a history that heals and a narrative of return to the dispossessed land. I end with a reflection on the decolonial methodologies engaged by scholars and activists in these projects, which might be useful for researchers doing intersectional work across historical periods to unearth the deep history of a region.

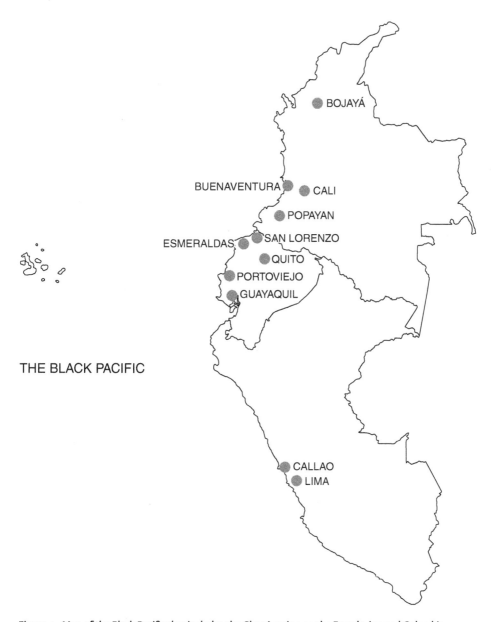

THE BLACK PACIFIC

Figure 4. Map of the Black Pacific that includes the Chocó region on the Ecuadorian and Colombian Pacific and extends into the Peruvian coasts.

Colonial Narratives of Conquest

In the very conception of Esmeraldas as an early modern Spanish colonial frontier in the Pacific coast, there are racial and gendered tensions that relate to the silencing of Black women in Latin-American postcolonial history. Esmeraldas generated a great number of documents surrounding its pacification, from chronicles to petitions and from rectifications to court statements. One such petition reads,

> Tiene puertos en la costa de mar del sur . . . convendría abrirse por [Esmeraldas] camino para desde el Reyno de tierra firme de Quito y echar de allí a un negro cimarrón que está gobernando en lo que de la dicha provincia está descubierto . . . también porque se entiende que en ella hay muchas minas de oro y de esmeraldas y otros aprovechamientos de que la Real Hacienda de Vuestra Majestad podrá ser acrecentada.

> Esmeraldas has ports in the Southern Sea. . . . It would be convenient to open a path [to Esmeraldas] from this landlocked Kingdom of Quito and chase out a *runaway slave* who governs the discovered lands of this province . . . and because there abound gold and emerald mines and many other resources that could increase Your Majesty's state. (spelling modernized, emphasis added)[17]

The *cimarrón* Spanish settlers wanted to "chase out" was Francisco Arobe, a free man who defied the *castas* system of racial categories that sought to dominate Black and Indigenous peoples.[18] He stood in the way of resource extraction. The *criollos* (creoles), as Spanish-American settlers were then called (today they go by *mestizos*), described the Arobe men as their tyrant enemy, an obstacle to the king's prosperity, dangerous fugitives who subjugated innocent Indigenous peoples.

The conquest of Esmeraldas was a vague attempt to conceal the sense of impotence among criollo settlers after Spain's king punished them at the consolidation of Quito's Spanish colonial order in the aftermath of the Alcabalas revolt. The fight had ensued between the president of the Real Audiencia de Quito, Manuel Barros de San Millán, and criollo *oidores* (member judges).[19] In 1585, Barros became president and overseer of the Real Audiencia de Quito, sent from Lima's Viceroyalty to supervise the town council bureaucrats who favored heavy taxation on Indians and their forced labor.[20] A graduate of the University of Salamanca, Barros was inspired by the humanist doctrine of the Dominican jurist Bartolomé de las Casas, who defended the self-governance of Indigenous nations. Barros opposed the town council's bureaucrats, who supported the claim of Las Casas's rival Juan Ginés de Sepúlveda that Indians were natural slaves while Spaniards were naturally predisposed to God.[21] Upon arriving to Quito, Barros brought criollo member judges to court, registering five counts against Pedro Venegas de Cañaveral as well as other accusations against Francisco de Auncibay. Next, Barros forbade peon labor and decreed Indigenous salaries should be commensurate with inflation, "cuando fuere creciendo el valor de las cosas, crezca el precio del sudor de los indios" (when the value of things increase, so does the value of Indian sweat).[22] While he proclaimed, "I have come to give you freedom in the name of the king,"[23] criollos accused him instead of reducing taxation and helping Indians "to the point of shame and temerity" (que daba atrevimiento y osadía).[24] Before serving as president, Barros had already escaped the stake twice for homosexuality, *pecado nefando*, so Quito's bureaucrats reacted against his immoral Indigenist policies in a land "que antes estaba rica y próspera, se iba acabando" (previously rich and prosperous, and now eroding and suffering), and accused him of "*mal gobierno, poca cristiandad y mala conciencia*" (bad government, poor Christendom, and a foul conscience).[25]

Barros's fiercest enemy was member judge Lic. Cabezas de Meneses. First, he ridiculed Las Casas's Dominican sympathizers by writing libelous, satirical verses. Then, he wrote a letter to the king denouncing Barros for failing to recognize the king's authority while claiming to be a descendant of the Incas and their historic leader Túpac Amaru.[26] Cabezas closed his epistle accusing Barros of having said that "el turco con ser infiel hacía más justicia que su Majestad siendo cristiano" (Turks as infidels do more justice than Your Majesty who is a Christian) and other "scandalous words."[27] When Barros renewed *alcabala* taxation, following the orders of Lima's new viceroy Don García Hurtado de Mendoza, Cabezas found the perfect excuse to end him: he schemed a murder complot, an incident that in 1592 unleashed the crisis of the Alcabalas, described as follows.[28]

Barros's murder attempt began with a city covered in posters addressed to Quito's councilmen, warning them against a president who inflicted pain on people: "Mira bien que os trae engañados equeste eunuco maldito" (Look carefully who has deceived you, this damned eunuch).[29] After surviving his murder attempt, Barros imprisoned several councilmen, which led to a siege of his palace until he released the criollo prisoners. Convinced of their victory, the councilmen celebrated Saint Jerome the next day with jousting and bullfights, "con toros y cañas," while Barros secretly wrote to Viceroy Mendoza in Lima, a military expert who sent General Arana to crush Quito's elite and "put criollos on their knees."[30] Cabezas's enemies from Loja to Riobamba in the South of the Audiencia joined Arana in his military advance to Quito. When they finally arrived on the eve of Palm Sunday 1593, Arana unleashed unprecedented tyranny and horror.[31] Daily at the main square (Plaza Mayor), he hanged decapitated bodies and demanded "public celebrations" for Easter Sunday—celebrations for his triumph over Quito's criollos. King Philip II forbade Quito's councilmen to hold elections for 108 years.[32] This blow revived the criollos' desire to reach the sea and pacify Esmeraldas to circumvent Lima's taxation and freely export Quito's goods, like Otavalo textiles.

Esmeraldas was a diverse region of Indigenous and *palenque* nations who worked to control the maritime trade passing by Cape San Lorenzo and on the way from Panama to Lima. Indigenous caciques, many of them hailing from the Chibcha cultural region, spanning Colombia and Ecuador from Portoviejo to Popayán, had allied with the cimarrones and Francis Drake to sink trading ships passing by Cape San Lorenzo.[33] Meanwhile, the precolonial Tolita of Esmeraldas controlled overland trade throughout the Pacific region.[34] Through alliances with Chibcha caciques and Tolita communities, Esmeraldas's cimarrones gained access to impressive human and cultural capital. Two Afro-Sevillian men, Don Alonso de

Yllescas and Francisco de Arobe, rose to be prominent leaders a generation after the first shipwrecks in the 1540s and 1550s. They adopted the clothing of Indigenous people and married *cacicas*, women with political power.[35] Esmeraldas's cimarrones and caciques used the bays to ambush Spanish ships carrying gold and silver to the Caribbean, silks and spices from Asia, and enslaved men to the Andes. The Spanish king clearly had an interest in pacifying Esmeraldas.

The failed attempts to conquer Esmeraldas include Tomás López's in 1559, Captain Diego de Zúñiga's, who left *"desbaratado"* (unhinged),[36] and Andrés Contero's, with powers from both Viceroy Toledo as well as Quito's Audiencia.[37] Contero fled right back to Guayaquil city.[38] After such defeats, the king personally selected Rodrigo de Rybadeneira to enter with 190 men, more men than those present in Pizarro's conquest of Cuzco, the Inca capital; he even ordered 150 men without proof of blood,[39] "sin pedir información ninguna," to be sent to the Esmeraldas front.[40] Religious failed attempts to conquer Esmeraldas feature Miguel Cabello Balboa's alliance with Cayapa caciques to establish communication with the African *dones* and settle Mercedarian towns in the 1570s,[41] and a faint advance by the Trinitarian bachelor Espinosa.[42] Upon his crowning in 1598, Philip III authorized another pacification of Esmeraldas, this time under Barrios de Sepúlveda, the member judge appointed to replace Cabezas after the Alcabalas crisis. Barrios entered with two Mercedarian friars, Fr. Gaspar de Torres and Fr. Francisco de Burgos, hoping to "convert the savages" by means of philosophical persuasion, so that the three dones of Esmeraldas, Francisco de Arobe and his two sons, "salidos de la selva" (out from the jungle), traveled with them to Quito, letting criollos believe they had been pacified.[43] The bishop himself baptized the Arobes in the cathedral. While these Esmeraldas leaders could not exert real political power in a mostly matriarchal Tolita society, they could play the script of a Spanish theatricality of power to unsettle the masculinity of the criollo elite. They succeeded. Barrios commissioned Indigenous artist Andrés Sánchez Gallque, from the Dominican Guild of the Rosary to paint their portrait (a genre reserved for nobles and saints until the seventeenth-century works by Rubens or Velásquez).

But Gallque's painting articulated a discourse of resistance that countered the colonial order through scattered encoded messages that, in turn, also reflected his own autonomy and masculinity as Indigenous. Educated in Spanish, Kichwa, and Latin, he had a privileged position to do so. The portrait features Don Francisco de Arobe, then fifty-six years old, at the center with his two sons by his side. They wear fine Asian silks. This orientalist gaze reveals an expanding anxiety over a fragile colonial identity that emerges in the Andean landscape by complying with Counter-Reformation binaries whereby Christian men defeat enemies from the "Orient,"[44] the "epitome of lechery, debauchery, sodomy, and a whole battery of assorted treacheries."[45] This gendered religious difference racialized early modern bodies under the logic of a just war against Islam. But the dones also wear gorgets like those in Mali's wooden figurines from Central West African, a region where many of the enslaved people in Spanish America came from. His African lineage contradicts his status of nobility in the honorific *Don*, which purportedly granted him Spanish *privilegios de honra*, the right to bear weapons and own property, which no African could exercise in Christian Iberian lands whether in Seville or the Americas. In his right hand, Francisco holds a black-palm spear, "a characteristic garment among the savage Indians all over South America."[46] With his left hand he holds a Spanish hat with copper borders, perhaps removed as sign of reverence to the king, but his son's hat faces inward, breaking the protocol of salute. Arobe's right hand trumps his left. Similarly, his sons Pedro, twenty-two, at his right, and Domingo, eighteen, at his left, ignore altogether the viewer/king and look straight into their father's eyes. Arobe looks straight ahead and does not bow.

On top of the canvas features a banner that reads, in Latin, "Philippo 3 Catholico Regi Hispaniar Indiar Q3 Dño Svo Doctor Joanes Del Barrio A Sepúlveda Avditor Sve Cancillería del Quito Svis Expensis Fie Ri Cvravit Anno 1599" (Doctor Juan del Barrio de Sepúlveda, Judge of the Real Audiencia de Quito, commissioned this painting at his expense, and that of the Indies). Gallque signs his name in caps and in larger font, ADR SHS GALQ, and in small shorthand he writes, "*nt. de qto. ft.*" (made by a Native from Quito). Like the men depicted, the painter refuses his colonial subjugation. While using aesthetic techniques and styles demanded by his masters, he still managed to subvert this hierarchical relation with layered images of early modern masculinities whereby neither Indians nor Africans stood below Spanish criollos. Free men do not fit into terms like *negro* or *indio*. As performative as Quito's criollo power was, no one respected it, not Lima, not Esmeraldas, not Gallque. Indeed, this criollo triumph over Esmeraldas was short-lived. Settler colonialism failed at every turn and the province remained a free *palenque* until the close of the eighteenth century. *Los dones de Esmeraldas* reveals this tension over governance in early modern Quito and questions this frail Spanish triumph over Andean souls.

For criollos in Quito, Esmeraldas represented more than just a place: it was the land of salvation, the promise of riches, and the gate to its liberation from Peru. This colonial tension is revealed behind the painting of *Los dones de Esmeraldas*, sent to Spain as a gift for the inauguration of King Philip III. In a letter signed in Valladolid in 1602, soon after receiving the portrait, Philip III acknowledged the importance of opening a path from Quito to Esmeraldas.[47] Upon receiving Gallque's portrait, Philip III had irrefutable proof of his triumph over the cimarrones, so he went ahead and authorized the government of Quito to open its desired path to the sea.

The Esmeraldas shipwrecks from the 1540s and 1550s are considered the most famous episodes in the colonial history of the Pacific. Among their survivors were the Arobe and Yllescas families, but they were only an example of many more *zambos* and mulattos who joined the local caciques,[48] claiming their freedom and

Figure 5. *Los dones de Esmeraldas* (1599), gorget and spear detail.

Figure 6. *Los dones de Esmeraldas* (1599), Francisco de Arobe, detail.

Figure 7. *Los dones de Esmeraldas* (1599), Pedro, detail.

Figure 8. *Los dones de Esmeraldas* (1599), Domingo and text, detail.

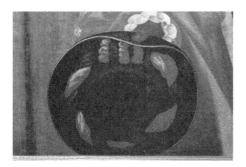

Figure 9. *Los dones de Esmeraldas* (1599),
Franscisco's hat, detail.

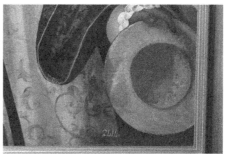

Figure 10. *Los dones de Esmeraldas* (1599),
Domingo's hat, detail.

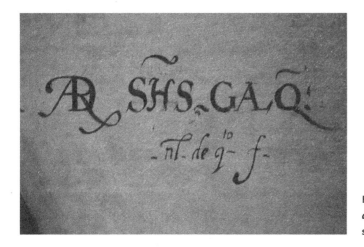

Figure 11. *Los dones
de Esmeraldas* (1599),
signature, detail.

living together in *palenques* as lords of their world, "amos y señores de sus mundos."[49] This colonial story celebrates the mixing of the brown races, the *zambaje* that results from a Black man and an Indigenous woman, excluding Black women who, generation after generation, have the burden to whiten their progeny. In Ecuador's mestizo racial grammar, Black women have no place, and lighter Black women are treated more favorably than their darker relatives. There is a constant pressure to mix into *zambaje* or *mulataje* and leave Blackness behind. This pressure is centuries long. We know nothing of Francisco de Arobe's wife nor if he had any daughters, but chances are he did. What we do know is that the 1778 census reports that the Chocó was already mostly Afro descendant by then, with 45 percent free Blacks and 22 percent slaves. In 1808, on the eve of South American independence from Spain, free Blacks totaled 61 percent of the Chocoan population.[50] At its peak, the Colombian Pacific was 90 percent Black by the end of the nineteenth century. By 1918 and after the implementation of a Latin American discourse and mestizo identity, only 56 percent of the Colombian Pacific was Black, and another 22 percent include mestizos and mulattos. Whether 60, 70, 80, or 90 percent of the population in Chocoan communities are of the African diaspora, half of them are women. Yet no one speaks about women's role in the Black Pacific's history.[51] To flesh out the history of Chocoan women, we must redirect our gaze away from the dones and toward the women who fought to end the slave trade in the South Pacific and who prove that women's voices can be retrieved from smaller colonial archives, even if they seem absent in the archives of Seville.

Liberation Struggles among Enslaved Women in the Colonies

Enslaved women have always been at the vanguard of liberation processes in the Americas. During appearances at court hearings, women demanded their freedom in many forms. Among them, Marcela took her enslaver to demand her liberation on moral grounds; María Juana, previously Paula Diepa, demanded better living conditions; María Guía Calzadilla argued she could not possibly be sold due to her ugly aspect, which made her worthless by white standards.[52] Together, these enslaved women in Venezuela weave a narrative for their right to liberty in eighteenth-century Spanish America in conversation with the enlightened language of freedom, human rights, and bourgeois aesthetics. In Colombia in 1777, De María Gertrudis de León depended solely on her testimony to keep her freedom, because she had no letters to show for. She argued, "To have letters is not the same as wealth, but not having them is tantamount to misery" (Tener carta no es riqueza, pero no tenerla sí es mucha pobreza).[53] In 1782, Andrea demanded her freedom and her daughter's, Juana,[54] while in 1796 at the slave market, Carmela Vera wanted the opposite: "I am free and have come to enslave myself!" (he venido a esclavizarme).[55] Together, these women call out a complex structure of oppression: illiteracy, poverty, unemployment, rejection, objectification. Unfortunately, African diaspora women are still fighting some of the same forms of oppression today.

Black women have always been protagonists in the liberation struggles against these common forms of oppression going back generations, which is why Castriela Hernández finds it necessary to study orality as archive of memory.[56] She discusses a "sexed-gendered-modern-colonial-racialized" system that "explains the ways in which different forms of subjugation and the control of Black women and their sexuality get configured within a matrix of power and domination that began in colonial times and that extended to the Republic."[57] She describes strong scenes of resistance against all kinds of injustices in Colombia, after the proclamation of the Ley de Vientres (1814) that liberated babies born from enslaved women, and after the official abolition of slavery in 1851.

In the Spanish postcolonies, Afro-descendant women's invisibility persists in a perpetual coloniality of gender that Maria Lugones defined as what lies at the "intersection of gender/class/race as central constructs to a capitalist system of power."[58] Sexuality is another transversal axis, like gender, class, and race, that must be analyzed to understand the complex systems of domination. Ochy Curiel, member of La Tremenda Revoltosa drum collective, believes that Black feminism in Colombia is conceived as theory and must include sexuality as an integral element of a critical analysis.[59] La Tremenda Revoltosa began in 2012 to repurpose art for political use to denounce patriarchal violence and weave activist networks across Colombia. For Betty Ruth Lozano, Black feminisms "vindicate traditional practices such as midwifery and sisterhood which under the leadership of Black women weave tight the community in a context of conflict over the territory through which diverse mechanisms and strategies attempt to individualize and separate people."[60] She concludes that Black feminism is necessarily linked to the defense of the territory, so it forges a feminism *in-place* as opposed to the non-place that a white memory affords to Black women. Aurora Vergara-Figueroa and Katherine Arboleda define "Afrodiasporic feminism" as "a complex, contradictory, broad, and heterogenous perspective on thought, political action, and life as they emerge from the realities in which Black women are protagonists in different moments in history and geographic spaces."[61]

There were 20 million people brought to this continent, and today there are 200 million Afro-Latinxs in Latin America.[62] After 350 years of slavery, Brazil today has the largest Black population in the world after Nigeria.[63] The Great Chocó has the largest diaspora in the Americas after Brazil. Yet scholars have yet to fully lay to rest multiple, ongoing myths in Latin America related to mestizaje, the postcolonial, post-racial identity. When speaking of race in this region, conversations fall into the trap of the language of mestizaje and colorism, a discourse that is blind to colonial structural differences. This myth of racial democracy dominates public discourse, eclipsing the lived experience of racialized people who demand we speak about race.[64] In the absence of inclusive policies, activists weave a more nuanced critique of structural and institutional racisms that requires communities and allies to gather discrete data themselves and disseminate everywhere information on the inner workings of structural, institutional, state, and interpersonal racisms.

Over a century after the discourse of mestizaje emerged in Latin America in the hope of crafting a modern citizenry equal to the Global North, those who endure poverty and exploitation are still racialized, just like those drowning in the Mediterranean in total dispossession. My concern here is that those welcomed migrants of North Atlantic descent or the mobility of the upper or "floating" middle class are what makes this new identity of the Afropolitan possible.[65] This echoes the project of whitening the nation at the close of the nineteenth century in Spanish America, a migration and a concept that came with the dispossession of ancestral lands and a rhetoric of whiteness that still fuels mestizaje (mixing with whiteness for upward mobility). An Afropolitan mobility and international education does not resonate with the lived experience of women in the Chocó. Not talking about race has not helped overcome racism and might even have helped strengthen racial inequality.

The struggle for the defense of a free territory against global neoliberal capital points to the shortcoming of an Afropolitanism that does not represent the whole experience of the African diaspora and that stubbornly ignores the enslavement of their own people, with its long effects in the Americas. On the contrary, Chocoan women evoke a local feminism that has a translatable outlook and that redefines the African diaspora experience, foregrounding Blackness and femininity.

The accumulation of violence on Black women "undermine[s] their traditions of solidarity and mutual help" and their political enunciations that oppose the discourse of violence that presume people in the territory are "each against all and all against each other" (socavan sus tradiciones de solidaridad y ayuda mutual . . . a cada uno contra todos y a todos contra cada uno).[66] In the Chocó, women struggle for a dignified life; their lives are in danger, yet they continue to lead collective processes for fundamental rights and for life. This was the case of Francia Márquez, who has lived with death threats for decades for her leadership in the Communitarian Council of La Toma. The reason: her fight against illegal mining. Many, including those in Francia's surrounding areas, have fallen prey to paramilitarism in the name of development. Márquez received the 2018 Goldman Prize for her environmental activism and brought some attention to the region. The Chocó is under fire!

The Power of Memory, Autonomy, and Oral Histories in the Chocó

The territory has its own symbolic interpretation for women in the Black Pacific. Besides being *palenques, quilombos, mambises, mocambos, ladeiras*, or whatever other term used to recognize self-liberated Afro-descendant nations, for women in the Chocó their communities also reconstitute geography through a politics of "appropriation, defense, and reconstructions of place."[67] Mamá Cuama, a land defender who has become a symbolic representation of elder women in the Black Pacific, says, "The territory is everything: life, food, labor, sustenance . . . it's where we are happy . . . without the territory it is like going back to slavery."[68] Betty Ruth Lozano explains that the Colombian Pacific (Buenaventura, Tumaco, Quibdó, as in Esmeraldas) has always been left out, conceived as outside the Andinocentric state, at its borders at best, so, in practice, the territory has always been defined by Black women in-place. Lozano says, "This rootedness to the territory has been possible historically through the home established by Black women, because Black men are mobile, but Black women are fixed to their homes, in each specific river, enabling the sense of belonging in which a matrilineality has played a prominent role."[69]

If we believe Lozano, there is little Afropolitan mobility for the women in the Black Pacific. There, women oversee religious festivities, farming cycles, and the sowing of medicinal plants, as well as the recreation of ecosystems and the fishing economy. This local economy is threatened by an extractivist development (shrimp farms, large-scale mining, and palm and coca plantations) with its deadly consequences: deforestation, the loss of mangroves, pollution, and displacement. Albán

Achinte's concept of *re-existence*, the daily life practices that constitute a true decolonial praxis, defy a system where "Black, Indigenous, *raizales*, Roma peoples . . . must accept the conditions of a project whose patterns assimilate them as minorities, stigmatized," with a strategy "to reinvent life daily" and defy the constant premise of the non-existence of Black people in every space.[70] Local communities mobilize memory for the re-existence of peoples and the sustainability of nature and the territory in multiple ways.

In the case of Bojayá, in the northern Colombian Chocó, a group of mourning singers, mostly women, gathered to craft rag dolls and used them to rummage into the collective memory of a place-in-healing. The *alabaoras* belonged to a performing group called Grupo de Alabao de Pogué, in Bojayá.[71] The project sought to strengthen local artistic practices and use oral memory to tell the story of the effects of armed conflict in their territory. After reflecting on their art of praise, singing to lead dying souls into their final place of rest, these women employed mortuary hymns to collectively denounce the massacre that took place in Bellavista, Bojayá's municipal seat, on May 2, 2002, when eighty people were murdered inside a church where women and children sought refuge from ongoing paramilitary violence, and another forty people were killed and found scattered through town. Orality here makes room for a peaceful return and functions as a shield for the (protection of) truth, "escudos de la verdad."[72] The *alabaoras* used the emotional effectiveness of their testimonial chants to mobilize memory for Black cultural and political life and to fight oblivion: when all people can talk about is the death surrounding them, they sing so that people can talk about things that make life joyful, "cosas que alegran la vida."[73] In doing so, Chocoan women produce a language beyond the trope of crisis.

Like many Afropoetic practices in the Black Pacific, *alabao* chants have a dialogic structure in which one woman sings a stanza, the next improvises an answer, another makes a comment, and someone else adds a detail. This collective weaving of memory shapes truth together to fully capture the complexity of events with their layered symbolic dimensions, because "making memory is more than remembering; it is rebuilding ourselves over and over" (hacer memoria no solo es recoraer; es volver a hacernos).[74] The dolls are much more than objects to invite singers into a conversation about the past. They bring back a time long gone, their childhood before paramilitary violence. The dolls *Maria Esperanza* (Mary Hope), *Juan no me Olvides* (Forget-me-not John), and *Juana Paz* (Jane for Peace) represent positive characters who live in a land with clean rivers and fruit trees. The dolls and recorded songs function as storytelling objects (*objetos-relato*) that prompt a narrative with driving metaphors to denounce violence while composing a picture of a thriving territory as imagined by women returning from exodus.

In the Chocó, the political and cultural heritage of women is rewriting the history of the Black Pacific by developing communities for a joyous life and defying the inevitable fetishizing of their people and culture in the process of representation. Oral history projects denounce the various forms of racisms, but they also tell a story that counters the discourse of forced displacement, of the territory as an imperial frontier, and of its land and people ready for extraction.

The autonomous re-existence in Bellavista, La Toma, Esmeraldas, and Quibdó seeks social and environmental justice and demands the creation of infrastructure that would allow these communities to live a dignified life as per constitutional rights.[75] Like their ancestors, Black women seek cultural and historical vindications as well as political and economic sustainability. Juan García Salazar conceives Esmeraldas's oral heritage as the philosophy and doctrine for life and death, "filosofías y doctrinas para la vida y para la muerte," and culture as the accumulation of daily practices that are stored in the hearts and souls of *palenque* territories.[76] García concludes that "resistance, memory, and word are born out of this rich culture. . . . The guardians of tradition, with their music, poetry, healing knowledge, agricultural techniques, and a thousand other secrets on life and death, come to be again . . . born from the diaspora in the land of Esmeraldas."[77]

Women are at the core of creating life and meaning while facing neoliberal impoverishment that comes from states' policies, which are certainly necropolitical.[78] Statistics bear this out: closed hospitals, lack of doctors, no running water, food insecurity, a collapsed civil registry. For Ecuador's mestizo elite, Esmeraldas is "barely anything," its culture mere "entertainment" and its people "color added to public feasts and celebrations."[79] Afro-Esmeraldas's "oraliterature," its oral archive of memory, "points to a re-creation" of ancestral knowledges in the rural communities of the "Gran Comarca" of Esmeraldas.[80] The Comarca was first incorporated in 1997 by Black communities in Borbón at the border with Colombia.[81] It symbolized the cultural and political alliance of transnational *palenque* communities directly affected by migration and neoliberal development. This alliance sought to protect mangrove forests that sustain Esmeraldas's economy against predatory fishing and farming, long before the mining threats that communities face today. In each generation, Esmeraldas must be defended with all it takes against the threat of an "extractivist logic that devours territories."[82] While a colonial view of Esmeraldas reduces it to its natural resources, the Comarca offers an imagination of a land complete with its peoples and their histories. Colombian paramilitary violence displaces millions each year, and Chocoans have founded entire villages in Esmeraldas's borderland counties, villages that then have become important posts of resistance, as was the case during the Comarca organizing of the 1990s, which echoes today's collective mangrove fisheries, recently re-unionized.

The knowledge to win this fight against extractivist development and restore Esmeraldas is recorded in oral memory, not in the archives of the colonies or the metropole. An obvious example of this orality is marimba music, a well-known cultural re-existence practice of the Black Pacific dominated by male performers such as Lindberg Valencia and Papá Roncó. Other Chocoan genres include *curru-laos*, *arrullos*, and other forms of poetry, whose scholarly studies mostly leave out women. Laura Hidalgo, for her part, collected Esmeraldas's *décimas*, a poetic form that Yaima Lorenzo Hernández identifies as hosting the repertoire of magical-religious practices, and more common among women poets.[83] Other genres, such as Esmeraldas's *arrullos*, *chigualos*, and *rondas*,[84] and many other spiritual songs, are often performed by women, who also tell "the thousands of stories . . . teachings on how to organize and engage in dialogues with power."[85] This is "valuable material to learn about living memory indoors, *casa adentro*, while forming an intercultural identity to the outside world, *casa afuera*."[86] Here are extracts from *décimas* compiled by García during the 1980s shrimp-farm development:

Como ignorante que soy
Me precisa preguntar
Si el color blanco es virtud
Para mandarme blanquear[87]

(Ignorant as I am
I must ask
If whiteness is a virtue,
To go and make myself white)

La tierra se está muriendo
Con un dolor sin fronteras
Porque se están destruyendo
Los bosques de la madera[88]

(The earth is dying
Of a pain beyond borders
Because they are destroying
The wooded forests)

Yo me abarqué a navegar
En una concha de almejas
A rodear el mundo entero
Pa'a ver si hallaba coteja[89]

(I embarked myself to sail
On top of a mussel shell
To skirt the whole world
Looking for someone to love)

Poet-singers reveal tensions surrounding the genocidal logic of progress and the defense of their territory against an extractivist development that produces death and a forever misunderstood, wandering diaspora. This is hardly the Afropolitan global and mobile diaspora, educated to mimic whiteness in a racialized territory open for extraction.

Oral history triangulates the past, its current manifestations, and ideations of a future, moving away from an individual into a collective memory that exceeds the present of a narrator and extends into a legacy from the longer memory of the mangrove, where 80 percent of migration in Esmeraldas begins. Orality can slow the exodus of Esmeraldas's youth by recomposing an image and a meaning in-place, which gives them an opportunity to live in the Pacific region from a sustainable economy. While Bojayá *alabaoras* mixed oral history with objects to weave a memory for re-existence, women in Esmeraldas are taking the opposite path and starting with oral histories to ground memory in cultural products that help them imagine a development to counter extractivism and state violence. Mujeres de Asfalto, a collective of Black feminists in Esmeraldas, combines decolonial oral history and critical feminist geography to defend communities, territories, and memory against the violence of capitalism and a genocidal state.

In the Ecuadorian Chocó, Mujeres de Asfalto are having intergenerational dialogues to develop platforms for Afro-Ecuadorian women and their experiences. Using oral history as a decolonial tool, they ground collective memory in the recognized experience and knowledge of Black women's heritage by promoting research skills in local communities and gathering oral histories to amplify Black women's voices; they understand how state violence operates on their bodies and document the role Black women have in the making of the history of Esmeraldas. In one project, *#LaRutaDeLasCimarronas*, one of the participant sings: "I know what I have to learn: let us talk about my own history and hold it dearly in our memory. How I wish that Black teachers could impart teachings of our history! Black women teachers must do this, because history will be written with Black handwriting!"[90]

A second project, RECLAMA (Recuperando y Celebrando la Herencia de las Mujeres Afroecuatorianas), seeks to sow Black women's memory by conducting oral histories in Esmeraldas's seven counties. Young researchers map extractivist and state violence on their territories and their bodies while they record the historical legacy of Black women in each county for the reconstitution of time-space and of life, "without having to adjust for another the way we speak."[91] A decolonial oral history practice should not try to resemble a Western historiography that leaves colonial power structures intact, but speak in *palenque* language, often creolized, about a history as remembered by its people.

RECLAMA combines mapping and oral history methods to document the gendered patterns of violence in Esmeraldas while still telling another story, of joy and happiness. For example, each workshop opens, develops, and closes with collective singing. During the first workshop, which took place in the absence (or virtual presence) of academic researchers, communitarian researchers had training in oral history methods, ethics, and examples. Before they could get into any of that, they had to compose a song of encounter, a joyful tune for the celebration of a shared heritage and a "banquet of sorority." The chorus goes,

Venimos, venimos,
de diferente lugar
a sentir la cultura
como signo de unidad.

(We have come, we have come
from a different place
to feel culture
as a sign of unity.)[92]

The painful conversations that took place *casa adentro* are not what Mujeres de Asfalto chose to showcase on RECLAMA's website, but the uplifting singing that empowers the participants. Simply put, without Marimba, there is no encounter.

The newly trained communitarian researchers were activists in their counties but had never met each other. Now that they were together, they proudly wore identical shirts that read, "Yo soy una cimarrona" (I am a *cimarrona*). After reflecting on a decolonial language of storytelling and insisting on speaking the way they do without having to comply with foreign Spanish grammar rules, the participants agreed on something: they would collectively tell an *historia bonita*, a joyful story woven from each territory, where the oral histories of elder women chosen by the communitarian researchers could serve as guides and legacy for the younger generations, a legacy much deeper than violence or victimhood. Later, in the mapping exercise, participants identified the shared experience of a lack of infrastructure (hospitals, sewage, running water, employment) and the migration routes of ancestors that come and go through the Chocó. They end with rituals of healing and with the marimba, naturally. Women who had never met suddenly felt like family.

During the second workshop, when researchers met to share what they had heard and build a vision of a future together, they began with marimba, then spoke in an assembly. They separated in working groups according to four themes, each with a timetable for the cultural production of Esmeraldas's heritage: (1) food sovereignty with farms of the identified plants and shared seeds (many of which only exist in the borderland counties), collected in a documentary for communitarian screenings; (2) unapologetically Black aesthetics with fashion shows of dresses and turbans, and hair-styling competitions featured in a self-produced documentary still under production; (3) oral poetic forms from *décimas* to the river procession of Saint Martin de Porres, the Black saint who protects Chocoan fishermen and celebrated at the Island of Canchimalero every November in a day of laughter, singing, and dancing, with transcribed musical and poetic repertoire from all counties; and (4) a revival of ancestral medicine with recipes, techniques, and practices gathered in a zine.

Using the knowledge collectively systematized, the new researchers identify topics of interest and imagine sustainable solutions. Several subprojects have emerged from this collective effort to reconstruct Esmeraldas's memory, among them ancestral farming with the guarding and sharing of seeds, the retelling of magical-religious practices and the composition of verse, training in mangrove medicine (crucial during COVID), and a serious aesthetic conversation on fashion design. Two elements stand out: demands for self-representation and for territorial and cultural sovereignty. By playing with the concept of "body-territory," women relate their lived experiences to the patterns of development and mark the spaces that can be redefined through daily practices of re-existence, like praising, cooking, farming, and sowing.

The mobilization of memory for a local articulation of Esmeraldas's history can have a real economic impact. This second workshop included researchers and narrators, was truly intergenerational, and successfully built the space of intimacy that is required to share stories, heal, re-exist, and thrive. On the final night, every woman, from the youngest to the eldest, walked the runway. They were happy, felt beautiful, laughed wholeheartedly. They were writing a new chapter in the joyful history of Esmeraldas. Much remains to be done, but Mujeres de Asfalto will not stop working until it happens. This type of feminist, anti-racist oral historiography goes beyond participatory research and fully centers knowledge in the needs and memory of local communities.

Through workshops, interviews, and creative outputs, young women engage with memory in significant ways that will positively impact the development of their communities using ancestral environmental and libertarian practices retrieved from the oral archive of elder women. The collection of their legacy in the seven counties has revived the spirit of the Comarca. RECLAMA is at the front line of a communitarian resistance to historical violence on Black women's bodies in Esmeraldas. Mapping the patterns of violence in local communities and on women's bodies is a tool increasingly used by feminists in a region wracked with patriarchal violence.[93]

Conclusion

RECLAMA crafts an analysis of race that features a world created by Black women for the sustenance of life, a joyful life that defies silence and oblivion as well as the dooming death of extractive capitalism and the neocolonial state. This decolonial oral history contradicts the usual methods that come from discussions around the researcher's fear of failure, power relations, and self-criticism in ethics.[94] Esmeraldas's collective project has no room for individual concerns and instead recenters research methods on existing communitarian practices that combat the "bloody-mangrove narrative."[95] In Esmeraldas, memory and history are inseparable.[96] The theory and practice of history making in a project where women have total control of the design, implementation, and use of oral history points to our failure as Eurocentric researchers to recognize the intellectual work of oral cultures. Orality is itself the archive that stores cultural forms connecting past, present, and future in each utterance of resistance. Memory and history in the Black Pacific attest to that re-existence. Ashé.

Antonia Carcelén-Estrada teaches orality and postcolonial literature with a focus on interculturality at Universidad San Francisco de Quito. She is also a translator and an activist for the revitalization of Indigenous languages and for environmental rights of racialized peoples. Her academic interests include translation, colonial and postcolonial Abya Yala, political philosophy, cultural studies, art history, and orality.

Notes

1. Because of the white mestizo ordering of the state, statistics on racial and ethnic groups are scarce and inconsistent. Groups gather discrete data themselves to counter the whitening of the National Census, but these statistics are equally unreliable and volatile. For example, the majority Indigenous population appears as just over 10 percent (up from a mere 7 percent in the 2010 census), but organizations' numbers vary from 30 percent to 70 percent of the country, depending on who is counting and who gets counted. The latest census also puts the Afro-descendant population at 7 percent (one point less than the 8 percent in the 2010 census), so that statistically Ecuador is over 80 percent white. Of the self-identified Black population, 70 percent live in Esmeraldas. In this province, there is limited access to services (23 percent), education (15 percent illiteracy rate), and work (85 percent live in poverty).
2. Gutiérrez Usillos, "Nuevas aportaciones."
3. EFE, the name of letter *F* in Spanish, began in Burgos in 1939, hometown of the dictator General Franco, so it could refer to his initial, or the initials of the news agencies united under EFE: Fabra, Faro, and Febus. The name is not an acronym. Today it continues to be the flagship agency for Spanish news, like the BBC for Great Britain.
4. EFE, "Museo Nacional de Ecuador recibe obra virreinal 'Mulatos de Esmeraldas.'"
5. Carneiro, "Ennegrecer el feminismo."
6. Trouillot, *Silencing the Past*, 45.
7. Trouillot, *Silencing the Past*, 82.
8. Trouillot, *Silencing the Past*, 106.
9. Mikhail Bakhtin defined *chronotope*, or time-space, as "the intrinsic connectedness of temporal and spatial relationships that are artistically expressed" (*Dialogic Imagination*, 84), but I prefer to think of a material manifestation of these complex relationships that fix meanings of time and space in our collective memory.
10. Bartra, *La jaula de la melancolía*.
11. Ho, "Afropolitanism and Social Class," 771.
12. Mbembe, "African Modes of Self-Writing."
13. After the globalization of contemporary Africa, not all people living there are of African descent, and this breaks the synonymity of Africa with Blackness—Taiye Selasi defines

Afropolitans as "Africans of the world" in "Bye-Bye Babar"—and of Blackness with nativism, with a recognition of Africans' long dispersal East and West and as main actors in the "weaving of worlds" (Mbembe, "Afropolitanism," 59).

14. Francis et al., "Decolonising Oral History."

15. Gikandi, "Foreword: On Afropolitanism."

16. Balakrishnan, "Afropolitanism and the End of Black Nationalism," 580.

17. Acerca del descubrimiento y población de la provincia de Esmeraldas y Puerto Viejo, June 6, 1585, Quito 1, no. 14, Consulta del Consejo de Indias, Archivo General de Indias, Seville, Spain.

18. Whereas *marronage* has a connotation of illegality, the Spanish *cimarrón* denotes freedom, autonomy, and the possibility of a Black utopia. See Quintero Rivera, "La cimarronería como herencia y utopía."

19. Established by Spanish Royal Decree in 1563, the Real Audiencia de Quito operated under the supervision of Lima's Viceroyalty, the highest office after the king.

20. Murra, *El mundo andino*, 435.

21. For an excellent analysis on the consequences of the Valladolid debates (1550–51) between Las Casas and Sepúlveda in Spanish America, see López-Baralt, *Para decir al otro*.

22. Descalzi, *La Real Audiencia de Quito*, 300.

23. Descalzi, *La Real Audiencia de Quito*, 291.

24. "Acerca de lo que resulta contra el doctor Barros, Presidente y Visitador de la Audiencia de Quito," May 4, 1590, Quito 1, no. 31, Consulta del Consejo de Indias, Archivo General de Indias, Seville, Spain.

25. "Acerca de lo que resulta contra el doctor Barros."

26. Túpac Amaru (Royal Snake) was the last Inca monarch, captured in the Amazon while escaping Viceroy Toledo's persecution and brought to Cuzco, where he was beheaded in 1572.

27. "Acerca de lo que resulta contra el doctor Barros."

28. This was a 2 percent sales tax on luxury goods such as tobacco and alcohol, which King Philip II hoped would pay for maritime protection of Spanish ships.

29. Descalzi, *La Real Audiencia*, 308.

30. Descalzi, *La Real Audiencia*, 312.

31. Vargas, *Biografía de Fray Pedro Bedón*, 42.

32. Vargas, *Biografía de Fray Pedro Bedón*, 43.

33. Hernández Ascencio, "Los límites de la política imperial," 331. Caciques are Indigenous leaders in the Spanish colonies.

34. The Tolita culture were masters of metallurgy and were unique in their use of platinum, besides gold and silver, but they were also notorious for their skills as sailors and traders. A Tolita sun mask is the most prominent object used to represent Ecuador and is the logo of its national bank, Banco Central del Ecuador. For a full study of this culture before Columbus and before the African diaspora, see Scott, "The La Tolita-Tumaco Culture."

35. Hernández Ascencio, "Los límites de la política imperial," 332.

36. "Sobre confirmar al capitán Diego López de Zúñiga el título de un regimiento de Quito que le dio el marqués de Cañete," February 22, 1598, Quito 1, no. 69, Consulta del Consejo de Indias, Archivo General de Indias, Seville, Spain.

37. "Contestación a la resolución de la consulta de 14 de julio de 1584." June 6, 1585, Quito 1, no. 14. Consulta del Consejo de Indias, Archivo General de Indias, Seville, Spain.

38. Hernández Ascencio, "Los límites de la política imperial," 330.

39. Spanish kings controlled the American masses by separating peoples according to blood quantum, a practice inherited from the surveillance of Jewish and Muslim blood during the Christian conquest of the Iberian Peninsula. Since the American conquest was a Catholic pursuit, people of polluted lineage (namely Muslims and Jews) were not allowed to travel into the continent, but this rule was not always followed.

40. "Ynstancia de Andres Diaz Rivadeneyra, sobre el asiento para el descubrimiento de la Ysla de las Esmeraldas," October 2, 1590, Contratación, 5873, Papeles Singulares, Archivo General de Indias, Seville, Spain.

41. Hernández Ascencio, "Los límites de la política imperial," 334.

42. Friar Alonso Espinosa was a Portuguese bachelor given the task of pacifying Esmeraldas after Zúñiga's defeat.

43. Navarro, *El arte de Quito*, 26.

44. Edward Said did this work in the French context of Enlightenment, but the Orientalist gaze precedes the formation of both French and Spanish Christian kingdoms and yet it is inescapable to both. Said, *Orientalism*.

45. Said, *Orientalism*, 62.

46. Navarro, *El arte de Quito*, 28.

47. Lane, *Quito 1599*, 22.

48. Lane, *Quito 1599*; Beatty-Medina, "Caught between Rivals."

49. García Salazar, "La cultura afroecuatoriana en Esmeraldas."

50. Wade, *Race and Ethnicity in Latin America*, 128.

51. Hoffmann, *Comunidades negras en el Pacífico Colombiano*, 52.

52. Cosme and Vergara-Figueroa, *Demando mi libertad*.

53. Arboleda, "María Gertrudis de León," 118.

54. González, "La defensa de una mujer afrodescendiente," 133–71.

55. Sánchez, "¡Soy libre y vengo a esclavizarme!, 1796," 154.

56. Hernández, "Aproximaciones al Sistema de Sexo-Género en la Nueva Granada en los Siglos XVIII y XIX," 31.

57. Hernández, "Aproximaciones," 33.

58. Lugones, "Toward a Decolonial Feminism," 747.

59. Curiel, "Crítica poscolonial"; Curiel, *La nación heterosexual*.

60. Lozano, "Feminismo negro-afrocolombiano," 44.

61. Vergara-Figueroa and Arboleda, "Feminismo afrodiaspórico," 113.

62. Laó-Montes, *Contrapunteos diaspóricos*, 55.

63. De la Fuente and Andrews, *Estudios afrolatinoamericanos*, 12.

64. For a pioneering analysis of the impact of mestizaje on Black women that informs my own, see Caldwell, *Negras in Brazil*.

65. Ho, "Afropolitanism and Social Class," 772.

66. Lozano, "Feminismo negro-afrocolombiano," 33.

67. Ruth Lozano, "Feminismo negro-afrocolombiano," 24.

68. Lozano, "Feminismo negro-afrocolombiano," 25. Mamá Cuama's real name is Rosana Cuama Caicedo; she is a renowned leader from Buenaventura.

69. Lozano, "Feminismo negro-afrocolombiano," 27.

70. Albán Achinte, "¿Interculturalidad sin decolonialidad?," 71, 85. Roma people are associated with Europe and *raizales*, with the root, or the African diaspora.

71. *Alabar* is to praise the lord, and the women who praise through singing are *alabadoras*, but the *d* is dropped in the Spanish of the Pacific region so that they are known as *alabaoras* and their chants as *alabaos*.

72. Herrera et al., "El objeto-relato," 29.
73. Herrera et al., "El objeto-relato," 33.
74. Herrera et al., "El objeto-relato," 33.
75. Adolfo Albán Achinte conceives daily practices of re-existence as a way to write a narrative, different from the colonial narrative "where Blacks, Indians, Maroons, and Roma . . . must adopt behaviors from a project that assimilates them in conditions of stigmatization and as minorities" ("¿Interculturalidad sin decolonialidad?," 71).
76. García Salazar, "La cultura afroecuatoriana."
77. García Salazar, "La cultura afroecuatoriana."
78. Mbembe, *Necropolitics*.
79. García Salazar, "La cultura afroecuatoriana."
80. The word *Comarca* translates as "shire" and connotes a utopian conception of space that requires a community of care. García Salazar, "Cuentos afroecuatorianos," 42.
81. Pabón, "Ora-literatura afroecuatoriana," 109.
82. Pabón, "Ora-literatura afroecuatoriana," 99.
83. Lorenzo Hernández, "Imaginarios cimarrones."
84. There are many genres of spiritual chants among Afro-descendants. In the Black Pacific, *arrullos* are chants for children's funerals and are joyful and fast-paced, *chigualos* are playful chants for baby Jesus during Christmas and Carnival, and *rondas* are nurseries with the poetic structure of Medieval romance written in octasyllabic verse.
85. García Salazar, "La cultura afroecuatoriana."
86. García Salazar, "La cultura afroecuatoriana." *Casa adentro* means behind closed doors, or within the communities, while *casa afuera* refers to the space beyond the territory.
87. García Salazar, "Poesía negra en la Costa del Ecuador," 37.
88. García Salazar, "La cultura afroecuatoriana."
89. García Salazar, "Decimas y argumentos recopilados en diferentes localidades de Esmeraldas," 12.
90. Colectivo Mujeres de Asfalto, "#LaRutaDeLasCimarronas."
91. RECLAMA, "Un pequeño vistazo a nuestro primer taller."
92. RECLAMA, "Un reencuentro entre el saber y la experiencia."
93. Colectivo de Geografía Crítica del Ecuador, *Geografiando para la resistencia*, 27.
94. Sheftel and Zembrzycki, "Who's Afraid of Oral History?"
95. Francis et al., "Decolonizing Oral History," 266, 268.
96. Mahuika, Rethinking Oral History and Tradition.

References

Albán Achinte, Adolfo. "¿Interculturalidad sin decolonialidad? Colonialidades circulantes y prácticas de re-existencia." In *Diversidad, interculturalidad y construcción de ciudad*, edited by Wilmer Villa and Arturo Grueso Bonilla, 64–96. Bogotá: Universidad Pedagógica Nacional, 2008.

Arboleda, Katherine. "María Gertrudis de León: Una parda libre y propietaria en la Nueva Granada." In *Demando mi libertad: Mujeres negras y sus estrategias de resistencia en Nueva Granada, Venezuela y Cuba, 1700–1800*. Edited by Carmen Cosme and Aurora Vergara-Figueroa, 109–31. Cali: Editorial Universitaria ICESI, 2018.

Bakhtin, M. M. *The Dialogic Imagination: Four Essays*. Translated by Caryl Emerson and Michael Holquist. Austin: University of Texas Press, 1982.

Balakrishnan, Sarah. "Afropolitanism and the End of Black Nationalism." In *Routledge International Handbook of Cosmopolitanism Studies*, 575–85. London: Routledge, 2018.

Bartra, Roger. *La jaula de la melancolía: Identidad y metamorfosis del mexicano*. Mexico City: Grijalbo, 1987.

Beatty-Medina, Charles. "Caught between Rivals: The Spanish-African Maroon Competition for Captive Indian Labor in the Region of Esmeraldas during the Late Sixteenth and Early Seventeenth Centuries." *Americas* 63, no. 1 (2006): 113–36.

Caldwell, Kia Lilly. *Negras in Brazil: Re-envisioning Black Women, Citizenship, and the Politics of Identity*. New Brunswick, NJ: Rutgers University Press, 2007.

Carneiro, Sueli. "Ennegrecer el feminismo." *Movimiento, Agencia Cubana de Rap*, no. 7 (2009): 47–50.

Colectivo de Geografía Crítica del Ecuador. *Geografiando para la resistencia: Los feminismos como práctica espacial*. Quito: Colectivo de Geografía Crítica del Ecuador, 2008.

Colectivo Mujeres de Asfalto. "#LaRutaDeLasCimarronas." Facebook video, January 26, 2020. https://www.facebook.com/watch/?v=112651856814623.

Cosme, Carmen, and Aurora Vergara-Figueroa, eds. *Demando mi libertad: Mujeres negras y sus estrategias de resistencia en Nueva Granada, Venezuela y Cuba, 1700–1800*. Cali: Editorial Universitaria ICESI, 2018.

Curiel, Ochy. "Crítica postcolonial desde las prácticas políticas del feminismo antirracista." Nómadas, no. 26 (2007): 92–101. https://www.redalyc.org/pdf/1051/105115241010.pdf.

Curiel, Ochy. *La nación heterosexual: Análisis del discurso jurídico y el régimen heterosexual desde la antropología de la dominación*. Bogotá: Brecha Lésbica, 2013.

De la Fuente, Alejandro, and Georges Reid Andrews, eds. *Estudios afrolatinoamericanos: Una introducción*. Buenos Aires: CLACSO, 2018. http://biblioteca.clacso.edu.ar/clacso/se/20181206023201/EstudiosAfro_ES.pdf.

Descalzi, Ricardo. *La Real Audiencia de Quito, claustro en los Andes*. Barcelona: Seix y Barral, 1978.

EFE. "Museo Nacional de Ecuador recibe obra virreinal 'Mulatos de Esmeraldas' de 1599." YouTube video, May 16, 2019. https://www.youtube.com/watch?v=8PUjMaetAnA.

Francis, Hilary, Inge Boudewijn, Antonia Carcelen-Estrada, Juana Francis Bone, Katy Jenkins, and Sofia Zaragocín. "Decolonising Oral History: A Conversation." *History* 106, no. 370 (2021): 265–81.

García Salazar, Juan. "Cuentos afroecuatorianos." *Letras del Ecuador*, no. 184 (2002): 40–51.

García Salazar, Juan. "Décimas y argumentos recopilados en diferentes localidades de Esmeraldas." *Cuadernos afroecuatorianos* 4 (1985): 1–60.

García Salazar, Juan. "La cultura afroecuatoriana en Esmeraldas." Conferencia Ecuatoriana de Religiosas y Religiosos, Vida Religiosa Afro, June 1, 2011. https://www.vidadelacer.org/index.php/comisiones/vr-afro/1492-la-cultura-afroecuatoriana-en-esmeraldas-una-aproximacion.

García Salazar, Juan. "Poesía negra en la Costa del Ecuador." *Desarrollo de base* 8, no. 1 (1984): 30–37.

Gikandi, Simon. "Foreword: On Afropolitanism." In *Negotiating Afropolitanism: Essays on Borders and Spaces in Contemporary African Literature and Folklore*. Edited by Jennifer Wawrzinek and J. K. S. Makokha, 9–10. Amsterdam: Rodopi, 2011.

González, Edna. "La defensa de una mujer afrodescendiente: El caso de Andrea, 1782." In *Demando mi libertad: Mujeres negras y sus estrategias de resistencia en Nueva Granada, Venezuela y Cuba, 1700–1800*. Edited by Carmen Cosme and Aurora Vergara-Figueroa, 133–71. Cali: Editorial Universitaria ICESI, 2018.

Gutiérrez Usillos, Andrés. "Nuevas aportaciones en torno al lienzo titulado Los mulatos de Esmeraldas: Estudio técnico, radiográfico e histórico." *Anales del Museo de América* 20 (2012): 7–64.

Hernández, Castriela. "Aproximaciones al Sistema de Sexo-Género en la Nueva Granada en los Siglos XVIII y XIX." In *Demando mi libertad: Mujeres negras y sus estrategias de resistencia en Nueva Granada, Venezuela y Cuba, 1700–1800.* Eited by Carmen Cosme and Aurora Vergara-Figueroa, 29–75. Cali: Editorial Universitaria ICESI, 2018.

Hernández Ascencio, Raúl. "Los límites de la política imperial: El oidor Juan de Barrio y la frontera esmeraldeña a inicios del Siglo XVII." *Institut français d'études andines* 37, no. 2 (2008): 329–50. https://doi.org/10.4000/bifea.3179.

Herrera, María Paola. "El objeto-relato como dispositivo de la memoria: El caso del Grupo de alabaos de Pogue, Bojayá, Chocó." In *Lugares, recorridos y sentidos de la memoria histórica: Acercamientos metodológicos.* Edited by Laura Fonseca, Diana Vernot, Tatiana Rojas, Laura Giraldo Edwin Corena, and David Luquetta, 27–47. Bogotá: Universidad de la Sabana.

Ho, Janice. "Afropolitanism and Social Class." *PMLA* 136, no. 5 (2021): 770–77.

Hoffmann, Odile. *Comunidades negras en el pacífico colombiano.* Bogotá: Instituto Francés de Estudios Andinos, 2007.

Lane, Kris. *Quito 1599: City and Colony in Transition.* Albuquerque: University of New Mexico Press, 2002.

Laó-Montes, Agustín. *Contrapunteos diaspóricos: Cartografías políticas de Nuestra América.* Bogotá: Universidad Externado de Colombia, 2020.

López-Baralt, Mercedes. *Para decir al otro: Literatura y antropología en Nuestra América.* Madrid: Iberoamericana, 2005.

Lorenzo Hernández, Yaima. "Imaginarios cimarrones: Orígenes de la cosmovisión y prácticas mágico-religiosas de los afroesmeraldeños." *Revista del Colegio de San Luis* 6, no. 12 (2016): 95–113. http://www.scielo.org.mx/scielo.php?script=sci_arttext&pid=S1665 -899X2016000200258.

Lozano, Betty Ruth. "Feminismo negro-afrocolombiano: Ancestral, insurgente y cimarrón; Un feminismo en-lugar." *Intersticios de la política y la cultura: Intervenciones latinoamericanas* 5, no. 9 (2016): 23–48.

Lugones, Maria. "Hacia un feminismo decolonial." *Hypatia* 25, no. 4 (2010): 742–59.

Mahuika, Nepia. *Rethinking Oral History and Tradition: An Indigenous Perspective.* New York: Oxford University Press, 2019.

Mbembe, Achille. "African Modes of Self-Writing." *Public Culture* 14, no. 1 (2002): 239–73.

Mbembe, Achille. "Afropolitanism." *Nka: Journal of Contemporary African Art* 46, no. 1 (2020): 56–61.

Mbembe, Aquille. *Necropolitics.* Durham, NC: Duke University Press, 2019.

Murra, John V. "El Doctor Barros de San Millán: Defensor de los ́señores naturales ́ de los Andes." In *El mundo andino: Población, medio ambiente y economía*, 426–38. Lima: Pontificia Universidad Católica del Perú, 2002.

Navarro, Gabriel. *El arte de Quito en el Siglo XVI.* Quito: Editorial Casa de la Cultura Ecuatoriana, 1958.

Pabón, Javier. "Ora-literatura afroecuatoriana: Narrativas insurgentes de re-existencia y lugar." *Latin Americanist* 60, no. 1 (2016): 95–115. https://doi.org/10.1111/tla.12062.

Quintero Rivera, Ángel. "La cimarronería como herencia y utopía." In *Antología del pensamiento crítico puertorriqueño contemporáneo.* Edited by A. Santory and M. Quintero Rivera, 91–116. Buenos Aires: CLACSO, 2019. http://biblioteca.clacso.edu.ar/clacso/se /20190614031101/Antologia_Puerto_Rico.pdf.

RECLAMA (Recuperando y Celebrando la Herencia de las Mujeres Afroecuatorianas). "Un pequeño vistazo a nuestro primer taller." Website, July 12, 2021, video, 3:45. https://proyectoreclama.wixsite.com/reclama/post/un-peque%C3%B1o-vistazo-a-nuestro-primer-taller.

RECLAMA (Recuperando y Celebrando la Herencia de las Mujeres Afroecuatorianas). "Un reencuentro entre el saber y la experiencia." Website (blog), June 11, 2021. https://proyectoreclama.wixsite.com/reclama/post/un-reencuentro-entre-el-saber-y-la-experiencia-oralidad-m%C3%A9dula-espinal-de-cultura-afroesmeralde%C3%B1a.

Said, Edward. *Orientalism*. New York: Vintage Books, 1978.

Sánchez, Angélica. "¡Soy libre y vengo a esclavizarme!, 1796." In *Demando mi libertad: Mujeres negras y sus estrategias de resistencia en Nueva Granada, Venezuela y Cuba, 1700–1800*. Edited by Carmen Cosme and Aurora Vergara-Figueroa, 153–71. Cali: Editorial Universitaria ICESI, 2018.

Scott, David. "The La Tolita-Tumaco Culture: Master Metalsmiths in Gold and Platinum." *Late American Antiquity* 22, no. 1 (2011): 65–95.

Selasi, Taiye. "Bye-Bye Barbar." *Callaloo* 36, no. 3 (2013): 528–30. (Reprint of "Bye-Bye Babar," *LIP Magazine*, March 3, 2005.)

Sheftel, Anna, and Stacey Zembrzycki. "Who's Afraid of Oral History? Fifty Years of Debates and Anxiety about Ethics." *Oral History Review* 43, no. 2 (2016): 338–66.

Trouillot, Michel-Rolph. *Silencing the Past: Power and the Production of History*. Boston: Beacon Press, 1995.

Vargas, José María. *Biografía de Fray Pedro Bedón O.P.* Quito: Editorial Santo Domingo, 1965.

Vergara-Figueroa, Aurora, and Katherine Arboleda. "Feminismo afrodiaspórico: Una agenda emergente del feminismo negro en Colombia." *Universitas humanística*, no. 78 (2014): 109–34. http://dx.doi.org/10.11144/Javeriana.UH78.fafn.

Wade, Peter. *Race and Ethnicity in Latin America*. London: Pluto Press, 2010.

Blackness out of Place

Black Countervisuality in Portugal and Its Former Empire

Patrícia Martins Marcos

The grammar of black feminist futurity is a performance of a future that hasn't yet happened but must. It is an attachment to a belief in what should be true, which impels us to realize that aspiration. It is the power to imagine beyond current fact and to envision that which is not, but must be. It's a politics of pre-figuration that involves living the future *now*—as imperative rather than subjunctive—as a striving for the future you want to see, right now, in the present.
—Tina Campt, *Listening to Images*

When does racial "unconsciousness" or awareness of race enrich interpretive language, and when does it impoverish it? What does positing one's writerly self, in the wholly racialized society that is the United States, as unraced and all others as raced entail? What happens to the writerly imagination of a black author who is at some level always conscious of representing one's own race to, or in spite of, a race of readers that understands itself to be "universal" or race-free? . . . Living in a nation of people who decided that their world view would combine agendas for individual freedom and mechanisms for devastating racial oppression presents a singular landscape for a writer. When this world view is taken seriously as agency, the literature produced within and without it offers an unprecedented opportunity to comprehend the resilience and gravity, the inadequacy and the force of the imaginative act.
—Toni Morrison, *Playing in the Dark*

Radical History Review
Issue 144 (October 2022)   DOI 10.1215/01636545-9847830
© 2022 by MARHO: The Radical Historians' Organization, Inc.

Figure 1. Kiluanji Kia Henda, *Redefining the Power*. Digital photographs mounted on aluminum, 2010. A monument in Angola through its various temporal iterations: colonial, postcolonial, and countervisual quilombismo, the time of self-definition, selfhood, and new collective imaginaries. Courtesy of the artist.

Quilombismo and the Afropolitan

Despite the ubiquitous presence of Black subjects in Portugal's historical past and its (post)colonial imaginaries, both Blackness and Afro-diasporic peoples remain systematically elided from Portuguese political life and public participation. Indeed, until 2020, when the legal criteria regulating access to Portuguese citizenship first made all Afro-descendants born in Portugal after 1984 eligible, the legal path to political participation remained barred to most.[1] This omission was no accident. Rather, it speaks to an enduring strand of anti-Blackness in Portuguese postcolonialism: a hegemonic, albeit historically contingent, universalism that promised to assimilate all citizens equally into the national body. However, Portuguese claims of universal, colonial color blindness were always rather elusive. While early modern Catholicism used the doctrine of "spiritual equality available to everyone who converted" to legitimize and uphold slavery,[2] later iterations of universalism—be it *lusotropicalismo* or republicanism—recapitulated the same logic of Black assimilation into whiteness.[3] All universal promises of Black inclusion ultimately entailed its extinction. By equating color blindness with the normalized experiences of Western white men, Black subjecthood was rendered unthinkable to the nation's imaginary. Hence, Blackness—equated with race—was positioned as inherently foreign and therefore incompatible with citizenship.

This reflective essay excavates the production of a Portuguese national imaginary that can neither conceive Black agency nor accommodate Blackness outside of racializing tropes. Because of Portugal's enduring myths of colonial color

Figure 2. Patrícia Lino, *Portugal, 2019*, visual poem. The poem explores how borders create enclosure and separate peoples through ethnocentric concepts of belonging, and how such moves to separate or sort life into nation-state categories that reify whiteness, coloniality, and racial citizenship.

blindness, Afro-descendants remain incommensurate with the Portuguese body politic, figuring as "bodies in but not of."[4] Against this mold, practices of Black countervisuality—or what I am calling *countervisual quilombismo*—constitute a method of historical retelling and an aesthetic practice that cuts across the epistemic limits of colonial essentialisms.[5] Performative, ephemeral movements reject the fixity of colonial monuments and rupture their stone-chiseled ambitions of eternity. Rather, Black subjects assert liberation as praxis and, in doing so, offer new imaginaries for Black life. Yet, because they suggest *marronage* or escape, specifically from slavery, these knowledge-making acts enacted as surrealist, poetic, and visual performances remain illegible to Western epistemes.[6] Black people in motion affirm diasporic personhood and expose the silences encoded in the sterilized white spaces of Portuguese imperial glorification.

In developing the practice of liberation, or what bell hooks called "a visual politics" and a "black vernacular," countervisual enactments refuse fixity and subvert both rigid canons and conventions.[7] In other words, they manifest what Neil Roberts termed as "freedom as marronage."[8] Performers use embodied movement to expose the curated whiteness of Portuguese colonial monuments and reveal geographies of racial exclusion.[9] In doing so, artists like the Angolan Kiluanji Kia Henda, or the Afro-Luso-Brazilian diasporic trio Aurora Negra, use their work to refuse the ethnographic reduction of Blackness to *a body*. Unlike the Western sciences, they aim not for universality but to affirm Blackness outside of colonial teleologies, that is, to assert Blackness rather than the mere "fact" of a Black body. At the same time, diasporic citizens like Joacine Katar Moreira intentionally deploy their physical presence in political spaces to enact "theory-in-praxis."[10] Moreira, in the photograph depicting her that will be discussed below, refuses the fetishist objectification of colonized peoples as racialized bodies and affirms her status as a historical and political agent.

As a method, countervisual quilombismo is diasporic. It weaves together Brazil, Cape Verde, Guinea-Bissau, Angola, Mozambique, and Portugal, but as an epistemology of marronage, it is also designed to evade detection. Unlike the captivity of Portuguese colonial epistemes and its attending geographic enclosures, these artists and activists demonstrate radical knowledge-making imaginaries for Black life. They enact transnational solidarity, political self-determination, and historical autonomy—or a history of Black being—outside of the narrative of slavery.[11] Such practices enact "freedom as marronage" and are diasporic at heart. They begin with physical movement as a site of resistance and progress toward marronage as the practice of collective liberation. This formulation draws on Beatriz Nascimento's research on Afro-Brazilian maroon communities, or *quilombos*, and her rich theoretical elaboration of the nexus between flight, body, recovery, spatial liberation, and community.[12] For Nascimento, the quilombo was the crux of Black life.[13] Quilombos signified the possibility of historical autonomy and created spaces to imagine Black being before and beyond colonial domination.[14] Contingent over time, quilombos were at once metaphors and material spaces—a heuristic for freedom and liberty embodied in each fugitive act and person.[15] Both as a symbol and concept, quilombismo also became a wider cultural and political Afro-Brazilian movement in the 1970s and 1980s. Articulated by Abdias Nascimento, quilombismo represented an Afrocentric revolutionary worldview that sought Black liberation and novel "cognitive maps of the future."[16] Through art, aesthetics, religiosity, and cultural memory, Nascimento challenged Brazilian fictions of "racial democracy" and placed Black aesthetics at the crux of political kin and sovereignty.

This protean conception of quilombismo informs my formulation of Black autonomy and my approach to the radical, countervisual methods of self-definition explored here. To decipher Black sovereignty and self-determination entails eschewing liberal fantasies of the individual and "proprietorial notions of the self."[17] Rather, sovereignty elicits the power of asserting Black being without an external or Western referential. This entails the affirmation of Black historical subjecthood beyond the story of enslavement and colonial domination; the right to

African, Black, and diasporic histories whose chronologies and conventions interrupt Eurocentric temporality; the avowal of self-defined epistemes devised to operate outside of Western knowledge-making formulas; and the pronouncing of Africans as theorists and knowledge makers of their own realities. This vision reaches beyond emancipatory imaginaries because, as Beatriz Nascimento argued, it resets the default settings of the Black past, present, and future to liberty rather than liberation. Ushering the potentiality of histories where Black being and kinship exist without the overdetermined narrative of struggle from slavery, the centering of Black sovereignty forces the suspension of coloniality.[18]

In this reflection, *countervisual quilombismo* refers to aesthetic practices developed by Afro-Luso-Brazilians to figure Black autonomy rather than presenting it as a reaction to whiteness.[19] This concept of countervisual quilombismo, as an epistemic and visual departure, disrupts official Portuguese narratives of universal, unmarked whiteness; and in doing so, it confronts silences and expands the range of sanctioned protagonists permissible in the nation's history—indeed, it may even demand letting go of the nation as the key vessel for history.[20] Moreover, drawing from an Afropolitan sensibility, countervisual Black production also challenges the assumption of assimilation and pursues instead what Pamila Gupta calls "decolonization as diaspora-making."[21]

This exploration of diaspora as method and quilombismo as a world-making episteme seeks a dialogue with Achille Mbembe's conception of the Afropolitan, specifically his call for "new images for thought."[22] But it also addresses some notable exclusions. Despite Mbembe's extensive engagement with mobility and displacement—particularly inasmuch as they integrate the *longue durée* of African history, therefore challenging modernity, the naturalization of borders, and the nation-state—his essays on Afropolitanism hardly engage marronage and diaspora as analytics. In addition, Afro-Luso-Brazilian spaces are also relatively neglected, while the contributions of Black feminist theory and of the Black radical intellectual and anti-colonial tradition are also somewhat overlooked.

Countervisual quilombismo addresses these silences while, following bell hooks, it also thinks about lived experience as a mechanism to theorize liberation as praxis.[23] By enlisting these wider solidarities through traditions of Black thought and knowledge making, perhaps Afropolitanism could skirt the accusations of upper-class bias that mired the concept in long polemical debates.[24] For that reason, this reflection offers avenues to establish a dialectic between Afropolitanism, diaspora, and quilombismo.

Perhaps Mbembe's declared Pan-African skepticism—or what he sees as the present exhaustion of Cold War imaginaries for a view of decolonization based on models of racial and transnational solidarity, *and* internationalist and anti-imperialist solidarity—animates his Afropolitan orientation to underplay these historically significant traditions of Black emancipation. However, it is also necessary to acknowledge that the new imaginaries and "images for thought" Mbembe so ardently desires hardly constitute a new evocation. Indeed, they were already constitutive of various established traditions of Black liberation, both in thought and action. Within this context, diaspora and marronage offer models capable of equating freedom with anti-colonial refusal and the struggle for self-definition outside of colonial and Western-centric analytical dichotomies. If, however, Mbembe's Afropolitan desire for a tabula rasa entails a radical departure from maroon world making and diasporic Black resistance, then a further elaboration on how to concretize it and why it is different from others seems imperative. As it is presently framed, especially when considering the role that movement and dislocation play in his Afropolitan "aesthetic sensitivity," these omissions create some perplexity.[25] Be it through Mbembe's evocative images of "worlds-in-movement," his appeal for the "interweaving of worlds," or his stress on "itineracy, mobility, and displacement," the Afropolitan hardly seems possible without diasporas and fugitivity.

Maroon Epistemes and the Weapon of Theory

To note such inconsistencies does not render the concept of the Afropolitan moot. Fundamentally, Mbembe pursues a paradigm of sociality situated beyond the Pan-African gravitational pull toward the nation-state. His effort lies with rejecting "enclosures" and in producing the "unbordering" of the world by reimagining a commons of itinerant belongings, with identities unmoored to either biocentrism or the nation-state. Through a focus on Africa's heterogeneous pluralities, as Mbembe puts it, his Afropolitan view "deuniversalizes" Western epistemes. This move demands the reinvention of theory and a critique of liberal humanism that can excavate how science was "shaped by the eclipsed priorities of a Western mind."[26]

Stressing mind here is vital because the identification of reason with the West was critical to legitimate colonial extraction and codify "black objecthood" both as a scientific problem and an imperial fiction. In knowledge-making contexts, the reduction of Blackness into a corporeal ontology depleted Black people into quantifiable, racial data that, as Frantz Fanon noted, was "overdetermined from without."[27] But this identification of theory and Logos with specific dominant "genres of being human" cannot be separated from racial capitalist and colonial regimes.[28] After all, the reduction of people into racialized bodies was crucial to create labor and sustain the expendability of Black life through the Middle Passage. Thus, the crafting of "black fungible bodies" cannot be separated from Western technoscience, medicalization, and the ethnographic invention of human rank.[29]

Because Black autonomy and self-determination are incommensurate with the same colonial epistemes that were fashioned to confine Blackness to the status of object, any Black intellectual analysis that eschews taxonomy for radical self-definition is, therefore, bound for illegibility. In other words, because theory is the "West's attempt at domesticating contingency," as Mbembe noted, any emancipatory and maroon epistemology centered on Black being and liberation is bound to transcend the enclosed limits of Western knowledge.[30] After all, how could an epistemic and social order built to rank and govern difference achieve any other conclusion? Afrocentric theory, Afropolitan or other, mounts a fundamental challenge to whiteness, because any affirmation of Black autonomous life suggests an existence outside of colonial matrices. Put differently, maroon epistemes constitute a form of "oppositional knowledge."[31] Standards designed to objectify Blackness cannot recognize marronage as a legitimate way of knowing—especially since theory and praxis are inextricable. Racialized knowers are therefore often construed as unreasoned, unable or unwilling to adhere to procedure, and consequently ill prepared for self-determination. For instance, Portuguese colonial authorities delegitimated anti-colonial world making by labeling critics of Portuguese colonialism such as Amílcar Cabral (fig. 3) and others as "terrorists."[32] Cabral, a revolutionary from Guinea-Bissau, became an essential figure of the wars of African liberation against Portuguese colonialism fought from the 1960s until his murder in 1973. While Cabral was a key theorist of liberation, his ideas also led to action.[33] Specifically, among all three military insurgencies the Portuguese faced in Africa—including in Angola and Mozambique—Guineans not only challenged "the more powerful and better-equipped Portuguese army, [but] they also [laid] the groundwork for a postcolonial state."[34] Yet, propped up by fictions of universal reason, Portuguese colonialism cast Africans' desire for sovereignty as illogical. The wars of African Liberation (1961–74) epitomized this system of Western coloniality. Consequently, for Cabral, freedom for Guinea-Bissau and Cape Verde entailed as much economic liberation as it did cultural, political, historical, and epistemic emancipation.[35]

In Havana in 1966, Cabral offered an African reading of Marx in a speech known as "The Weapon of Theory."[36] Provincializing Marxism avant la lettre, Cabral presented an African reading of revolutionary struggle that challenged class as the vector of historicity. His critique of Marxist Eurocentrism stressed how the primacy of class excluded colonized peoples from history, rendering them as "proper" historical subjects only after "they were subjected to the yoke of imperialism."[37] Among other things, imperial domination usurped colonized peoples' freedom by negating their access to historicity. Thus, Cabral concluded, "The national liberation of a people is the regaining of the historical personality of that people, its return to history through the destruction of the imperialist domination to which it was subjected."[38] While history was a precondition for freedom, liberation became unthinkable without dismantling colonial oppression. In this manner, Cabral eschewed universal proclamations for the concrete analysis of specific cases of colonial domination—a move that required balancing theory and concrete experience. Specifically, it meant that each colonized people had to forge their own unique approach to liberation, since each emancipatory struggle created novel

Figure 3. Amílcar Cabral in Cuba with Fidel Castro during the 1966 Tricontinental Conference, at which Cabral presented his speech "The Weapon of Theory."

historical possibilities. To that end, no revolution could ever succeed without the support of a sound revolutionary theory, because theory and concrete action were inextricable to African liberation.

By bringing together revolutionary thought and praxis, Cabral reimagined intellectual work and expanded the meaning of revolution as a knowledge maker. But also, in articulating an umbilical tie between ideology and practice, Cabral evoked a long-standing tradition in Black thought: how knowledge drawn from lived experiences of oppression and resistance informed theoretical comprehension as well as self-recovery and collective liberation.[39] Through this resignification of theoretical labor—a defining feature of Afrocentric emancipatory conscience—Cabral exposed the elisions of universal reason and rebuffed Western epistemic conventions. This was tantamount to an epistemic *aquilombamento*. This transformation of *quilombo* from noun to verb—that is, from a place to an action, with the suffix *-mento* indicating the outcome of an act that occurred in a specific place—makes an overture to the "broad-mindedness" of "intellectual life in Africa" that Mbembe discussed. "Afropolitan culture," he adds, can thus be the outcome of a transnational exploration of new "possibilities in art" by configuring "a philosophy [and] an aesthetics that can say something new and meaningful to the world in general."[40] Given his stress on non-nativism, the absented dialogue with either diasporic or maroon traditions raises some questions. For, be it through forced dislocation or flight, Black people have constantly reinvented their grounds and pushed against imposed narratives.[41] Both quilombismo—the aesthetic Afro-Brazilian movement—and Cabral's stress on the pivotal role of culture in national emancipation exemplify the possibilities of maroon epistemes. Linking the Afropolitan with these Afro-Luso-Brazilian traditions can only expand such decolonial agendas. And, while Mbembe's desire to think without or outside of Pan-African nationalism is understandable, both Cabralism and quilombismo constitute two important intellectual traditions of anti-colonial solidarity, developing kin beyond ethnocentrism or borders.

Refusing Ethnography: The Power of Black Countervisuality

Black presence seems unthinkable in postcolonial Portugal because of the ways racial ideologies, empire, and the resulting myth of racial democracy interact. First, the dominant idea of "imperial whiteness," defined race (*raça*) as a hereditary "defect" inherent *only* to non-Christians.[42] As a result whiteness remained unmarked in the Portuguese metropole. Second, the rejection of whiteness as a racialized position, and the omission of colonialism from Portuguese national history, positioned Africa and Blackness outside the nation.[43] With Blackness serving as the ultimate metonym for race, diasporic people were configured in Portuguese national imaginaries as bodies out of place—frozen in ethnographic types and marked as inherently foreign. Finally, the visual power of imperial whiteness and the ideology of Lusotropicalism presuppose an adherence to the fiction that Portuguese colonial methods were color-blind and foundational to the Brazilian ideology of "racial democracy."[44]

The colonial ideology of *lusotropicalismo*, developed by the Brazilian Gilberto Freyre, declared Portuguese colonialism exceptional by stressing "miscegenation" and how sexual congress between "masters and slaves" led to "the creation" of the *mulatto*—the embodiment of color blindness.[45] However, this tale negated the ubiquity of racial and sexual violence as well as all power asymmetries inherent to any slave society.[46] Hence, for *lusotropicalismo*, Blackness remained viable only inasmuch as it was biologically and culturally diluted and assimilated into whiteness. Abdias Nascimento's formulation of quilombismo rebuked such tacit adherence to lusotropical "whitening" (*branqueamento*) as the visual and epistemic standard, and articulated how *mestiçagem* (miscegenation) was nothing but a technology of Black extinction.[47] Lélia Gonzalez and Beatriz Nascimento, among other Black feminists, also offered critiques not just of assimilation into whiteness but of the role of gendered violence. Gonzalez, in particular, began theorizing in the 1970s and 1980s about the intersecting oppressions endured by Black women, coining analytics like *améfricanidade*, which became critical for Black, diasporic, and feminist thinkers.[48]

More than ideology, *lusotropicalismo* also laid out the aesthetic base for Portuguese imperial visual culture.[49] This visual complex elevated white masculinity as the hypervisible emblem of prototypical humanity (fig. 4), encoding it into monuments, art, museums, and the idea of urban life. Intent on representing the collective Portuguese past as white, upper class, and male, the Oliveira Salazar regime—during the Estado Novo (1933–74) dictatorship—confined Blackness to the trope of "savagery." These dynamics of visual coloniality find their epitome in Belém, Lisbon's westernmost borough. First imagined in the 1500s by King Manuel I to celebrate the Portuguese arrival in India (1498) and Brazil (1500), Belém was subsequently subject to multiple visual-monumental interventions over the centuries. The most recent and comprehensive interventions date to the 1940s and 1960s—respectively, the "Exhibit of the Portuguese World" and the five-hundred-year anniversary of Prince Henry the Navigator, both organized by Salazar's colonial-fascist regime.[50] The 1940 exhibit's spatial layout, in particular, encoded racial hierarchies onto the production of space. Whereas Belém's "noble" areas, near the early modern Monastery of Jerónimos and the Tower of Belém, were imagined by the regime as spaces of white heroism, racialized subjects—especially but not exclusively Africans—were confined to the Tropical Botanical Garden and physically enclosed in the Colonial Ethnographic Section (Secção Etnográfica Colonial), where they were put on display. Prefiguring "a human zoo," this section confined Blackness to objecthood and carcerality (fig. 5).[51]

I propose the concept of countervisual quilombismo to upend these visual representations of racial hierarchy by highlighting African resistance to rigid Western biocentric taxonomies. Black diasporic performers disrupt the colonial frame with their insurgent movements, thus manifesting histories of Blackness as life. Kiluanji Kia Henda's *The Discovery* (fig. 6) exposes Belém as a "transparent space" by revealing imperial visuality and the labor needed to sustain Black exclusion.[52] Henda's subjects—all young men from Lisbon's underserved, racialized peripheries—appear as a corporeal interjection by standing and sitting on the monument as if to suggest "the managers of history cannot erase us."[53] Before Henda composed the photograph, and while each performer began to claim their place in Belém's Square of Empire (Praça do Império), the police confronted the young men and demanded their identification cards.[54] In this moment encapsulating the exclusions of imperial visual regimes, police scrutiny reduced their Blackness to a sign of criminal threat by coding their Black subjecthood as existing "out of place." Through this act of surveillance, police power reenacted what Joaquín Barriendos calls the "coloniality of seeing."[55]

Similar examples, this time improvised and with African children as protagonists, can be found in Ernst Schade's 2005 photograph from Cachéu, Guinea-Bissau (fig. 7), and in the still from Celso Luccas's film 25 (1975) (fig. 8). While the former rendered the statue of the "colonial hero" unimportant through

Figure 4. The sculptor Leopoldo de Almeida and several workers, *Henry the Navigator* (detail). There are no known portraits of the prince and thus, as Trouillot noted, "The Monument to the Discoveries had to invent a face for the Prince, just as Europe had to invent a face for the West" (110). Avenida da Índia Atelier, by Estúdio Mário Novais (1940). Fundação Calouste Gulbenkian, CFT003.061375.ic.

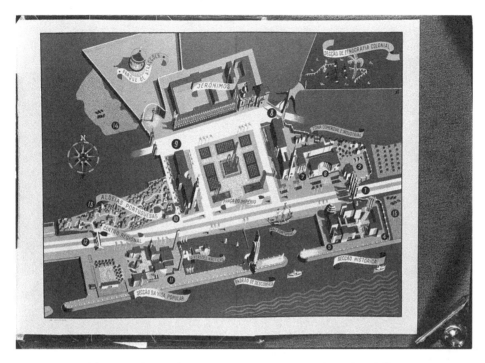

Figure 5. *Map of the 1940 Exhibit of the Portuguese World.* Perspective by Fred Kradolfer (1940). By Estúdio Mário Novais, Fundação Calouste Gulbenkian, CFT003.023751.ic. The white space of imperial visuality.

nonchalance, by placing himself above the white hero in the composition, the latter raises his hand in victory, standing atop an inverted Portuguese coat of arms in riotous celebration of Mozambique's independence. Each composition is rendered all the more powerful because we can observe the resignification in action: these symbols of imperial visuality are refashioned as instantiations of Black being and countervisual sovereign praxis.

To unlearn the preassigned hierarchies of spectatorship demands subverting the conventions of imperial visuality in multiple ways. Countervisual quilombismo pursues just that. These methods present abolitionist technologies and facilitate the crafting of more polyphonic pasts—for example, the representation of Black, Indigenous, Crip, or Queer histories.[56] Performative and visual methods also configure different modes of resistance or being that rupture established silences. For example, the play *Aurora Negra* (Black Dawn) (fig. 9), the first production by three Black women staged at Portugal's National Theater, challenges narratives of citizenship and belonging through song, dance, music, words, laughter, and unruly movement. Through this method, the performers resignify Blackness as joy and hope: "My body, I authorize you to occupy any place." A dialogue that places Queen Maria II—the first monarch to be born in Brazil, whose name was displayed on the façade of the

Figure 6. Kiluanji Kia Henda, *A descoberta*, 2007. Before the performance and shoot, the Lisbon police racially profiled the protagonists of the photograph. By demanding to see their IDs in that space of prototypical whiteness, the police deemed them as bodies out of place and continued to enforce the regime of imperial visuality as the "correct order." The performers belonged to the Association TDK (bairro do Lumiar, Lisbon).

Figure 7. *Africa, Guinea-Bissau, Cacheu* (2005). Photo by Ernst Schade, De Beeldunie. A boy sits on top of a statue of the Portuguese colonial explorer Nuno Trisao. After independence in 1974 this and other statues were removed from the capital of Bissau and dumped in a field near the village of Cacheu. Courtesy of the artist.

Figure 8. *25, A Revolução de Moçambique*, dir. Celso Luccas and José Celso Martinez Corrêa, 1975–76. Screenshot from the film depicting the Mozambican transition to independence in 1976.

theater—the conversation among the characters, in Creole and Chokwe, draws contrasts between the Queen's identity as Portuguese and their position as "foreign."[57] In the second act, two characters relay their stories of migration and arrival in Portugal. Departing, respectively, from Cape Verde and Angola, they recalled reaching a destination that suspected their motives, facing the border police interrogation, and spending suspended time at the airport "detention" as children in custody. The last character, however, did not need to arrive. She was born in Portugal—unlike the Queen—yet her Blackness made her legible as an unnatural presence.

Braiding each other's hair as they practice intimate kinship onstage, suddenly an external narrator interrupts their personal accounts. Questioning the mise-en-scène, a disembodied voice rejects their subjectivity and clamors for the familiar. Instead of Black women's intimacy and kinship making, the voice demands a recapitulation of platitudes about the African "exotic." This face-off between the white, colonial frame and a self-defined Black gaze brings the play to an inflection point.[58] The white habitus of confining Blackness to discrete categories and legible

Figure 9. *Aurora Negra.* Photo by Felipe Drehmer, body art by Tony Cassanelli, 2020. Depicted: Bruno Huca, Cleo Diára, Isabél Zuaa, Mauro Hermínio, Nádia Yracema, and Paulo Pascoal.

classifications is upended by the diasporic assertion of Édouard Glissant's "right to opacity."[59] As diasporic women, they refuse the enclosure of ethnographic frames. And by threading Guinea-Bissau to Cape Verde, Angola, Portugal, and Brazil, they assert new models of relation and existence, refusing the taxonomies of Black confinement. In doing so, *Aurora Negra* cultivated onstage a quilombo that celebrated ancestors, honored diaspora, and affirmed a commitment to Black being, irrespective of nation or place of birth.

In January 2019, similar displays of diasporic solidarity took place in the streets of Lisbon. It was a one-of-a-kind protest; first because it was not planned; second, the participants were not activists but teenagers and young adults, many of whom were ineligible for Portuguese citizenship; and last, the crowd spanned the diaspora. Raquel Borges and Yane Brazão were two of the many participants. Depicted in a photograph, they emerge against the whiteness of an old monastery— a site of Catholic universalism—evoking Black conscience and internationalist solidarity with their coordinated Black Power gesture (fig. 10). While Borges and

Figure 10. *Raquel Borges and Yane Brazão.* Photo by Nuno Ferreira Monteiro, Público, January 27, 2019.

Brazão may not be citizens—since, like many others in attendance, the citizenship law valid at the time of the protest rendered most Afro-descendants born in Portugal between 1984 and 2019 nearly ineligible for citizenship—they nevertheless projected themselves as self-determined and fully political subjects.[60]

Though Afro-diasporic assertions of political and historical autonomy are not always oriented to the telos of citizenship, the protest in January 2019 marked a crucial turning point in Portuguese history. Months later, in October, this momentum was fortified in the election of three Black women—another first in Portugal's democratic history. Joacine Katar Moreira was one of them (fig. 11). Moreira, born in Guinea-Bissau and a historian of gender and colonialism, deliberately composed this photograph with her defiant self-presentation in mind. Standing in the Parliament's Noble Hall (Salão Nobre), Moreira rises against colonial murals, which not only represent or visualize colonialism but in fact are colonialism in action.[61] Painted in 1940, the year of the Exhibit of the Portuguese World, the murals prefigure what art historian Inês Beleza Barreiros conceptualized as the Portuguese imperial visuality complex.[62] Yet Moreira refuses to be reduced to Black objecthood. Her gravitas is unapologetic, her gaze defiant. With her arms crossed, standing against a background of prostrate, racialized bodies depicted as welcoming the purportedly salvific arrival of Portuguese colonization, it is she who observes us—and in doing so, she upends every convention of institutional and gendered portraiture. Her self-determined subjecthood ruptures the assumed transparency of

Figure 11. *Joacine Katar Moreira.* Photo by Daniel Rocha, Público, 2019. Picture taken shortly after Katar Moreira's election and placed on the front page of Portugal's largest newspaper of record. She wrote the inscription for the image herself: "In the grand hall of the Assembly of the Republic, countering the colonial logic and the exposed and institutionalized subalternization [inherent] to colonialism and slavery [imposed] in this space."

that space's exclusionary designs and hegemonic imperial visuality. By confronting the historical fiction encoded in that room, Joacine Katar Moreira claimed her own right to historicity and self-determination. And just like that, other pasts, a different present, and many more futures became possible *in that moment*, through acts of seeing and being seen. Freedom as marronage was embodied in the grammar of one's own self-defined liberty because ultimately, the weapon of theory lies within.

Patrícia Martins Marcos (UCLA—UC Chancellor's Postdoctoral Fellow) is a scholar of Portuguese colonialism and postcolonialism working at the intersections of history of race, science, medicine, and visual culture in the Afro-Luso-Brazilian Atlantic. She is associate editor of the *History of Anthropology Review*. Her work has been supported by the Consortium for the History of Science, Technology, and Medicine; the Huntington Library; American Philosophical Society; the John Carter Brown Library; the Folger Shakespeare Library; and the Center for Black, Brown, and Queer Studies.

Notes

In memory of Trisha Tschopp, a generous colleague and the voice of steadfast pursuits

1. As long as parents resided in Portugal for a year prior to birth and were not expats working for a foreign government. "Lei Orgânica n.º 2/2020," *Diário da República*, no. 219/2020, 2–15, https://dre.pt/dre/detalhe/lei-organica/2-2020-148086464.
2. Rowe, "After Death, Her Face Turned White," 728.
3. *Lusotropicalismo* is a theory articulated by the Brazilian social scientist Gilberto Freyre, who argued that Brazilian "racial democracy" was the by-product of Portugal's benign colonial methods of racial mixing between colonizer and colonized. Entirely oblivious to power, sexual abuse, and the violence of colonial domination, Freyre argued the "uniquely Portuguese way of existing in the world" was premised on racial and cultural mixing. For decades, the Portuguese dictatorship (1928–74) used Freyre's words to reinvent a colonial policy capable of enduring the decolonial tides pushing through Africa between the 1950s and the 1970s. Freyre, *The Portuguese and the Tropics*; Freyre, *Aventura e rotina*; Freyre, *O luso e o trópico*; Castelo, *O modo português de estar no mundo*.
4. Moten and Harney, "The University and the Undercommons."
5. Morrison, *The Source of Self-Regard*.
6. For definitions of the West and its historicization, see Trouillot, *Silencing the Past*; and Mignolo, *Darker Side of the Renaissance*.
7. hooks, *Art on My Mind*.
8. Roberts, *Freedom as Marronage*.
9. Mirzoeff, "Artificial Vision."
10. Barreiros and Moreira, "'To Decolonize Is to Perform.'"
11. Weinbaum, *The Afterlife of Reproductive Slavery*.
12. Beatriz Nascimento was a critical figure of the Afro-Brazilian Black and feminist movement from the 1970s until her murder in 1995. Nascimento, "O conceito de quilombo"; Nascimento, *Uma história feita por mãos negras*; *Ôrí* (documentary, dir. Raquel Gerber, Brazil, 1989). Alongside Beatriz, Abdias Nascimento also elaborated on

the concept of quilombo as a form of Black aesthetic resistance since the 1970s and until his death in 2011. Nascimento, *O genocídio do negro brasileiro*; Nascimento et al., *O quilombismo*; Nascimento, "Quilombismo."

13. The quilombo was originally a precolonial West Central African (Imbangala and Ovinbundu) institution brought to the Americas through transatlantic forced dislocation. In colonial Brazil, it evolved throughout centuries of Portuguese colonization, continuing to change well into Brazilian independence. At the end of the 1800s, the quilombo became gradually codified as an ideological unit and a symbol of Afro-Brazilian resistance. In the 1970s and 1980s, it became a critical symbol of the Black liberation struggle. Nascimento, "O conceito de quilombo." Lara, *Palmares & Cucaú*.

14. Wynter, "1492: A New World View."

15. Smith, Davies, and Gomes, "'In Front of the World'"; Smith, "Towards a Black Feminist Model."

16. Nascimento et al., *O quilombismo*; Kelley, *Freedom Dreams*.

17. Hartman, *Scenes of Subjection*, 6.

18. *Ôrí* (documentary, dir. Raquel Gerber, Brazil, 1989); Quijano, *Ensayos en torno a la colonialidad del poder*.

19. Morrison, *The Source of Self-Regard*.

20. My elaboration of imperial visuality and countervisual resistance draws on Mirzoeff, *The Right to Look*. While I articulate a hegemonic method of organizing space by placing the onus of historical agency on a white, heteropatriarchal model of the human, Mirzoeff expresses methods that oppose imperial authority through claims to autonomy and assertions of the right to become visible. Countervisuality thus formulates a challenge to "the real" codified in hegemonic imperialist visual conventions. It is a form of visual abolitionism. For unmarked whiteness, see Frankenberg, "The Mirage"; and Martins Marcos, "Producing the Fiction."

21. Gupta, "Ethnographies of the Lusophone Indian Ocean."

22. Mbembe, *Out of the Dark*.

23. hooks, "Theory as Liberatory Practice."

24. Bwesigye, "Is Afropolitanism Africa's New Single Story?"; Dabiri, "'Why I Am (Still) Not an Afropolitan'"; Santana, "Exorcizing Afropolitanism"; Tveit, "The Afropolitan Must Go."

25. Mbembe, "Afropolitanism."

26. Tallbear, "Science and Whiteness."

27. Fanon, *The Wretched of the Earth*.

28. Wynter, "Unsettling the Coloniality."

29. King, *The Black Shoals*.

30. Mbembe, *Out of the Dark*.

31. Hill Collins, *Black Feminist Thought*.

32. Portugal, "'Para Angola e em força.'"

33. Serequeberhan, "The African Anti-colonial Struggle."

34. Tomás, *Amílcar Cabral*, 1–2.

35. Cabral, *Documentário*.

36. Cabral, "The Weapon of Theory."

37. Cabral, *Unity and Struggle*.

38. Cabral, "The Weapon of Theory."

39. hooks, "Theory as Liberatory Practice."

40. Mbembe, "Afropolitanism."

41. Torres-Saillant, *An Intellectual History of the Caribbean*.
42. For imperial whiteness, see Hussain, "Race, Gender, and Beauty." For the definition of race as the possession of "defect," exempting white Christians, see *Regimento do Santo Officio*.
43. Paraphrased from Stoler, *Duress*, 12.
44. Freyre, *Aventura e rotina*; Dávila, "Raça, etnicidade e colonialismo"; Dávila, *Hotel Trópico*; Graham, *Shifting the Meaning of Democracy*.
45. Freyre, *Casa-grande & senzala*.
46. Aidoo, *Slavery Unseen*.
47. Nascimento et al., *O quilombismo*.
48. *Améfricanidade* aimed for the liberation of diasporic Black people across the Americas and laid crucial stress on the connection between Black and Indigenous struggles. Gonzalez, *Por um feminismo afro-latino-americano*; Perry and Sotero, "Amefricanidade."
49. Barreiros et al., "O padre António Vieira." Barreiros, "As pinturas murais"; Barreiros, "Assembleia da república."
50. "Colonial-fascismo" was a designation coined by Hélio Jaguaribe in Brazil and adopted by the liberation fighters who opposed Portuguese colonialism in Africa to designate Portugal's political regime. See Jaguaribe, "Brasil."
51. Castelo, "Simulação e dissimulação do império colonial."
52. "Transparent space" is the idea that space "just is, and the illusion that the external world is readily knowable and not in need of evaluation, and that what we see is true" (McKittrick, *Demonic Grounds*, xv).
53. The expression "the managers of history" is borrowed from Trouillot's *Silencing the Past*, especially from chapter 4, "Good Day, Columbus," which starts in Belém and provides an analysis of the palimpsest of myths and silences enforced in and by that space.
54. Personal communication from Dr. Marta Lança, who was with Henda when this happened. Article 250 of the Portuguese Penal Code allows the police to request identification if suspicious of illegal presence in national territory.
55. For Barriendos, the coloniality of seeing "acts as a hierarchic pattern of domination . . . [or a] visual matrix" used to order and make visible the inferior status of "savage" and "primitive" peoples, who are rendered into objects, racialized, and placed into a hierarchy of being ("La colonialidad del Ver").
56. Sandahl, "Queering the Crip or Cripping the Queer?"
57. On stage, they speak Cape Verdean Creole, Guinean Creole, and Chokwe, a language spoken by the Chokwe (Chokwe) people whose territory is located in present-day Angola.
58. Campt, *A Black Gaze*.
59. Glissant, *Poetics of Relation*.
60. On this point, see note 1. For Yane Brazão and Raquel Borges's interview, see Henriques, "Estrearam-se numa manifestação."
61. Barreiros, "As pinturas murais."
62. Barreiros, "As pinturas murais."

References

Aidoo, Lamonte. *Slavery Unseen: Sex, Power, and Violence in Brazilian History*. Durham, NC: Duke University Press, 2018.

Barreiros, Inês Beleza. "As pinturas murais do Salão Nobre da Assembleia da República: Documento do colonialismo ou o colonialismo (ainda hoje) em acção?" *Buala*, October 31, 2021.

Barreiros, Inês Beleza. "Assembleia da República: A entrada do corpo negro." *ReMapping Memories Lisboa–Hamburg*, Goethe Institut Portugal, September 2021. https://rb.gy /hslfnw.

Barreiros, Inês Beleza, and Joacine Katar Moreira. "'To Decolonize Is to Perform': The Theory-in-Praxis of Grada Kilomba." In *Challenging Memories and Rebuilding Identities: Literary and Artistic Voices That Undo the Lusophone Atlantic*, edited by Margarida Rendeiro and Federica Lupati, 56–81. London: Routledge, 2019.

Barreiros, Inês Beleza, Patrícia Martins Marcos, Pedro Schacht Pereira, and Rui Gomes Coelho. "O padre António Vieira no país dos cordiais." *Público*, February 2, 2020. http://tiny.cc /anacronismocordiais.

Barriendos, Joaquín. "La colonialidad del Ver: Hacia un nuevo diálogo visual interepistémico." *Nómadas*, no. 35 (July 2011): 13–29.

Bwesigye, Brian. "Is Afropolitanism Africa's New Single Story?" *Aster(ix) Journal*, November 22, 2013. https://asterixjournal.com/afropolitanism-africas-new-single-story-reading-helon -habilas-review-need-new-names-brian-bwesigye/.

Cabral, Amílcar. *Documentário: (Textos políticos e culturais)*. Edited by António E. Duarte Silva. Lisboa: Cotovia, 2008.

Cabral, Amílcar. *Unity and Struggle: Speeches and Writings*. Texts selected by the Partido Africano da Independência da Guiné e Cabo Verde; translated by Michael Wolfers. New York: Monthly Review Press, 2016.

Cabral, Amílcar. "The Weapon of Theory: Presuppositions and Objectives of National Liberation in Relation to Social Structure." In Cabral, *Unity and Struggle*, 119–37.

Campt, Tina. *A Black Gaze: Artists Changing How We See*. Cambridge, MA: MIT Press, 2021.

Castelo, Cláudia. *"O modo português de estar no mundo": O luso-tropicalismo e a ideologia colonial portuguesa (1933–1961)*. Porto: Edições Afrontamento, 1998.

Castelo, Cláudia. "Simulação e dissimulação do império colonial português em Belém, Lisboa (1940/2020): A secção colonial e o jardim botânico tropical." *Anais do Museu Histórico Nacional* 54 (2021): 1–24. https://repositorio.ul.pt/handle/10451/49405.

Dabiri, Emma. "'Why I Am (Still) Not an Afropolitan.'" *Journal of African Cultural Studies* 28, no. 1 (2016): 104–8.

Dávila, Jerry. *Hotel Trópico: Brazil and the Challenge of African Decolonization, 1950–1980*. Durham, NC: Duke University Press, 2010.

Dávila, Jerry. "Raça, etnicidade e colonialismo português na obra de Gilberto Freyre." *Desigualdade & Diversidade*, no. 7 (2010): 153–74.

Fanon, Frantz. *The Wretched of the Earth*. 1961; repr., translated by Constance Farrington London: Penguin Books, 2001.

Frankenberg, Ruth. "The Mirage of an Unmarked Whiteness." In *The Making and Unmaking of Whiteness*, edited by Birgit Brander Rasmussen, Eric Klinenberg, Irene J. Nexica, and Matt Wray, 72–96. Durham, NC: Duke University Press, 2001.

Freyre, Gilberto. *Aventura e rotina*. Lisboa: Livros do Brasil, 1953.

Freyre, Gilberto. *Casa-grande & senzala: Formação da família brasileira sob o regimen de economia patriarchal*. Rio de Janeiro: Maia & Schmidt, 1933.

Freyre, Gilberto. *O luso e o trópico: Sugestões em torno dos métodos portugueses de integração de povos autóctones e de culturas diferentes da europeia num complexo novo de civilização: O luso-tropical*. Lisboa: Comissão Executiva das Comemorações de V Centenário da Morte de Infante D. Henrique, 1961.

Freyre, Gilberto. *The Portuguese and the Tropics: Suggestions Inspired by the Portuguese Methods of Integrating Autocthonous Peoples and Cultures Differing from the European in a New, or Luso-tropical Complex of Civilisation.* Translated by Helen M. D'O., Matthew and F. de Mello Moser. Lisbon: Executive Committee for the Commemoration of the Fifth Centenary of the Death of Prince Henry the Navigator, 1961.

Glissant, Édouard. *Poetics of Relation.* Translated by Betsy Wing, Ann Arbor: University of Michigan Press, 1997.

Gonzalez, Lélia. *Por um feminismo afro-latino-americano: Ensaios, interenções e diálogos.* Rio de Janeiro: Jorge Zahar, 2020.

Graham, Jessica Lynn. *Shifting the Meaning of Democracy: Race, Politics, and Culture in the United States and Brazil.* Oakland: University of California Press, 2019.

Gupta, Pamila. "Ethnographies of the Lusophone Indian Ocean." Webinar, the Research Centre for Luso-Asian Studies (CIELA), University of Macau, November 11, 2021.

Hartman, Saidiya V. *Scenes of Subjection: Terror, Slavery, and Self-Making in Nineteenth-Century America.* Oxford: Oxford University Press, 1997.

Henriques, Joana Gorjão. "Estrearam-se numa manifestação por causa do Jamaica. 'Podia ser a minha mãe.'" *Público*, January 27, 2019. https://www.publico.pt/2019/01/27/sociedade /reportagem/geracao-instagram-primeira-manifestacao-causa-bairro-jamaica-mae -1859323.

Hill Collins, Patricia. *Black Feminist Thought: Knowledge, Consciousness, and the Politics of Empowerment.* New York: Routledge, 2000.

hooks, bell. *Art on My Mind: Visual Politics.* New York: New Press; distributed by W. W. Norton, 1995.

hooks, bell. "Theory as Liberatory Practice." *Yale Journal of Law and Feminism* 4, no. 1 (1991): 1–12.

Hussain, Mobeen. "Race, Gender, and Beauty in Late Colonial India c. 1900–1950." PhD diss., Cambridge University, 2021.

Jaguaribe, Hélio. "Brasil: Estabilidade social pelo colonial-fascismo?" In *Brasil: Tempos modernos*, edited by Celso Furtado, 49–76. Rio de Janeiro: Paz e Terra, 1968.

Kelley, Robin D. G. *Freedom Dreams: The Black Radical Imagination.* Boston: Beacon Press, 2003.

King, Tiffany Lethabo. *The Black Shoals: Offshore Formations of Black and Native Studies.* Durham, NC: Duke University Press, 2019.

Lara, Silvia Hunold. *Palmares & Cucaú: O aprendizado da dominação.* São Paulo: Editora da Universidade de São Paulo, 2021.

Martins Marcos, Patrícia. "Producing the Fiction of Unmarked Whiteness: Unarchiving Race and the Making of Difference in Portugal." Lisboa: Buala, 2021. https://www.buala.org/en /to-read/portugal-race-and-memory-a-conversation-a-reckoning.

Mbembe, Achille. "Afropolitanism." *Nka: Journal of Contemporary African Art* 46, no. 1 (2020): 56–61.

Mbembe, Achille. *Out of the Dark Night: Essays on Decolonization.* New York: Columbia University Press, 2021.

McKittrick, Katherine. *Demonic Grounds: Black Women and the Cartographies of Struggle.* Minneapolis: University of Minnesota Press, 2006.

Mignolo, Walter. *The Darker Side of the Renaissance: Literacy, Territoriality, and Colonization.* Ann Arbor: University of Michigan Press, 2003.

Mirzoeff, Nicholas. "Artificial Vision, White Space, and Racial Surveillance Capitalism." *AI & Society* 36 (2021): 1295–1305. https://doi.org/10.1007/s00146-020-01095-8.

Mirzoeff, Nicholas. *The Right to Look: A Counterhistory of Visuality*. Durham, NC: Duke University Press, 2011.

Morrison, Toni. *The Source of Self-Regard: Selected Essays, Speeches, and Meditations*. New York: Vintage International, 2020.

Moten, Fred, and Stefano Harney. "The University and the Undercommons." *Social Text* 22, no. 2 (2004): 101–15.

Nascimento, Abdias do. *O genocídio do negro brasileiro: Processo de um racismo mascarado*. Edited by Florestan Fernandes, Wole Soyinka, and Elisa Larkin Nascimento. São Paulo: Perspectiva, 2016.

Nascimento, Abdias do. "Quilombismo: An Afro-Brazilian Political Alternative." *Journal of Black Studies* 11, no. 2 (1980): 141–78.

Nascimento, Abdias do, Kabengele Munanga, Elisa Larkin Nascimento, and Valdecir Nascimento. *O quilombismo: Documentos de uma militância pan-africanista*. 3rd rev. ed. São Paulo: Perspectiva, 2019.

Nascimento, Beatriz. "O conceito de quilombo e a resistência cultural negra." *Afrodiáspora* 3, nos. 6–7 (1985): 41–49.

Nascimento, Beatriz. *Uma história feita por mãos negras*. Rio de Janeiro: Zahar, 2021.

Perry, Keisha-Khan Y., and Edilza Sotero. "Amefricanidade: The Black Diaspora Feminism of Lélia Gonzalez." *LASA Forum* 50, no. 3 (2019): 60–64.

Portugal, Rádio e Televisão de. "'Para Angola e em força': Guerra Colonial eclodiu há 60 anos." Discurso de Salazar. Arquivo RTP. Lisbon: RTP, 1960. https://www.rtp.pt/noticias/pais/para-angola-e-em-forca-ha-60-anos-salazar-fazia-o-discurso-que-marcou-o-inicio-da-guerra-colonial_v1312060.

Quijano, Aníbal. *Ensayos en torno a la colonialidad del poder*. Buenos Aires: Ediciones del Signo, 2019.

Regimento do Santo Officio da Inquisição dos Reynos de Portugal: Ordenado Por Mandado do Illmo & Revmo. Snor Bispo Dom Francisco de Castro, Inquisidor Geral do Conselho d'Estado de S. Magde. Lisboa: Manoel da Sylva, 1640.

Roberts, Neil. *Freedom as Marronage*. Chicago: University of Chicago Press, 2015.

Rowe, Erin Kathleen. "After Death, Her Face Turned White: Blackness, Whiteness, and Sanctity in the Early Modern Hispanic World." *American Historical Review* 121, no. 3 (2016): 727–54.

Sandahl, Carrie. "Queering the Crip or Cripping the Queer? Intersections of Queer and Crip Identities in Solo Autobiographical Performance." *GLQ* 9, no. 1 (2003): 25–56.

Santana, Stephanie Bosch. "Exorcizing Afropolitanism: Binyavanga Wainaina Explains Why 'I Am a Pan-Africanist, Not an Afropolitan' at ASAUK 2012." *Africa in Words* (blog), February 8, 2013. https://africainwords.com/2013/02/08/exorcizing-afropolitanism-binyavanga-wainaina-explains-why-i-am-a-pan-africanist-not-an-afropolitan-at-asauk-2012/.

Serequeberhan, Tsenay. "The African Anti-colonial Struggle: An Effort at Reclaiming History." *Philosophia Africana* 6, no. 1 (2003): 47–58.

Smith, Christen Anne. "Towards a Black Feminist Model of Black Atlantic Liberation: Remembering Beatriz Nascimento." *Meridians* 14, no. 2 (2016): 71–87.

Smith, Christen, Archie Davies, and Bethânia Gomes. "'In Front of the World': Translating Beatriz Nascimento." *Antipode* 53, no. 1 (2021): 279–316.

Stoler, Ann Laura. *Duress: Imperial Durabilities in Our Times*. Durham, NC: Duke University Press, 2016.

Tallbear, Kim. "Science and Whiteness." Presented at the Symposium DNA and Indigeneity, Simon Fraser University, October 22, 2015.

Tomás, António. *Amílcar Cabral: The Life of a Reluctant Nationalist*. Cambridge: Cambridge University Press, 2021.

Torres-Saillant, Silvio. *An Intellectual History of the Caribbean*. Basingstoke: Palgrave Macmillan, 2006.

Trouillot, Michel-Rolph. *Silencing the Past: Power and the Production of History*. Boston: Beacon Press, 1995.

Tveit, Marta. "The Afropolitan Must Go." *Africa Is a Country* (blog), November 28, 2013. https://africasacountry.com/2013/11/the-afropolitan-must-go/.

Weinbaum, Alys Eve. *The Afterlife of Reproductive Slavery: Biocapitalism and Black Feminism's Philosophy of History*. Durham, NC: Duke University Press, 2019.

Wynter, Sylvia. "1492: A New World View." In *Race, Discourse, and the Origin of the Americas*, edited by Vera Lawrence Hyatt and Rex Nettleford, 5–57. Washington, DC: Smithsonian Institution Press, 1995.

Wynter, Sylvia. "Unsettling the Coloniality of Being/Power/Truth/Freedom: Towards the Human, After Man, Its Overrepresentation—An Argument." *CR: The New Centennial Review* 3, no. 3 (2003): 257–337.

Urban Iconographies

Gender, Hair, and Afro-Parisian Consumerism

Dawn Fulton

In the Francophone literary tradition, the intersection of fashion and transnational African culture finds one of its most widely recognized depictions in Alain Mabanckou's 1998 novel *Bleu-Blanc-Rouge* (*Blue White Red*). This groundbreaking text brought the informal economies of "Congolese dandies" to the attention of a new audience, illuminating the subversive potential of performance, inscribing transnationalism as a cultural practice and identity, and affirming the interpretive authority of marginalized spaces and subjects in a carefully coded subculture.[1] Yet, despite the links between this rendering of a late twentieth-century practice and millennial notions of Afropolitanism, *Bleu-Blanc-Rouge* also exposed the *limited* mobility and concrete conditions of poverty experienced by these apparent proto-Afropolitans. Moving forward a decade to the works of such writers as Léonora Miano, Rokhaya Diallo, and Lauren Ekué, we find Franco-African narratives that echo Mabanckou's in their emphasis on self-presentation and Parisian space, but foreground instead the middle-class status and consumerism of their female protagonists. In this respect, these later narratives seem to extol the excesses of materialism and apoliticism for which Afropolitanism has come under critique. But I would argue that through an attention to gender, and specifically to the representation and inscription of the Black female body in Paris, these writers probe the latent historicism of Afropolitan experience in the Francophone context. In this article, an initial consideration of how hair, space, and consumerism intersect in works by Miano and Diallo will

Radical History Review

Issue 144 (October 2022)   DOI 10.1215/01636545-9847844

© 2022 by MARHO: The Radical Historians' Organization, Inc.

bring me to a focus on the less well-known writer Lauren Ekué, whose fiction at once flaunts the extremes of stereotypical Afropolitanism and offers a pointed critique of political indifference and of the imbrication of gender in consumerist culture.

Alain Mabanckou's *Bleu-Blanc-Rouge* dramatizes the practice of *la sape*, a youth culture linking Brazzaville and Kinshasa to European fashion capitals. The movement, whose name indexes the French slang word for clothes (*la sape*) and the playful acronym denoting the Society of Trendsetters and Elegant People (Société des ambianceurs et personnes élégantes), foregrounds the acquisition and display of expensive clothing in defiance of economic conditions. Indeed, the mythology surrounding the Congolese dandies, or *sapeurs*, draws much from the stark contrast between the material and cultural capital they perform and the backdrop of extreme poverty against which this performance occurs. The triumph of the sapeur is a triumph of self-presentation over economic reality, of narrative over experience, and ultimately an ascent to interpretive authority in the face of social and cultural disdain in both European and African societies.[2] While the idealization of Paris is central to their practice, the sapeurs nonetheless re-center hermeneutic authority by locating it in their audiences at home rather than in Europe. The "product" they perform may be French, but the arbiters of that product's value are young Congolese men living on the African continent. In Mabanckou's *Bleu-Blanc-Rouge*, the destitution and marginalization experienced by the sapeurs in Paris are erased and eclipsed by the carefully adorned bodies and shimmering tales of social success, an exuberant refusal of social, class, and geographic hierarchies.

In comparison, twenty-first-century Afropolitanisms suggest a celebration of a socioeconomic status that is inherited rather than acquired, and assert the epistemological authority of an already elite class. The major critiques of Afropolitanism that have emerged since the publication of Achille Mbembe's "Afropolitanism" and Taiye Selasi's "Bye-Bye Babar" target its elitism, commodification, and lack of political conscience.[3] The writer Emma Dabiri, for example, deplores the "rapacious consumerism of the African elites claimed to make up the ranks of the Afropolitans" and asks, "While Afropolitans talk and talk about what it means to be young, cool and African, are many of them concerned with addressing the world beyond their own social realities, to the issues that concern other Africans?"[4] Similarly, as S. Okwunodu Ogbechie notes, the African continent itself tends to function primarily as a referent rather than as a site of cultural practice.[5] Although Mabanckou's novel might, at first glance, be taken as an exemplary story of Afropolitanism, its evocation of class hierarchy begs a key question: Is *Bleu-Blanc-Rouge* a "miserabilist" or pessimistic text?[6] The refusal of what in French is termed *misérabilisme* and in the African context connotes a singular narrative of victimhood and destitution has been a crucial ingredient in twenty-first-century formulations of Afropolitanism.[7] Mabanckou's novel, though its celebration of style and materialism echoes this defiance of victimhood, also exposes the performed socioeconomic status of the sapeurs as an illusion through the eyes of its narrator, Massala-Massala. The character's failure to read the Parisian landscape effectively enough to join the community of the sapeurs means that the novel weighs in ambiguously on the question of Afro-pessimism.

Many of the writers and artists who explore the experiences of contemporary Afro-Parisian women, by contrast, confirm the Afropolitan impulse in explicitly rejecting "miserabilist" narratives. Ekué, for example, in an interview with *Amina* about her first novel, *Icône urbaine* (*Urban Icon*), affirms that her goal was to write "a book in French with a heroine who was Black, strong, and free of miserabilism."[8] There is a tension—one we could see as fundamental to the contemporary debates around Afropolitanism—between the urge to reject singular "ethnic" victim narratives and the concern for all that might be left out, forgotten, or dismissed in that same gesture: history, inequality, politics. A question generated by this tension, and by the larger debate, is whether anti-pessimist narratives of Black experience are necessarily apolitical. The works I examine here suggest that it is possible to reject miserabilist narratives while raising a critique of apoliticism; but their focus on the cultural practices of Black women in the French capital also demands an attention to the role of gender as crucial to understandings of the relationship between Black cosmopolitanism and historicism.

Public Spaces, Private Maps: Afropolitanism in Paris

Léonora Miano's work signals a break from canonical narratives of African immigration to France. Her probing considerations of the notions of "Afropeanism" and "border identities" imagine a transcendence of categories of race and nation, while her portraits of the Black middle class in Paris foreground a new politics of belonging and ownership in the City of Light.[9] Her 2010 novel *Blues pour Élise* (*Blues for Elise*), in particular, offers a vision of Black France that, in contrast to the tales of urban disenfranchisement, clandestine existences, and abject poverty that dominate twentieth-century narratives of Francophone migration, presents characters who are staunchly bourgeois, resolutely carving out their spaces in the city through a hybrid consumerism blending French, African, and African American products, services, clothing, art, and music.[10] The novel serves to disrupt the "miserabilist clichés" mentioned on its book jacket that have fed and continue to feed the anti-immigrant political platform in France.[11] But this representational break with the past is also a shift that speaks to a gendered narrative of African migration and Afropean identity. Miano's primarily female characters map a vision of the Parisian cityscape that is very much inflected by their gender, in that they are consciously pulling away not only from the social and economic conditions of an earlier generation of Africans in France but also from the rigid gender roles prescribed by those communities. As a result, the particular Afropean habitus projected by these women does not reject African cultural identification outright but has an ambiguous and nuanced relationship to visibility that suggests a novel form of urban practice.

The trope of generational rupture is signaled in the book's epigraph, taken from the translation of Haruki Murakami's novel *After Dark*: "The new day is almost here, but the old one is still dragging its heavy skirt." Evoking the liminal space between two contrasting yet fundamentally linked narratives of African identity in Paris, the phrase foregrounds with its reference to feminine dress the particular weight of the past on women of African origin in Paris. In fact, as Nicki Hitchcott and other scholars have noted, Miano's characters put into question the very category of "women of African origin," realizing in their social and family relationships the politics elaborated in the author's collection of essays, *Habiter la frontière* (*Living in the Border*), with a firm refusal to endorse singular genealogies or to choose between notions of "African" or "French" identity.[12] Miano's adoption of the term *Afropean* in her critical and fictional works, and her emphasis on music of the African diaspora as a crucial medium of cultural exchange and practice, present Paris as a manifold, pliant space where middle-class Black women are free to pick and choose the patterns of their daily lives without necessarily subscribing to a particular national or ethnic affiliation.

One space in particular that produces some of the most memorable passages on post-Obama racial politics in France is the African beauty salon Coco Prestige in Paris's Tenth arrondissement. Here the protagonists of *Blues pour Élise* inhabit a site that seems entirely theirs: they judiciously weigh their choices as consumers in light of their middle-class economic constraints, their desire for social mobility, and the myriad ways in which their hairstyle choices will be judged by their white employers and colleagues, by the men they are dating, by their mothers, by the African community at large, by themselves. The salon is situated in the symbolic neighborhood of Château d'Eau on the boulevard de Strasbourg, the hub of African hair and beauty salons in Paris, that seems to offer a concentrated site for the expression of their Afropean community in all its contradictions. The dialogic moment staged in this site is compelling in its dramatization of a claim to urban space, redefined through the lens of women's experiences outside familiar identity politics. But the scene is also notable for two reasons: first, the specificity of women's narratives of economic and social mobility as articulated through their hairstyle choices; and second, the place of the salon in the women's mappings of the city. Coco Prestige offers an informative glimpse, in other words, of both the urban practice and the urban geography of these characters.

The heavily charged ideological implications of hair for women of African descent are well documented, situated at the crossroads of racial and class politics, women's self-image, and cultural belonging. In Miano's description, European standards of beauty figure as a specter hovering over the entire neighborhood, as upon exiting the metro at Château d'Eau her characters confront an array of wigs and products in storefront windows, all designed, as Miano puts it, to help them through an affliction borne across the ages: "Paris, boulevard de Strasbourg. Every street corner tells of the Black woman's eternal torment, her private obsession: to feel beautiful with kinky hair."[13] Inside the salon, the women passionately affirm the right to forge their own paths through this calvary—from Akasha, who frames her choice to wear her hair naturally as in keeping with millennial trends toward organic, natural products and lifestyles rather than a position specifically marked as African, to Kimmy, who, in her desire to hold on to a hard-won job, follows her superior's advice not to look "too ethnic," and Élise, who decries the "Afro-terrorists" seeking to "give out lessons in racial pride."[14] Along with the range of politicized choices represented by this group of women, the scene presents a striking contrast between the interior, relatively private terrain of this dialogue on African identity politics and the inhumanity of the public world outside the salon, which is interpellated by those very conversations. Throughout the novel, women's hair and bodies figure as key points of reference in the pursuit—and critique—of social and class mobility.[15]

At the chapter's close, our urban heroines leave the salon, returning to their jobs or homes scattered across the city. Miano presents their departure as a moment of transition between worlds specifically marked by gender: "Black women of the third millennium are trying to find their place in an uncertain realm between alienation and a quest for identitarian purity. In an hour or two, they'll pay Coco, get back on the metro, and try to just be women."[16] The image is almost a diasporic one, suggesting the scattering of these young women into unconnected new spaces, once again vulnerable to the potential hostilities of a world where theirs is not the dominant narrative. The sense of loss connoted by this conclusion points to the temporary status of the vibrantly complicated Afropean community space they have created in the salon, and to the fact that—although Château d'Eau forms part of a symbolic site of African visibility—the salon itself is a space otherwise shielded from public view, where identity and relationships are deliberated in relative privacy. The dispersion across the cityscape at the end of this scene is not accidental; the novel's characters pay careful attention to the locations of their domestic spheres, making sacrifices to live away from the classic sites of Afro-Parisianism, away from their parents, or simply at "a good address."[17] One character, for example, tenaciously chooses a tiny studio in the fashionable Marais district over a larger apartment elsewhere, cherishing her newly acquired view onto the rue de Bretagne, epicenter of the coveted Parisian *bobo* lifestyle.[18]

This disjuncture between consumerism and inhabitance, between the spaces where the characters shop and where they live, is in many ways symptomatic of what we could call a twenty-first-century Black Paris. Urban sociologists have observed this trend in Château-Rouge in particular, the Montmartre neighborhood whose concentration of African food and products draws a majority of consumers from other neighborhoods in Paris or from other European cities.[19] In a French Republican context, in which the formation of a Black community is explicitly at odds with national narratives, it is striking that, even as the visibility of such a community may be on the rise, the priority of space—specifically public space—in that community formation seems to have shifted to other arenas.[20] While the "Paris Noir" of twentieth-century African American writers and artists was a visually inflected moment in the history of the city, closely tied to place and to the public practice of Black intellectualism and culture, the evocations of twenty-first-century Black Paris offered by Léonora Miano are not anchored to specific sites as much as to less immediately visible urban practices.[21] Her characters intersect with the nostalgic sites of Black identity in Paris primarily as consumers, selecting in a highly individualized way the products, services, and cultural narratives available in those locations, without necessarily forming or reinscribing collective "sites of memory" in Paris.[22]

While her focus is not explicitly on consumerism, Rokhaya Diallo offers a parallel set of reflections on the historiography inscribed in and by the Black female body in the contemporary French capital. An activist, journalist, author, and filmmaker, Diallo is one of the most widely recognized French Afro-feminists on the international stage and has deployed a range of media to express her views on racism and race relations in France.[23] Among Diallo's many points of interest is textured hair—her graphic novel *Pari(s) d'amies* (*Paris Girlfriends*) includes an autobiographically inspired character who returns from the United States with a "capillary obsession," having cut off her straightened hair—and she places this concern at the heart of her 2015 book *Afro!* The text is a tribute to the visibility of natural textured or frizzy hair in the urban landscape of the French capital. In a series of over one hundred portraits accompanied by photographs by Brigitte Sombié, Diallo offers testimonies from Parisians of African descent—some well known, some not—narrating and sometimes theorizing their relationships with their own hair. "Women and men of African origin writ large—sub-Saharan, Caribbean, Arab, Berber . . . —tell their stories through their hair," writes Diallo in her preface. "Photographed in their environment, they embody a snapshot of twenty-first-century Paris."[24]

The space of Paris was especially important to Diallo in this project, she notes, because with her book she could present an alternative vision of her home city, one that contradicts what she sees as its persistent association with a lack of racial diversity: "The French capital is too often seen as a sublime but monochromatic city, whereas New York and London have asserted themselves on the international stage as dynamic and multiracial spaces."[25] In a way that echoes Miano's literary texts, Diallo deftly weaves musical interludes into her collection, and the multimedia is ever present in her choice of subjects, who include bloggers, filmmakers, media artists, and fashion models. References to the key role of the Internet and social media in the formative moments of the turn to natural hair appear again and again in the portraits, with particular attention to the questions of visibility and access.[26]

The brief narratives and captions that accompany each image confirm this attachment to place. Interviewees are specific in their self-mappings in the French capital, giving addresses, neighborhoods, and daily routines, which are also reflected in the visual presentation of their bodies in mostly exterior sites in the city. The filmmaker Alice Diop, for example, photographed with her young son in front of the Stravinsky Fountain near the Pompidou Center in the Fourth arrondissement, deems the fountain a "symbol of a kind of modernity, of contemporaneity in the heart of Paris, where we inscribe our presence" (fig. 1).[27] And writer Leïla Slimani calls the Ninth arrondissement, where she's lived for six years, "my neighborhood": "Where I write, where I dream, where I go for walks, where I take my son to school" (fig. 2).[28] Both women are photographed in casual, comfortable poses that insist on the everyday quality of their presence in the streets of the French capital. In this "snapshot of twenty-first-century Paris," the visibility of Black women's experience brings together the materiality of hair as practice and the materiality of urban space.

As we saw earlier with Miano's work, however, this kind of urban mapping has less to do with monumentalizing certain sites of Black activism than with a notion of permeation, a claim to ubiquity that doesn't lose its hold on the particular, highly personalized definitions of home. The inscription of presence is connected to place in a dispersed model—not as a collective assertion of Black sites or site-based practices but as individual acts of taking up space, moving through the city, and being seen. The complexity of this relationship is perhaps best captured by a mode of digital production that dramatizes this interplay in commercial terms: the location-based service (LBS). If somewhat paradoxically, the LBS allows for a consumerism that at once privileges and transcends the local. The entrepreneur Rebecca Cathline, for example, created her location-based application *Ma coiffeuse Afro* (*My Afro Hairstylist*) in 2016 out of a frustration at the difficulty of finding salons in Paris where she could count on reliable expertise in Black hair.[29] Noting that none of the beauty schools in the city include training in styling textured hair, that the famous (or infamous) salons of Château d'Eau were overcrowded and rushed, and that her forays on eBay brought some unwelcome surprises, Cathline created her app to connect clients with specialized hairstylists, many available for in-home service. As in Miano's landscapes, this model envisions a remapping of Parisian space that turns toward private spaces even as it places a premium on visibility. The role of digital space in the unfolding of a twenty-first-century feminist Afropolitanism seems to be crucially connected to this kind of Janus-faced move: a way of envisioning an urban practice that is at once international, media savvy, and unmistakably intimate.

Mobility, Iconography, Historicity: Lauren Ekué's Literary Networks

Lauren Ekué, a French journalist, novelist, and blogger of Togolese descent, has asserted the dissemination of positive images of Black women as a pursuit that

Fontaine Stravinsky, IV ~ *Pour moi c'est le symbole d'une forme de modernité, de contemporanéité au cœur de Paris, dans laquelle nous inscrivons notre présence. C'est l'image de ce qu'est à mes yeux le mouvement* nappy, *ce retour au naturel, ce Paris jeune et contemporain.*

Figure 1. Alice Diop. Diallo, *Afro !*, 167.

Place Gustave-Toudouze, IXᵉ ~ *J'habite ici depuis six ans, c'est mon quartier. Là que j'écris, que je rêve, que je me balade, que j'emmène mon fils à l'école ou au manège. C'est mon petit village, je l'aime beaucoup.*

Figure 2. Leïla Slimani. Diallo, *Afro !*, 176.

undergirds her work. Claiming inspiration in US "chick lit" and branding her work as French-language hip-hop feminism, Ekué writes fiction that presents young, impossibly fashionable and beautiful Black women comfortably circulating among the African glitterati of Paris while maintaining ties to financially and politically powerful families on the African continent.[30] On her website, Ekué presents herself as a "native of Hauts-de-Seine," a Parisian suburb known primarily for its La Défense business district; her "remarkable genealogy" includes Afro-Brazilian heritage and Togolese royal ancestry.[31] While her blog has not been active since 2015, the topics raised there—fashion, style, and the rise of the African middle class—form the basis of a collection of interviews Ekué published in 2020. *L'industrie de la mode africaine* (*The Industry of African Fashion*) features the African musicians, curators, politicians, and celebrities who, she argues, have forged an often-overlooked fashion industry.

The assertion of class status seen in Miano's work is fundamental for Ekué as well. While Afropolitanism is not evoked by name in Ekué's fiction, her exaggerated depiction of consumerist culture seems constructed as a direct provocation of those who would lament Afropolitan hollowness. In her second novel, *Black Attitude #1: Ro$e*, for example, the portrait of her high-flying protagonists insists not only on the consumerist excesses of these Afropolitan elites but also on their apparent obliviousness to the political contingencies and consequences of their extravagance: "Still, we're proud of being Africans, divesting the continent of its goods for our own tremendous profit. What other land could furnish so many wonderfully precious raw materials to support our frivolous lifestyle with such impunity and indifference?"[32] The gleeful, tongue-in-cheek hyperbole in this passage proclaims no room for ambiguity in the rendering of luxury and social status on the part of Ekué's characters, and seems pitched to explicitly negate the kind of stark economic contrast so central to the code of the sapeurs.

Yet it is precisely the gleefulness—or we might say defiance—of this tone that suggests that something more may be going on under the surface of an ostensibly frivolous narrative. As in Miano's and Diallo's work, Ekué's emphasis on affirmative portraits of Franco-African lives aligns her with Afropolitanism's opposition to entrenched Afro-pessimism or miserabilism. When pressed about the potential lack of overlap between her experience and that of "other young people in the public housing projects," Ekué insists, "I don't think I'm part of a minority. My experience is not exceptional."[33] For Ekué, then, it is important not only to reject negative images of the African community in France but also to affirm the authenticity of the alternative images she renders in her fiction, and it is through this lens that we might interpret the seemingly endless social circles that wind through her novels.[34]

The author's political engagement is carefully calibrated against the cultural portraits she sketches out in her first two novels, *Icône urbaine* and *Black Attitude #1*. In both novels, Ekué shrewdly interrogates the Afropolitans-as-apolitical model

to which her characters are meant to conform. Flora d'Almeida, the autobiographically inspired protagonist of *Icône urbaine*, reflects openly on the generational
gap in the narrative of African migration to France that underpins this vision of
the contemporary Afropolitan: "The younger generation confronts the one that
came before. Born in France at the beginning of the decadent 1980s, I have never
known slavery, segregation, dictatorship, ethnic wars or apartheid. *Happy Few.* For
us, it's a different world. Well, almost. We carefully avoid stirring up stories from
the past. As far as we're concerned, Pandora's box will remain well sealed."[35] Even
in its apparent irreverence, this revealing passage pays tribute to the ancestors of
Afropolitanism, to the very history that must be obscured in order to maintain the
narrative of carefree cosmopolitanism and socioeconomic success that underpins
Afropolitan culture. The casually rendered caveat ("Well, almost") is typical of the
kind of discursive maneuver that Ekué employs in her work, affirming a fundamental historical awareness in the very act of dismissing it. The political impetus of
Ekué's novel is at once subtle and resounding, confirmed by claims to the contrary
within its pages.

The difficulty of reconciling fashion and flagrant consumerism with a political conscience has been key to many of the debates around Afropolitanism. Stephanie Bosch Santana writes in "Exorcizing Afropolitanism" that, while the emphasis on
style may not itself be a necessary target of criticism, it is "the attempt to begin with
style, then infuse it with substantive political conscience" that is problematic.[36] But
Amatoritsero Ede and others argue that the political impact of Afropolitanism could
lie precisely in the specificity of its hallmark consumerism.[37] Ekué's work, with its
resounding—if narcissistic—claims of self-confidence and cultural capital on the
part of its heroines, suggests such a logic. With Ede, Ekué might argue that "one
of the ways in which Afropolitanism becomes political is in its pressing of symbolic
capital towards self-empowerment and the enabling of human agency."[38] What is
interesting about Ekué's work is that the author goes further by parsing the specificity of gender in this attempted intersection between capital and ethics, illuminating the particular conditions—and pitfalls—of self-fashioning for Black women in a
hyper-consumerist society.

Media and mobility are key factors in this aspect of Ekué's vision.[39] *Icône
urbaine*'s Flora, the self-proclaimed "rising star" at the magazine *Afro-International*,
edits the section on hair and writes on beauty, music, and sports. Her discourse asserts
a fluency with celebrity and music culture: Flora seems to float from night club to
night club, swept away in limousines by stars of the hip-hop world (their names only
slightly altered from those of their real-world referents), on every VIP list and ever
alert to the latest career moves and fashion trends. In a novel structured like a play-
list, Ekué includes frequent reflections on the cultural and political impact of the
Pan-Africanist media, as when Flora wryly notes the cultural capital generated by
her magazine's unwavering elitism, which, she claims, has transformed the playing

field of the "ethnic" media: "Making the cover of the magazine has quickly become a must for international models. Actors, singers, athletes, diplomats, politicians, clerics, filmmakers, and tribal chiefs are lining up to be featured in one of our issues."[40] With this enumeration of sectors represented by the contemporary Black elite, Flora underlines the existence of a widespread network of social and economic power while at the same time foregrounding the internationalism of this network with another list that crosses from so-called First World to Third World economies: "in London, Nairobi, Cotonou, Yaoundé, and Pretoria, but also in Brasília and Haiti."[41]

Above all, Flora's professional acumen emerges as a keen awareness of the power of the image as a means and an object of manipulation. This awareness, in turn, illuminates the underlying tension between political activism and economic power, as Flora reflects on the reductive and disempowering force of the mass-produced image: "So much for dreams in this mercenary, ideal-crushing society; we sell what we are. But who are we? . . . Our image has evolved so little. Cliché after cliché, we are forever the token entertainers."[42] Despite the claims of historical amnesia cited above, Flora goes further to launch a political critique of the double bind of consumerist culture for Black celebrities: "Our people are the only ones to have been captured, sold, and subjected to forced reproduction on such a large scale. The chains may have been broken, but we've ended up marketing our image."[43] By invoking slavery as precursor to the commodification of Black cultural images, Flora cannily inscribes contemporary iconography, culturally affirming as it may be, into a historical narrative of racism. While such a critique has been made before, Ekué offers it here as a deft infusion of political consciousness into an overtly positive portrayal of Black media, culture, and consumerism.

The specificity of gender in this context emerges in Ekué's novel through a reflection on the Black female body as object of consumption. As Célia Sadai argues, *Icône urbaine* can be read as an invitation to Black women to wrest their image away from the clichés of hip-hop misogynism and replace it with their own formulation.[44] But while Flora performs the gestures of female empowerment, affirming the right to choose her sexual and romantic partners and to defy the entrenched sexism of dating customs on both sides of the Atlantic, she also acknowledges the treacherous terrain of forms of empowerment that depend on image. The attention to beauty in Flora's professional work, for example, affords a cynical reflection on the hierarchies internal to the Black female community: "BEAUTY. One word, six letters, billions of creams, countless hopes . . . dashed! But the cosmetics industry thrives . . . After all, beauty is first among all inequalities. . . . Women will still lose the war, but will never give up the fight. Bitter combat."[45] Here Ekué pits individual financial success against the beauty industry to interrogate the high stakes of image manipulation and consumption that threaten to eclipse all other facets of Black female experience. This reflection thus offers nuance to critiques of Afropolitanism that focus on the commodification of African culture, foregrounding the micromanagement of the female body that signals consumerist society's incursion from the public sphere into the private, from cultural performance into everyday life. In an uncanny nod to the sapeurs, whose somatic transformations also formed a part of their practice, the women in Ekué's portraits find their wallets "mutilated" by these relentless beauty regimens.[46]

In a book-length essay published in 2010, Ekué elucidates many of these points, focusing in particular on hair. The setting of *Carnet spunk* (*Spunk Notebook*) is Harlem on the night of Barack Obama's election in 2008. This geographical triangulation adds the US context to the Afro-Parisianism of *Icône urbaine* and affords an account not only of the importance of US Black culture globally—not least the exhilarating iconography of the country's new first lady—but also of the common "tyrannical canons of beauty" that afflict women in all communities.[47] While female agency is at the forefront here, Ekué pinpoints the ways in which the self-affirming hairstyle choices Black women make can nevertheless signal the persistent subjugation of their gender: "By way of straighteners and the rigorous use of extensions, Black women give themselves up to male fantasies of beauty."[48] There are strong echoes here of Miano's salon scene in *Blues pour Élise*, whose protagonist also points out that the politically motivated critiques of such practices only add to the subjugation of Black women: "This political take on beauty is designed . . . to hold back women who have already suffered enough at the hands of History."[49] While Miano's Élise opts for a hairstyle inspired by Naomi Campbell, Lauren Ekué notes that the supermodel's iconic status in the 1990s meant an unprecedented valorization of the Black female body whose straightened hair nonetheless reinforced "the hegemony of Western beauty."[50] *Carnet spunk*'s cover image portraying a woman's face split down the middle between the "natural" and the "artificial" (fig. 3) succinctly captures the dualities generated by these competing pressures of politics, culture, and self-determination.

If Ekué's unswerving eye exposes with bitterness and humor the many contradictions of Black female consumerist culture, ultimately this focused attention seems to be at the heart of her professional impetus as a writer: the tangled reckoning exhibited in her critical work and practiced by her fictional characters forms the very material of political and social change. Closing her essay with a nod to her "elder sisters" Zora Neale Hurston (also acknowledged in the work's title), Angela Davis, Toni Morrison, and Myriam Makeba, Ekué explicitly points to literature as a vehicle for political consciousness, adding to her tribute those future generations of women who will have "the audacity to plunge into French literature" and "who work on and will reflect on Black experience in the feminine."[51] The fraught exploration of the specificity of Black women's culture in a transnational, media-driven, consumerist society is thus framed here as a legacy of activism for the future.

Figure 3. Ekué, *Carnet spunk*, cover image.

Given the political underpinnings of her work, Ekué not surprisingly assigns primary status to the question of audience. The protagonist's readers are interpellated within three paragraphs in *Icône urbaine*, in a pronouncement that offers the author's signature blend of irony and sincerity: "You are MY readers, MY audience. I LOVE YOU."[52] When asked about the informality of her language in *Icône urbaine*, Ekué points out that she stands to lose an important sector of her potential readership with dense, lengthy prose: "I try to reach people who don't read as much as people who do. What has been gratifying about *Icône urbaine* is that even non-readers read it all the way through, when it's maybe been years since they last picked up a book."[53] At the same time, she cites inspiration from Hugo and Baudelaire, and characterizes the novel as "much more subversive than it appears" in that it reverses the dominant codes of readability with its implicit references to the world of hip-hop.[54] Above all, Ekué underlines the importance of an audience of peers who would not otherwise see their stories captured in literary form. Citing her inspiration in chick lit for her second novel, *Black Attitude #1: Ro$e*, she notes, "It's a book written for women by a woman,"[55] and speaking of *Icône urbaine* with *Planète Afrique*, she says, "I think novels can be a useful way of communicating ideas to people who would never read sociological essays, or history or economics. . . . This journal can serve as a message to young French women of immigrant parents: 'You're not alone!!!!'"[56] Beneath the apparent superficiality of Ekué's short sentences and abundant exclamation points lies a determination to forge a studied sociological landscape while merging vectors of readership across class, race, and education.

The trajectory of *Icône urbaine*'s narcissistic and witty protagonist suggests much of what Ekué might like her audience to glean from such a project. At the novel's conclusion, Flora d'Almeida seems poised to leave for the United States to found a new television station. Despairing of the endless clichés of objectified Black and female bodies she sees as she surfs impatiently through the channels on her TV, Flora raises the possibility of using her media expertise to change the image of Black women internationally.[57] What is striking about this vocation is not only the political conscience it suggests but also the intersection of individualistic and collective concerns in Flora's professional outlook: while the consumerism she flaunts may fall in line with critiques of Afropolitanism's hollow individualism, Ekué frames her character's self-promotion—and her own literary work—in a way that insists on fundamentally interrogating and redefining negative images in the media. Ekué inscribes herself and even her most ostensibly shallow characters in a line of women who are "working and reflecting on the experience of Black women."

To return to the comparison with Mabanckou's sapeurs, then, it seems clear that many of the elements that could be cited to attribute social and political value to the practice of *la sape* are missing in Ekué's representation of twenty-first-century Afropolitans. The centrality of Paris is reaffirmed, even if it is inscribed in a cosmopolitan configuration with restorative returns to African countries and commercial links to other "First World" capitals; poverty is all but nonexistent; and colonial history remains (mostly) sealed in its Pandora's box. The social, class, and geographical hierarchies so forcefully upended by the sapeurs, in other words, remain largely intact in Ekué's work. And yet Ekué's considered attention to her literary audience suggests that the ostensible frivolity of her work—inseparable as it may be from an outward apoliticism—is in fact part and parcel with her artistic ethical project. While her prose may reinscribe the absence of the "other Africans" lamented by Emma Dabiri, its claims of ahistoricism are haunted by the past. The vigor with which Ekué confronts the historically laden question of objectified Black female bodies is difficult to dismiss in the spirit of anti-Afropolitanist backlash. And while the individualism of the sapeur portrayed in Mabanckou's novel is crucial to the narrative's successful demystification of economic and cultural hierarchies, the self-fashioning highlighted by Ekué's Flora is embedded in a female literary genealogy and a vision of ongoing critical work and reflection on a collective scale. Much as Miano posits consumerism as the very mechanism for new social networks and a gendered Black Paris, Ekué claims hip-hop feminist literature as a site of political change for and by the millennial offspring of the not entirely forgotten African migrants who came before them.

Dawn Fulton teaches French and comparative literature at Smith College. Her recent publications include articles on urban space and colonial history in the works of Alain Mabanckou, Jean-Roger Essomba, Fabienne Kanor, and Michael Haneke.

Notes

I am grateful to Rosa Carrasquillo and Lorelle Semley for coordinating and hosting the October 2017 "Rethinking the Afropolitan" workshop, and to workshop participants for their thoughtful questions and comments on an earlier version of this article.

1.   Recent attention to this practice in the English-language media has favored the terms *Congolese dandies* or *Congo dandies*. See, for example, Stone, "Congolese Dandies"; and *Congo Dandies* (documentary, dir. Natalya Kadyrova, Russia, 2015).

2.   On the marginalization of the sapeurs at home and abroad, see Gandoulou, *Au cœur de la Sape*, 17–26. Additional resources on *la sape* include Gondola, "Dream and Drama"; and MacGaffey and Bazenguissa-Ganga, *Congo-Paris*.

3.   For summaries of this debate, see Eaton, "Eternal Blackness"; Gerhmann, "Cosmopolitanism"; and Toivanen, "Cosmopolitanism's New Clothes?"

4.   Dabiri, "Why I Am Not an Afropolitan."

5.   Ogbechie, "Afropolitanism." See also Mbembe, "Afropolitanism."

6.   Susanne Gehrmann points out Mabanckou's privileged status as the only Francophone writer to make the list of "Ten Afropolitan Writers You Should Know" published by the Black Entertainment Television platform in 2015 ("Cosmopolitanism," 64).

7.   Mbembe's definition of Afropolitanism envisions "a way of being in the world, refusing on principle any form of victim identity" ("Afropolitanism," 28–29). See also Gikandi, "On Afropolitanism," 9; and Dabiri, "Why I Am (Still) Not an Afropolitan," 105–6.

8.   Cristèle D., "Lauren Ekué." Similarly, in an interview about her 2020 documentary *Où sont les noirs?* (*Where Are the Black People?*), which recounts the challenges facing Black actors in the contemporary film industry, Rokhaya Diallo confirms an avoidance of negative stereotypes as the motivation for her emphasis on the esthetic: "We really wanted to focus on the esthetic and to avoid the miserabilism that usually characterizes this kind of subject" (Capot, "*Où sont les noirs?*"). Unless otherwise noted, translations are my own.

9.   See Miano, *Habiter la frontière*, 25–32.

10. Nicki Hitchcott has cast *Blues pour Élise* as a kind of Afropean *Sex and the City*, in which four intelligent, beautiful, financially independent young women share stories of love gained and lost, sex and sexuality, and family tensions: "Miano's women are not disenfranchised, marginalized 'immigrants' but rather enfranchised urbanites who participate in and appropriate the city spaces they inhabit" ("Sex and the Afropean City," 125).

11. The cover blurb of the Plon edition of *Blues pour Élise* promises a portrait of Black France that is "a long way from miserabilist clichés."

12. See Hitchcott, "Sex and the Afropean City."

13. Miano, *Blues pour Élise*, 39.

14. Miano, *Blues pour Élise*, 43, 47, 48.

15. The Coco Prestige scene resonates in many ways with the reflections of Aline Tacite, one of the seven women featured in Mame-Fatou Niang and Kaytie Nielson's documentary film *Mariannes noires* (France, 2016). According to her website, Tacite's salon is set to open in its new location in Paris's Thirteenth arrondissement in 2022. See https://www.bouclesdebenestudio.com (accessed January 10, 2022).

16. Miano, *Blues pour Élise*, 48.

17. See, for example, Miano, *Blues pour Élise*, 25, 134, 170–71.

18. *Bobo*, a contraction of "bourgeois-bohème" (bourgeois-bohemian), denotes a late twentieth-century iteration of middle-class status, noted for its emphasis on fashion.

19. See Bouly de Lesdain, "Château-Rouge"; and Chabrol, "Continuités d'usages."

20. See, for example, Ndiaye, *La condition noire*; Keaton, Sharpley-Whiting, and Stovall, *Black France/France noire*; and Tshimanga, Gondola, and Bloom, *Frenchness and the African Diaspora*.

21. See Stovall, *Paris Noir*; and Frund, "Site-ing Black Paris."

22. Nora, *Lieux de mémoire*.

23. When asked in an interview about the role of social media in antiracist activism, Diallo cites her Twitter account in particular and notes, "We can force the media to take on topics they would never bring up otherwise," highlighting the origins of the Black Lives Matter movement as a hashtag response to the killing of Trayvon Martin (Doucouré, "Rokhaya Diallo").

24. Diallo, *Afro!*, 9.

25. Diallo, *Afro!*, 9.

26. See, for example, Diallo, *Afro!*, 166, 175, 177. On the role of the Internet and social media in the affirmation of twenty-first-century Afro-French identities, see Niang, *Identités françaises*, 253–59.

27. Diallo, *Afro!*, 167.

28. Diallo, *Afro!*, 176.

29. As Célia Laborie notes in her profile of Cathline, this newly found political consciousness around images of Black female beauty is embedded in the digital sphere: "The digital did a lot to raise awareness. All the Black women youtubers, bloggers, and trendsetters are closely followed by the industry, because they're tastemakers who have the power to create consumer demand in the female market" ("Black (Hair) Is Beautiful").

30. Ekué's website foregrounds the role of chick lit and hip-hop feminism in her novels. See Ekué, *Lauren Ekué*, http://www.laurenekue.com/lauren-ekue/ (accessed December 1, 2021); Sadai, "*Chick lit novel*"; and Gehrmann, "Emerging Afro-Parisian 'Chick-Lit'"; see

Gupta and Frenkel, "Chick-Lit in a Time of African Cosmopolitanism," the introduction to a special issue of *Feminist Theory* on the topic.

31. Lauren Ekué, *Lauren Ekué*, http://www.laurenekue.com/lauren-ekue/ (accessed December 1, 2021). The economic prestige of the Hauts-de-Seine suburb contrasts strikingly with the bleak vision of the Parisian banlieue depicted as the protagonist's point of origin in *Icône urbaine*. See Ekué, *Icône urbaine*, 31.

32. Ekué, *Black Attitude #1*, 22.

33. See Cristèle D., "Lauren Ekué et son livre."

34. On the political engagement and implications of Ekué's work, see Volet, "*Icône urbaine*"; Sadai, "*Chick lit novel*"; Anyinefa, "*Icône urbaine*"; and Malela, "*Icône urbaine*." Mame-Fatou Niang recounts a similar pattern of skepticism among viewers of her film *Mariannes noires*, which features seven economically comfortable, professionally successful Black women in France. See Niang, *Identités françaises*, 208–10.

35. Ekué, *Icône urbaine*, 112.

36. Santana, "Exorcizing Afropolitanism."

37. See Ede, "Politics"; and Salami, "Can Africans Have Multiple Subcultures?"

38. Ede, "Politics," 91.

39. On the theme of mobility in Afropolitanism, see Eze, "We Afropolitans"; Gehrmann, "Cosmopolitanism"; and Mbembe, "Afropolitanism."

40. Ekué, *Icône urbaine*, 110–11.

41. Ekué, *Icône urbaine*, 112.

42. Ekué, *Icône urbaine*, 18.

43. Ekué, *Icône urbaine*, 18.

44. Sadai, "*Chick lit novel*."

45. Ekué, *Icône urbaine*, 42.

46. Ekué, *Icône urbaine*, 42. On the use of skin-lightening creams by the sapeurs, see Gondola, "Dream and Drama."

47. Ekué, *Carnet spunk*, cover copy.

48. Ekué, *Carnet spunk*, 44.

49. Miano, *Blues pour Élise*, 47. Like Miano's heroines, *Icône urbaine*'s Flora ventures to the African beauty salons of the boulevard de Strasbourg only as a short-term consumer, anxious to return to the sanctity of home after having her hair done (Ekué, *Icône urbaine*, 37–40).

50. Ekué, *Carnet spunk*, 49. Chimamanda Adichie makes a similar reference to the symbolic importance of Michelle Obama's hair in *Americanah* (367–78); on this topic see Cruz-Gutierrez, "'Hairitage' Matters."

51. Ekué, *Carnet spunk*, 67. The title is a reference to Zora Neale Hurston's short story "Spunk," published in 1925.

52. Ekué, *Icône urbaine*, 9.

53. Cristèle D., "Lauren Ekué et son livre." On the categorization of *Icône urbaine* as "popular" literature, see Anyinefa, "*Icône urbaine*"; and Sadai, "*Chick lit novel*." As Susanne Gehrmann points out, a similar point could be made about the relative accessibility of *Blues pour Élise* in Léonora Miano's oeuvre ("Emerging Afro-Parisian 'Chick-Lit,'" 218).

54. Ajavon, "Lauren Ekué." Polo Belina Moji examines how the "dense matrix of referentiality" in Ekué's novel crosses linguistic, cultural, and textual borders ("Divas and Deviance," 12). Similarly, Koffi Anyinefa points out the use of footnotes in *Icône urbaine*

that inscribe, for example, a readership familiar with Malcolm X but not with Frantz Fanon or Mayotte Capécia ("*Icône urbaine*," 113).

55. Dukunde, "La Black Attitude."

56. Planète Afrique, "Lauren Ekué: Icône urbaine." On the relationship between Ekué's work and "chick lit," see Anyinefa, "*Icône urbaine*"; Sadai, "*Chick lit novel*"; and Gehrmann, "Emerging Afro-Parisian 'Chick-Lit.'"

57. On this topic see Volet, "*Icône urbaine*."

References

Adichie, Chimamanda Ngozi. *Americanah*. New York: Anchor, 2013.

Ajavon, Naomi. "Lauren Ekué, l'interview." *La croisée des plumes*, December 2, 2015. www.naomi-ajavon.com (accessed October 22, 2017).

Anyinefa, Koffi. "*Icône urbaine*: L'esthétique 'populaire' de Lauren Ekué." In *Créativité intermédiatique au Togo et dans la diaspora togolaise*, edited by Susanne Gehrmann and Dotsé Yigbe, 103–20. Münster: LIT Verlag, 2015.

Bouly de Lesdain, Sophie. "Château-Rouge, une centralité africaine à Paris." *Ethnologie française* 29, no. 1 (1999): 86–99.

Capot, Clément. "*Où sont les noirs?* Rokhaya Diallo expose le racisme sur RMC Story." *SFR: ACTUS*, March 18, 2020. https://actus.sfr.fr/cine-series/tv/ou-sont-les-noirs-rokhaya-diallo-expose-le-racisme-sur-rmc-story-202003180003.html.

Chabrol, Marie. "Continuités d'usages et maintien d'une centralité commerciale immigrée à Château-Rouge (Paris)." *Les Annales de la recherche urbaine* 108 (2013): 96–107.

Cruz-Gutierrez, Cristina. "'Hairitage' Matters: Transitioning and the Third Wave Hair Movement in 'Hair,' 'Imitation,' and *Americanah*." In *A Companion to Chimamanda Ngozi Adichie*, edited by Ernest N. Emenyonu, 245–61. Suffolk: James Currey, 2017.

D., Cristèle. "Lauren Ekué et son livre 'Icône urbaine.'" *Amina* 432 (2006). https://aflit.arts.uwa.edu.au/AMINAekue06.html.

Dabiri, Emma. "Why I Am Not an Afropolitan." *Africa Is a Country* (blog), January 21, 2014. https://africasacountry.com/2014/01/why-im-not-an-afropolitan/.

Dabiri, Emma. "Why I Am (Still) Not an Afropolitan." *Journal of African Cultural Studies* 28, no. 1 (2016): 104–8.

Diallo, Rokhaya. *Afro!* Paris: Editions des Arènes, 2015.

Diallo, Rokhaya. *Pari(s) d'amies*. Paris: Delcourt, 2015.

Doucouré, Samba. "Rokhaya Diallo: À la télévision, j'ai l'impression d'être un élément perturbateur." *SaphirNews*, March 27, 2016. https://www.saphirnews.com/Rokhaya-Diallo-A-la-television-j-ai-l-impression-d-etre-un-element-perturbateur_a22158.html.

Dukunde, Ange. "La Black Attitude de Lauren Ekué." *Amina* 496 (2011). https://aflit.arts.uwa.edu.au/AMINAEkue11.html.

Eaton, Kalenda. "Eternal Blackness: Considering Afropolitanism as a Radical Possibility." *Africa Today* 65, no. 4 (2019): 1–17.

Ede, Amatoritsero. "The Politics of Afropolitanism." *Journal of African Cultural Studies* 28, no. 1 (2016): 88–100.

Ekué, Lauren. *Black Attitude #1: Ro$e*. Paris: Anibwé, 2011.

Ekué, Lauren. *Carnet spunk*. Paris: Anibwé, 2010.

Ekué, Lauren. *Icône urbaine*. Paris: Anibwé, 2005.

Ekué, Lauren. *L'industrie de la mode africaine*. Paris: Anibwé, 2020.

Eze, Chielozona. "We, Afropolitans." *Journal of African Cultural Studies* 28, no. 1 (2016): 114–19.

Frund, Arlette, "Site-ing Black Paris: Discourses and the Making of Identities." In Keaton, Sharpley-Whiting, and Stovall, *Black France/France Noire*, 269–86.

Gandoulou, Justin-Daniel. *Au cœur de la Sape*. Paris: L'Harmattan, 1989.

Gehrmann, Susanne. "Cosmopolitanism with African Roots: Afropolitanism's Ambivalent Mobilities." *Journal of African Cultural Studies* 28, no. 1 (2016): 61–72.

Gehrmann, Susanne. "Emerging Afro-Parisian 'Chick-Lit' by Lauren Ekué and Léonora Miano." *Feminist Theory* 20, no. 2 (2019): 215–28.

Gikandi, Simon. "On Afropolitanism." In *Negotiating Afropolitanism: Essays on Borders and Spaces in Contemporary African Literature and Folklore*, edited by Jennifer Wawrzinek and J. K. S. Makokha, 9–11. Amsterdam: Rodopi, 2011.

Gondola, Ch. Didier. "Dream and Drama: The Search for Elegance among Congolese Youth." *African Studies Review* 42, no. 1 (1999): 23–48.

Gupta, Pamila, and Ronit Frenkel. "Chick-Lit in a Time of African Cosmopolitanism." *Feminist Theory* 20, no. 2 (2019): 123–32.

Hitchcott, Nicki. "Sex and the Afropean City: Léonora Miano's *Blues pour Élise*." In *Francophone Afropean Literatures*, edited by Nicki Hitchcott and Dominic Thomas, 124–27. Liverpool: Liverpool University Press, 2014.

Hurston, Zora Neale. "Spunk." In *The New Negro: An Interpretation*, edited by Alain Locke, 105–11. New York: Atheneum, 1925.

Keaton, Trica Danielle, T. Denean Sharpley-Whiting, and Tyler Stovall, eds. *Black France/France Noire: The History and Politics of Blackness*. Durham, NC: Duke University Press, 2012.

Laborie, Célia. "Black (Hair) Is Beautiful." *CelsaLab*, May 25, 2017. https://celsalab.fr/longform/black-hair-is-beautiful/.

Mabanckou, Alain. *Bleu-blanc-rouge*. Paris: Présence Africaine, 1998.

Mabanckou, Alain. *Blue White Red: A Novel*. Translated by Alison Dundy. Bloomington: Indiana University Press, 2013.

MacGaffey, Janet, and Rémy Bazenguissa-Ganga. *Congo-Paris: Transnational Traders on the Margins of the Law*. Bloomington: Indiana University Press, 2000.

Malela, Buata. "*Icône urbaine*, premier roman de Lauren Ekué: La génération hip-hop écrit au féminin." *Afrikara.com*, February 14, 2007. http://www.afrikara.com/index.php?page=contenu&art=1604&PHPSESSID=0007fc905031796fae227fc427c3e560.

Mbembe, Achille. "Afropolitanism." In *Africa Remix: Contemporary Art of a Continent*, edited by Simon Njami, 26–29. Johannesburg: Jacana Media, 2007.

Miano, Léonora. *Blues pour Élise*. Paris: Plon, 2010.

Miano, Léonora. *Habiter la frontière*. Paris: L'Arche, 2012.

Moji, Polo Belina. "Divas and Deviance: Hip-Hop Feminism and Black Visuality in Lauren Ekué's *Icône urbaine* (2006)." *Agenda* 32, no. 3 (2018): 10–20.

Murakami, Haruki. *After Dark*. Translated by Jay Rubin. New York: Alfred A. Knopf, 2007.

Ndiaye, Pap. *La condition noire: Essai sur une minorité française*. Paris: Editions Calmann-Lévy, 2008.

Niang, Mame-Fatou. *Identités françaises: Banlieues, féminités et universalisme*. Leiden: Brill, 2020.

Nora, Pierre, ed. *Lieux de mémoire*. Paris: Gallimard, 1984.

Ogbechie, S. Okwunodu. "Afropolitanism: Africa without Africans." *AACHRONYM* (blog), April 4, 2008. http://aachronym.blogspot.com/2008/04/afropolitanism-more-africa-without.html.

Planète Afrique. "Lauren Ekué: Icône urbaine." *PlanèteAfrique.com*, August 26, 2005. http://
    www.planeteafrique.com/Amis/News_display.asp?ArticleID=567&rub=IciAilleurs
    -Thematique.

Sadai, Célia. *"Chick lit novel* ou fiction performative? Hétéronomie et amour de soi dans *Icône
    urbaine* de Lauren Ekué." *La plume francophone*, March 22, 2013. https://la-plume
    -francophone.com/2013/03/22/lauren-ekue-icone-urbaine/.

Salami, Minna. "Can Africans Have Multiple Subcultures? A Response to 'Exorcising
    Afropolitanism.'" *Ms. Afropolitan*, April 3, 2013. https://msafropolitan.com/2013/04/can
    -africans-have-multiple-subcultures-a-response-to-exorcising-afropolitanism.html.

Santana, Stephanie Bosch. "Exorcizing Afropolitanism: Binyavanga Wainaina Explains Why 'I
    Am a Pan-Africanist, Not an Afropolitan' at ASAUK 2012." *Africa in Words* (blog), February 8,
    2013. https://africainwords.com/2013/02/08/exorcizing-afropolitanism-binyavanga-wainaina
    -explains-why-i-am-a-pan-africanist-not-an-afropolitan-at-asauk-2012/.

Selasi, Taiye. "Bye-Bye Babar." *LIP Magazine*, March 3, 2005. https://thelip.robertsharp.co.uk
    /2005/03/03/bye-bye-barbar/.

Stone, Mee-Lai. "Congolese Dandies: Meet the Stylish Men and Women of Brazzaville—In
    Pictures." *Guardian*, August 27, 2020.

Stovall, Tyler. *Paris Noir: African Americans in the City of Light.* Boston: Houghton Mifflin,
    1996.

Toivanen, Anna-Leena. "Cosmopolitanism's New Clothes? The Limits of the Concept of
    Afropolitanism." *European Journal of English Studies* 21, no. 2 (2017): 189–205.

Tshimanga, Charles, Didier Gondola, and Peter J. Bloom, eds. *Frenchness and the African
    Diaspora: Identity and Uprising in Contemporary France.* Bloomington: Indiana
    University Press, 2009.

Volet, Jean-Marie. *"Icône urbaine*: Un roman de Lauren Ekué." *L'Afrique écrite au féminin*,
    December 6, 2008. University of Western Australia. https://aflit.arts.uwa.

Racial Storytelling in the Classroom
Subject and Method

Paulina L. Alberto

Storytelling is having a moment in US culture. Although stories have long been told across countless genres (with video games, YouTube, TikTok, Instagram, and other social media platforms only the latest additions), storytelling is coming into crisp focus as concept and practice, art and craft. The Moth, a live storytelling program that began in a New York City living room and alighted at the Nuyorican Poets Café and other alternative venues in the early 2000s, has since spread its wings across US (and global) stages and radio stations. Countless other self-consciously storytelling-based, nationally syndicated radio programs have followed suit, as have TED talks and an endless proliferation of podcasts. Nowadays, it seems, everyone from economists to sociologists to spiritual leaders embraces the idea that the key to finding happiness, satisfaction, and meaning lies in the "stories we tell ourselves."[1] In the political fray, President Barack Obama often quipped that having "a better story to tell" gave him the upper hand over domestic or international rivals.[2]

The word *narrative*, too, has become ubiquitous. It used to be a term of art used largely by specialists in certain academic fields or in journalism; today, the injunction to "control the narrative" suffuses US media and politics. In some contexts, references to "narrative control" help illuminate the importance of perspective in shaping reality and, above all, the power that flows from authorship (as when Broadway's Eliza Hamilton puts herself "back in the narrative" from which she was long excluded, for example). In other contexts, narrative's entanglements with

Radical History Review
Issue 144 (October 2022)   DOI 10.1215/01636545-9847858
© 2022 by MARHO: The Radical Historians' Organization, Inc.

power, control, and persuasion emerge in a much more cynical, even sinister light. In business and advertising, "controlling" or "disrupting" the narrative is shorthand for brand burnishing and reputation management.[3] In its counterinsurgency manual, the US military teaches its forces that insurgencies arise in places where leaders "build a compelling narrative that . . . mobilizes the population to support a violent social movement"; the manual cautions states to "suppres[s] the insurgency in a way that deters other potential rebels while avoiding contributing to the insurgent narrative and provoking wider resistance."[4]

From all this, it seems clear that a growing body of interdisciplinary research (across social and cognitive psychology, neuroscience, philosophy, and literary studies) has succeeded in teaching a cross-section of US audiences about "narrative persuasion" or "narrative impact": the disproportional power of story or narrative, compared to nonnarrative expository and argumentative forms, to shape beliefs and attitudes. According to this research, human brains process narrative through a quick, primarily affective system of cognition that is distinct from the slower cognitive elaboration (based on logic and reasoning) required for information presented in nonnarrative form. This difference in processing makes narratives—both fictional and nonfictional—uniquely convincing and extremely difficult to dispel even with compelling expository, nonnarrative information.[5] Indeed, narrative projection—using story to extend meaning from something we think we understand to something we do not—is central to how we acquire and organize knowledge, interact with other human beings, and navigate the world every day.[6]

The importance of narrative persuasion helps explain why attempts to retell US history with questions of slavery and racism at its very center, most notably the 1619 Project, have sparked so much attention from both admirers and critics. Despite all the bogeyman qualities detractors attribute to critical race theory, it is less the theory behind the 1619 Project than its gripping, textured, harrowing, and deeply humane storytelling that accounts for its resonance with a wide public. As the project creator Nikole Hannah-Jones thoughtfully argues, it's the "new origin story" about the United States—the uncomfortably unvarnished narrative paths it plots through five centuries of history and brings vividly into classrooms—that makes the project so powerful, and so threatening to conservatives.[7] As the power of narrative surfaces into collective consciousness alongside struggles over whether and how to grapple with the nation's experience of slavery and its present-day afterlives, the stakes around racial storytelling in the classroom—around which stories about race and belonging get told or cast aside—have become abundantly clear.

It may seem redundant to speak of "racial storytelling"; after all, ideas about race and processes of race making are always a set of stories about who people are and are not. Yet it is imperative to notice and name the special place of story and narrative in what Evelyn Brooks Higginbotham famously called "the metalanguage of race": the power by which race "speaks about and lends meaning to a host of terms and expressions, to myriad aspects of life."[8] Stories infuse racial terms and expressions with uniquely persuasive force, disseminating, naturalizing, and reinforcing them at the capillary levels of public discourse and across many areas of human experience.[9]

For educators at any level who wish to teach students to understand racism and to practice anti-racism, news of narrative's disproportional impact is both bad and good. Stories transport readers, mimicking experiences and encouraging suspension of disbelief while discouraging counterargument. This allows readers or listeners "to disappear into the story, to experience the emotions"—and, we might add, to absorb the ideologies—"intended by the writer."[10] Its affective qualities and reliance on characters make narrative particularly good at encouraging perspective taking (getting readers to put themselves in the place of and to feel with a particular character) and producing lasting associations between individual cases (characters) and the broader social categories to which they belong.[11] Narrative is also different from stereotype or schema, which function in a more abstract, structural way to sort and organize information in our minds. Stereotypes and schemata are doubtlessly influential, but often they are so obviously totalizing and flattening that they become relatively easy to spot and contest. Narrative's power lies instead in its dynamism, particularity, subtlety, and detail—its ability to insinuate itself as truth without seeming overtly ideological, to suppress or highlight information without calling attention to this process of selection.[12]

What matters, then, is how each of us chooses to deploy the power of racial storytelling. The power of stories to shape and naturalize beliefs can be mobilized for political or monetary gain, for military control, or for racist, dehumanizing, and even genocidal purposes.[13] The novelist Chimamanda Ngozi Adichie has eloquently cautioned against "the danger of a single story"—an impoverished, incomplete, dangerous account that "show[s] people as one thing, as only one thing, over and over again," until that becomes "the definitive story" of a person or people.[14] But educators can effectively teach students to become skeptical of existing racial stories and expose their disempowering mechanisms and effects. I think of this as teaching "racial storytelling as a subject of historical analysis." Educators can also harness the power of storytelling to teach students to construct new, carefully considered racial narratives, grounded in historical methods at once rigorous and imaginative and guided by anti-racist principles. This process is more challenging than teaching students to spot and deconstruct existing stories, but it is arguably a more important way to connect theories and practices of racial justice. I think of this as teaching "racial storytelling as a critical method for historical reconstruction."

Racial Storytelling as a Subject of Historical Analysis

At the University of Michigan, I am jointly appointed in the departments of history and Romance languages, and within the latter, I teach in the programs of Spanish and Portuguese. My teaching thus takes place at the intersections of several disciplines, methods, source materials, times, places, and languages. In one way or another, all of my classes explore the particular histories of race-making in Latin America in centuries past, always with an eye to teaching students to think critically about the constructedness of race and the contingencies of racial formation, and to relate these insights to their experiences of racialization in the present-day United States. In particular, my research and much of my teaching seek to historicize, and ultimately demystify, dominant myths of racial exceptionalism in two very distinct national contexts: Brazil, which has the largest population of African descent outside Africa and has long been characterized as a "racial democracy" founded on unparalleled racial mixture and harmony; and Argentina, whose official history has long presented it as a regional exception characterized by homogeneous whiteness and the effective "disappearance" of its substantial colonial-era African and Indigenous populations. In the classroom and in my own writing, I examine the laborious, contested, multi-voiced, and nonlinear processes that gave rise to these ideologies, highlighting the role of Afro-Latin Americans in shaping and resisting them and exposing their consequences for Afro-Latin American lives.

It was in the classroom, about a decade ago, that I learned the value of seeing racial storytelling as a subject of historical analysis—something to be placed under the microscope, examined, and classified. For years, I had been teaching a course titled "Writing Race and Nation in Latin America" that explored some of the foundational texts around which dominant narratives and powerful counter-narratives of race coalesced in various countries after independence. But around 2010, a new crop of historical fiction coming out of Argentina caught my attention: novels, many of them best-selling romances, that newly centered Indigenous, Black, or mixed-race characters and their experiences in the nation's past (and, less frequently, its present). At the turn of the twenty-first century, the advent of a center-left nationalist government, the official adoption of multiculturalism, the economic crisis that shattered deeply held certainties about Argentina's white, middle-class modernity, and the efforts of increasingly organized Indigenous and Afro-descendant movements combined to provide openings for a reappraisal of Argentina's narrative of white exceptionalism. These novels, and the innovative works of academic history that (loosely) inspired them, expressed alternative conceptions of the nation that embraced its non-white roots. This development in Argentina— novelists' late-breaking celebration of hybridity, out of sync with the "foundational fictions" of its sister republics by at least a century—seemed to merit its own course. I designed the seminar "Argentina in History and Fiction" to examine contemporary historical fiction and historical writing about race in Argentina alongside some of the foundational nineteenth- and twentieth-century texts (literary and historiographic) that provided the inspiration for those newer productions. Together, the students and I considered why it was so important for histories of race to be written and rewritten in contemporary Argentina, especially in the years surrounding the bicentennial (2010). What could fiction do in this regard that traditional history writing couldn't—and vice versa?

To give students the critical tools with which to answer the first set of questions, I assigned the works of historians and other social scientists working on race in Argentina's past and present. This scholarship consciously revised or debunked older myths of Argentina's racelessness or homogeneous whiteness, telling new histories in which racialized groups—Afro-Argentines and Native peoples, for example—never "disappeared" from Argentina, as earlier narratives claimed, but were, rather, rendered invisible, stereotyped into oblivion, or enfolded into other racial categories, while race itself was largely subsumed by discussions of class.[15] For the second question, I exposed students to the methodological considerations of creative writers, theorists, and historians working in the "history-fiction borderland": the space where history's inescapable entanglements with and debts to storytelling become most evident.[16] As practitioners of microhistory, experimental narrative history, and judiciously speculative histories have shown, storytelling techniques like Saidiya Hartman's "critical fabulation" or "narrative restraint" can shed new light on the historical experiences of people marginalized or silenced in Western or postcolonial archives.[17] Going further, as the historian and novelist Richard Slotkin puts it, writing fiction outright can assist disciplinary historians in understanding and reconstructing the past:

Precisely because the novel imaginatively recovers the *indeterminacy* of a past time, it is *not* bound simply to celebrate the mere outcome; but leaves the writer and reader free to explore those alternative possibilities for belief, action, and political change, unrealized by history, which existed in the past. In so doing, the novelist may restore, as *imaginable possibilities*, the ideas, movements and values defeated or discarded in the struggles that produced the modern state—may produce a *counter-myth*, to play into and against the prevailing myths of the nation.[18]

The idea that fictional stories about the past have important historical and historiographic truths to tell is not new in Latin America. Indeed, the region arguably birthed the "new historical novel," which, for at least half a century, has been using literary techniques—such as the conscious distortion of history, the demythification or symbolic dethronement of famous figures, an emphasis on unpredictability and cyclicality, parody, anachronism, heteroglossia, intertextuality, and metafiction (the narrator's referring to the creative process of their own text)—to symbolically refound national imaginaries and upend official histories.[19]

The novels we read in our class were mostly not of this literary and historical caliber. Moreover, the frequently uncritical celebration, by white novelists, of interracial love and racial mixture as a panacea for Argentina's white supremacist ills is redolent of myths of harmony that Indigenous and Black activists in other parts of the region have been debunking for decades. But these novels nonetheless play an important public role in national conversations through what the literary scholar Linda Hutcheon calls "historiographic metafiction": fiction that engages with contemporary historiographic debates and consciously represents and dramatizes for readers different strands of historical interpretation as well as their competing stakes.[20] These novels interpellate modern readers as active interpreters of the national past and its present-day political implications through narrative strategies including framing stories set in the present, embedded (ersatz) historical manuscripts, narrators-as-detectives, or flagrant anachronism (such as endowing the nineteenth-century heroine with twenty-first-century feminist sensibilities). In a similarly revisionist vein, the new crop of historical fiction spotlights the protagonism, rather than the erasure or subsidiary role, of Indigenous people, Black people, and mixed-race people in Argentina's past, implicating readers personally and politically in their fates. Above all, these authors make the process of historical revision central to their story lines. White heroes and heroines become historian-sleuths whose personal quests compel them to uncover the role of Indigenous people or Afro-Argentines in the nation's past (though rarely its present), exposing Argentine whiteness itself as the result of fictional storytelling. Historians, histories, documents, and bibliographies appear throughout, arming readers with the knowledge needed to revise their racial-historical imaginaries. Literary devices like characterization, through which heroes and heroines are endowed with views imagined as progressive and anti-racist while villains are portrayed as deeply racist, guide readers in identifying with or dissociating from certain political positions and provide lessons (albeit frequently celebratory and oversimplified) on the virtues of Argentina's shift from whiteness to diversity.

Two insights from this course reshaped my subsequent teaching and research. First, ideas about race are not (or not *just*) static schema, flattened ideologies, or formulaic discourse but dynamic stories: engrossing and transporting tales of interracial love, friendship, or violence, with recognizable plots, settings, morals, and characters. Stories about Afro-descendants, Native people, and others have been told and retold not just in Argentina but across the Americas, different in form and content but similar in purpose as pedagogies of race and nation. I realized that examining racial ideologies *as stories* was crucial to understanding how these ideas circulate, persuade, shape behaviors, influence life chances, and persist in the Americas and beyond.

Second, identifying and naming racial stories is a remarkably effective way to expose, defamiliarize, examine, and dismantle them. Here, I benefited from the fortuitous cross-pollination that sometimes occurs across very different teaching projects. For another class, I had been teaching Martin Bernal's *Black Athena*, which makes accessible an extraordinarily intricate revision of the ethnocultural underpinnings of Ancient Greece by clearly labeling preexisting interpretations (the "Ancient Model" and the "Aryan Model") as well as his own (the "Revised Ancient Model").[21] These "models" or historical interpretations become almost like characters who moved through history, shaped by human events and shaping them in turn. I had also been teaching the defamatory tale of Spain's unique cruelty and rapaciousness in the New World, which the Spanish historian Julián Juderías famously dubbed the "Black Legend."[22] As several scholars have shown, conceiving of these anti-Spanish attitudes as an overarching story, and labeling it, makes it possible to track its emergence, evolution, and shifting political inflections across centuries and nations—including recent Native critiques of the Black Legend's exclusive focus on European cruelty or agency, which rhetorically obliterates or renders invisible Native presences.[23] Together, Bernal's work and the scholarship on the Black Legend made a compelling case for a historical method that, by tracking and labeling racial stories as historical subjects or objects, made them easier to grasp, manipulate, and peer into.

Inspired by those works, I began to label, with my students, the various guiding myths of Argentine racial formation. This pedagogical strategy made it much easier to explain the particular affordances and pitfalls of these narratives, as well as their stubborn persistence and paradoxical resonance across the political spectrum. The myth of Black and Indigenous Argentines' annihilation in wars or epidemics, for example, could be dubbed a "black legend" of Argentine racial formation. Like the Black Legend of Spanish cruelty and genocide in the New World, that narrative could be invoked in tones of satisfaction, pious lamentation, or outright denunciation, but in all cases it resolves into indirect affirmations of the success of the settler-colonial endeavor—or in Argentina's particular case, the triumph of whiteness. It was similarly useful to identify countervailing "white" or "rosy" legends of Argentine racial formation: historical, political, or literary narratives that, from the mid-nineteenth century onward, celebrated or asserted Argentina's whiteness and Europeanness as part of a successful "civilizing" process. And gaining traction more recently, as evidenced by the novels we read, were several "brown legends" of harmonious hybridity, local variants of the ideologies of racial mixture and "racial democracy" that characterized national discourses in other Latin American countries.[24] To be sure, like all taxonomies or heuristics, this system of labeling racial ideologies flattens some complexity. But it also brings these ideologies out of hiding; like pouring fluorescent dye on a tissue sample, it renders their contours and inner workings more visible and makes them easier to dissect.

If these guiding myths or legends could be described as racial master *narratives*, the individual novels, memoirs, reportage, or images we examined in class could more properly be labeled racial *stories*—the granular, smaller-scale tales that prop up master narratives of race in everday print and oral culture.[25] Among these, none offered a clearer example of the power of racial storytelling to support master narratives than the tales surrounding Raúl Grigera, an Afro-Argentine man who rose to fame as a dandy and an eccentric icon of Buenos Aires' bohemian nightlife in the 1910s. Stories about Grigera proliferated in the city's burgeoning print and popular culture, and his likeness circulated in countless photographs, cartoons, and even in film. As an Afro-Argentine celebrity in a city that newly proclaimed its status as the glittering Paris of Latin America, he was a Black legend—perhaps, one might say, an Afropolitan avant la lettre (on which more below).[26] Yet, slowly after 1916 and precipitously after 1930, as sociopolitical upheavals expanded the meanings and threats of Blackness, storytellers demoted Grigera from Black legend in his own right to lead character in the Black legend of Afro-Argentine disappearance and demise. Grigera's public persona fell prey to dominant racial narratives that cast him as an aberration in the white nation: an uppity Black man who dared too much and flew too high and was thus doomed to fall into misery, despair, and oblivion. Storytellers recast his fame as infamy, predicted his fall, and declared him dead before his time, dismissing him as a racial anomaly. And life followed art: the defamatory racial stories about Grigera narrowed the kinds of personas he could assume or project in the city's nightlife, channeling his life trajectory toward a very few unsavory denouements. As his character's star fell in the public imagination, in the 1930s Grigera himself began a long decline into destitution and panhandling, periodic homelessness, repeated police detention, illness, and hospitalization. In 1942 he was confined to the mental institution in which he died in 1955.

The many stories about Raúl Grigera have become a cornerstone of my teaching about the power of racial storytelling. Indeed, I began to try to reconstruct his story in the classroom long before I knew it would become the subject of my newest book.[27] First, students examine the Black legend of Afro-Argentine disappearance through traditional sources: nineteenth-century images and statuary, fiction, histories, census essays, and memoirs, working to distill these narratives' key tropes, plotlines, and repeating vocabulary. They then read examples of the stories I gathered about Raúl Grigera—in particular, the increasingly flattened, patterned, and defamatory stories about him that emerged timidly in 1916 and ferociously after 1930. Placing the documents side by side in this way proves immensely clarifying: it reveals the scandalous degree to which the stories about Grigera, for all of their seeming individualization, texture, and particularity of detail, subserviently recapitulated the broader narrative of Afro-Argentine disappearance—itself a process of largely baseless, iterative, plagiarized storytelling. Students can observe how the individualization, texture, and particularity of detail in the stories—along with their plotline, seemingly specific to Grigera—made those stories so much more dangerously seductive and transporting than the dusty proclamations that constitute the original myth of Afro-Argentine disappearance. Perhaps even more forcefully than I have been able to demonstrate in my writing, this dynamic juxtaposition of racial stories and narratives in the classroom helps unmask as fictions what have long passed as naturalized or descriptive demographic "realities." From this case, finally, I ask students to extrapolate. What stories about racialized individuals, groups, or "types" work to prop up master narratives of race in the present-day United States?

Grigera's case also stands as an extreme, and extremely clear, example of the concrete, everyday effects of racial stories and narratives on individuals and communities. Imani Perry notes that in the United States, the power of racial narratives "can be measured much more easily in media than in many other contexts"; a media-based analysis is thus her main focus. Yet she expresses the desire to see "ethnographies of racial narratives in social life," where their impact on individual and collective lives could be examined in more depth.[28] The case of Raúl Grigera provides precisely this forceful example of an ethnography set in the past, exposing the role racial stories played in making his life trajectory converge with the sad outcomes imagined for him.

Approaching racial storytelling as a subject of historical inquiry, then, involves identifying specific stories about race, tracing their flow into and out of master narratives, labeling those narratives clearly, and tracking their gestation across time, place, and genres. Although rooted in the techniques of historical and literary analysis, this method (similar to qualitative research coding or discourse analysis) can be applied much more widely—just as the insights about storytelling have suffused so many areas of public life. Similarly, thinking about all sources—not just narrative texts—as "stories" unlocks pedagogical opportunities that can be applied across multiple teaching contexts. For example, when teaching with a historical image, I cue students to observe the image closely and to think of it in narrative terms, as if it were a movie or a novel. What story about race does it tell, what plotline does its creator intend to communicate? Students get remarkably good at thinking with and through stories—precisely because story is fundamental to how their minds, like all minds, make meaning.

Racial Storytelling as a Critical Method for Historical Reconstruction

If undergraduate students can become proficient in naming and identifying racial stories in literary texts and primary documents, exposing their mechanisms and effects, are they also able thoughtfully and judiciously to partake in the process of putting new stories in place? As Slotkin puts it, "Our collective consciousness is informed and shaped by mythic symbols and narratives. Analytical deconstructions of myth may undermine existing structures, but nothing can take the place of a myth but another myth, another story with the same historical resonance and moral authority . . . a *counter-myth*, to play into and against the prevailing myths of the nation."[29] We need critical counter-narratives informed by the work of historians, theorists, activists, and cultural creators—artists, novelists, and other imaginative rebuilders of past or possible worlds—in order to "shift the narrative." "Narrative shifting, at its best," Imani Perry explains (contra Slotkin's emphasis on the usefulness of myths), "is not the creation of myths but the telling of stories about groups in ways that are politically useful and true . . . it is invoking tradition, history, culture, and practice that provide powerful counterexamples to bigoted narrative."[30]

The challenge of engaging students in shifting a narrative animates another course I developed for Romance Languages: "Stories and Histories of Race in Brazil and Argentina." The course, taught in Spanish, Portuguese, and English, examines a range of fictional works alongside historical documents and the writings of historians themselves to understand how history and fiction have reflected and shaped ideas about race in each country, and how these national cases compare or differ. Throughout, the course spotlights the role of Afro-descendants in particular, not only as frequent objects of representation in these stories but as historical subjects and authors who shaped or contested these dominant narratives, and in recent decades, led the charge to put counter-narratives in their stead.

The major writing assignments for this course invite students to engage in precisely the sort of informed and judicious imaginative historical reconstruction and counter-narration that Slotkin and Perry call for. Early in the course, I introduce students to the dominant narratives of race in each country—what I call the "then" narratives (Argentina's "homogeneous whiteness" or Brazil's "racial democracy")—and to the transformational critiques and counter-narratives voiced, since the late twentieth century, by Black thinkers and activists: the "now" narratives. In small, scaffolded weekly assignments, I guide students toward understanding the content and stakes of the "now" critiques by posing the question in a storytelling mode—a question embodied in specific characters and situations rather than framed around an abstract set of principles. In the 1970s, for example, the famous Afro-Brazilian thinker, actor, artist, and activist Abdias Nascimento became a vocal critic of Brazil's discourse of "racial democracy" and harmonious intermixture, denouncing it (as many other Black thinkers at the time did) as a harmful "myth" that precluded the formation of a unified Black identity and a consciousness of oppression among Afro-descendant Brazilians. Students read key texts by Nascimento; they also read the results of a 1976 household survey in which Brazilians' responses to the question "What color are you?" generated 134 different color terms, the majority of which emphasized mixture and tended to downplay or evade Blackness.[31] In any other class, I would have students read both these documents and lead into our discussion with an abstract question about what this survey says about the persistent valorization of whiteness within Brazil's celebrations of mixture, and why that would pose a problem for a self-defined "Movimento Negro" that wished to unite Brazil's Afro-descendant majority around that term of racial ancestry. But because this class encourages students to use their historical imaginations and to project themselves into the past through narrative, I ask them to write a short piece on what they think Abdias Nascimento might have had to say about these survey results. Some students choose to write from Nascimento's perspective, imagining an article he might have published in an activist publication or a speech he might have prepared for a rally. Others answer the question in a more detached or speculative, third-person academic voice but arrive at similarly plausible, historically credible, position statements. Either way, by placing themselves within a hypothetical story with a historical setting, a character, and a dramatic situation, students begin to grasp the political implications—personal, collective, national—of Brazil's narratives of race mixture and are able to see their significant limitations from the perspective of a leading critic. As an exercise in perspective taking, this sort of small writing assignment prepares students for their own attempts at narrative shifting in the course's longer assignments.

For those papers, I ask students a version of the following question:

Drawing on what we know about a) changing dynamics of race in Argentina and Brazil ("then" and "now") and b) how fiction can be used to intervene in discussions about race, history, and politics, write a new story based on a "then" source (of your choice) that reflects the political and historical concerns of the "now" perspective. In other words, rewrite the old story in a way that reflects the "now" critique, demonstrates your understanding of what's at stake in that critique, and shifts the narrative or provides a counter-narrative to the "then" story.

One stated objective of this assignment is to engage students' abilities to recognize the power of stories to shape dominant national "myths" about race and identity in each country (and to consolidate their skills working with racial storytelling as a subject of historical analysis). Another major objective is to allow students to demonstrate their grasp of the historical transformations in racial discourses in each country, with attention to how and why these discourses changed, what exactly the "then" and "now" look like for their chosen country, and what the political implications of each are. In other words, before they can write a "counter-myth" they have to be sure to identify the original myth and its effects in historical context. If, as Slotkin argues, "myths do not have limitless powers of falsification," one of the most important things I can help my students identify is when, how, and under what conditions critics were able to erode that myth's hold on the national imaginary and to begin to replace it with a countermyth.[32] By asking students to dramatize and embody otherwise abstract processes or theoretical arguments about the past, this kind of storytelling assignment challenges them to work across social, cultural, and intellectual histories about race in Latin America.

The central objective of this assignment, however, is to teach students to identify and deploy the power of imaginative storytelling to present critical, alternative, or oppositional perspectives—to link theory to practice. Here I have proceeded with care (even trepidation): I am aware that inviting students to try their hand at racial storytelling as a critical method for historical writing could court disaster. One could easily imagine, for example, white students (from the United States, Latin America, or elsewhere) using their historical fiction simply to seek catharsis or a rosy resolution. This could be harmful or insulting to students who, because of their social position, have different relationships to the material. One can also imagine students misunderstanding and misrepresenting Latin American histories and cultures. There is a thin line, moreover, between using stories to bring a historical person (real or imagined) to life and engaging in ventriloquism. My own subject position presents its own challenges. As a white Latinx (Argentine-born) historian, I do not belong to the communities whose citizenship and belonging is most directly at stake in the telling and retelling of national racial stories. Although my syllabus is built around the thoughts and words of Afro-Latin Americans who shaped discussions about race in their societies, these men and women are not physically in the classroom. It is a delicate endeavor, not without pitfalls.

Yet, with a series of guardrails in place, teaching students to use racial story-telling to engage the past is both possible and worth doing. The idea is not that they will necessarily bring new, finished stories into the world but that they will experiment in ways that make them more sophisticated critics of how racial stories work and how complex the task of rewriting them can be. It would be dangerously ill-advised to build a highway overpass designed by undergraduate engineering students, but that does not mean that bridge design is not a good classroom exercise for them as a way of building insights and skills that can be subsequently applied in the world. Creating an environment conducive to this kind of respectful experimentation involves an open and often difficult discussion of my own and students' positionalities and an acknowledgment that there are subjectivities we can never fully imagine, let alone inhabit. It requires, moreover, teaching students to find the line between what is and isn't in their control as authors who seek responsibly to represent the past. Occasionally, students—rightly outraged by systems of racial slavery that reduced people of African descent to property or, if juridically free, deprived them of equal rights and full humanity—are tempted to create a world in which realities were otherwise, slavery did not exist, or at least did not in some way affect their protagonist. We have had searching, generative discussions about why this cannot be. Students are writing fiction for the purposes of history, and they cannot thereby falsify or soften the known historical record, the broad social dynamics historians know to have existed, even if they lament them. The objective of this exercise is pointedly *not* to give students (or myself) comfort by imagining an alternate world in which slavery and racism did not exist or were magically over-come. Instead, the objective is to teach students to understand some of the workings and constraints of slavery, racism, or homogenizing narratives of mixture or white-ness, exposing their real consequences.

At the same time, the assignment invites students, within these constraints, to imaginatively reconstruct the ways in which women, men, and children of African descent nonetheless lived creatively, their human experience shaped but not exhausted by their imposed status as "enslaved" or "Black."[33] To help students do this, the course exposes them to the ways in which innovative, imaginative scholarship has made available new narrative frameworks for understanding the experiences and actions of Black people in the Americas. In our conversations about Raúl Grigera, for example, I presented students with the defamatory stories about him alongside earlier sources (archival and journalistic) that tracked his rise to fame. In these sources, Grigera's own attempts at self-representation as a scintillating Black icon of Buenos Aires nightlife and the nascent Argentine tango are strikingly more apparent than in the later defamatory tales. I share with students the ways transformational concepts and categories of analysis, such as Black celebrity, Black dandyism, or Afropolitanism—in effect, complex racial counter-stories developed primarily by Black scholars and critics—can provide us with new ways to read these sources and to imagine how historical subjects might have narrated their own stories.[34] In particular, the idea of the "Afropolitan," with its emphasis on performative self-fashioning and urbanity and its rejection of victimization or "miserabilism," helps plot Raúl Grigera's life around his efforts at artistic, musical, and sartorial self-expression and self-making. This interpretation, in turn, helps shift the history of twentieth-century Argentina from one that stresses Black absences to one that centers Black presences. And it offers a compelling frame for connecting Grigera's public performances to other courageous strategies of Black self-invention across the Americas. Through this and other examples, students can use the narrative shifting that has taken place within academia to expand the horizons of their historical imagination and guide their own work of historical reconstruction.

Ultimately, these sorts of assignments only work in a classroom that holds students and the instructor mutually accountable to anti-racist pedagogies and processes of individual and collaborative critical self-reflection.[35] The course content is designed to systematically and gradually build up students' knowledge about the power of storytelling, its relationship to race and racism, and the specific historical contexts and processes of racialization in each country. Before students can begin drafting their counter-narratives, moreover, they meet with me to discuss possible topics and narrative strategies; they then submit detailed drafts, which I read and comment on extensively. Finally—and this, to me, is the most generative moment in the learning process—students engage in a peer-to-peer writing workshop. With the help of structured feedback forms, student-editors read their colleagues' work for awareness of historical context and situated processes of race making, engagement with scholarly and political transformations, and precisely the kinds of pitfalls and challenges, discussed above, that can easily emerge in the process of writing historical (meta)fiction about race.

I am consistently stunned and moved by the work students produce. The challenge of constructing their own stories as vehicles for contemporary anti-racist counter-narratives instills in students a deep sense of investment and responsibility. It pushes them to make thoughtful and judicious choices: Who to choose as narrator? (Is this child's viewpoint too limited to dramatize the historical point I want to make? Can I really know how this enslaved woman might have experienced this event?) Which character to center? (I want to make a point about the importance of intersectionality in anti-racism; should I choose a female character? a queer character?) And what plotlines to construct? (I do not want to sugarcoat the past by evading the realities of slavery and racism, but I do not want to fall into stereotype. How do I communicate agency within constraints?) These are the kinds of subtle but ultimately decisive questions of historical interpretation, representation, and narration that professional historians grapple with. And in openly discussing these choices with their peers, students are also grappling with the very real tensions among the subtle, messy, sometimes inconclusive historical interpretations produced by professional historians; the demands of fiction (especially popular, commercial fiction); and the representational strategies necessary for racial activism, which must often dispense with the never-ending questions, nuances, and multi-perspectival considerations so dear to historians and novelists, in favor of more forceful or categorical statements about the past issued with clarity, brevity, and conviction.

One surprising outcome of teaching racial storytelling as a method of historical reconstruction is how well most students do in a speculative historical fiction mode. I offer them the choice to write one of their two papers in a more traditional academic, expository voice, and invariably, two things happen: most students choose historical fiction, and these papers are overwhelmingly richer and more nuanced than the few more traditional ones. It seems that what Slotkin argues is true of professional historians might be true of students of history as well: they "often *understand* more about the stories they tell than can be *proved* according to the rules of the discipline."[36] We humanists and social scientists may fail to recognize—because of the kind of often stultifying writing we demand of our students—that they are better at creative rather than expository writing, better at *understanding* than at *proving* according to disciplinary rules, and that we can harness that creativity for the purposes of critical, social scientific, social-justice-inspired work.

Above all, teaching about, through, and with racial stories and narratives sharpens students' critical and creative faculties and their engagement with anti-racist work in the here and now. As the course progresses and our discussions about the various racial formations, forms of racial discrimination, and strategies of anti-racism in each country become increasingly complex—engaged in a three-way comparison among Argentina, Brazil, and, ultimately, the ever-present context of the United States—students achieve a level of nuance and sophistication in their understanding of these issues that I cannot quite reproduce in other classes. Students come to understand one of the most difficult lessons about anti-racist work: that it is never stable and never done; that there is no one perfect, pristine, permanent, or uncompromised position (or counter-story) against racism, precisely because racism itself is such a shape-shifting target, entangled with so many other forms of making and marking difference. And yet the takeaways for students (as far as I can tell from conversations, feedback, and evaluations) are not resignation, apathy, or acquiescence. They leave the course feeling empowered to join a public that can criticize harmful narratives and help amplify or uplift more just narratives. A few, perhaps, will feel emboldened to sketch out new private or public stories of their own.

Paulina L. Alberto is professor of history, Spanish, and Portuguese at the University of Michigan. Her books include *Terms of Inclusion: Black Intellectuals in Twentieth-Century Brazil* (2011), *Rethinking Race in Modern Argentina* (as coeditor, 2016), and most recently, *Black Legend: The Many Lives of Raúl Grigera and the Power of Racial Storytelling in Argentina* (2022). Her forthcoming coedited volume (with George Reid Andrews and Jesse Hoffnung-Garskof), a translated and annotated selection of articles from the Afro-Latin American press, is *Voices of the Race: Black Newspapers of Latin America, 1870–1960*.

Notes

1. Shiller, "Narrative Economics"; Henricks, "Stories We Tell Ourselves"; Holloway, *Stories We Tell Ourselves*.
2. See, for example, Kleber, "Obama: We Have the Better Story"; NPR, "Transcript: Obama's Speech"; and *Columbian*, "Obama: Dems Have 'Better Story.'"
3. See, for example, Citroën, *Control the Narrative*; and Gervais, "Disrupt Your Own Narrative."
4. US Department of the Army, *Insurgencies and Countering Insurgencies*, 4-3, paragraphs 4-14 and 4-11.
5. For an overview of this literature, see Brock, Green, and Strange, "Power beyond Reckoning."
6. Turner, *Literary Mind*; Schank, *Dynamic Memory Revisited*.
7. MSNBC, "Changing the Narrative, with Nikole Hannah-Jones." See also Hannah-Jones et al., *1619 Project*.
8. Higginbotham, "African-American Women's History," 255.
9. For further discussion, see "Introduction: Racial Stories," in Alberto, *Black Legend*.
10. Quoted in Green and Brock, "Role of Transportation," 703.
11. On this literature and its overlap with empathy studies, see Harrison, "The Paradox of Fiction." On narrative and out-group empathy or identification, see also Batson et al., "Empathy and Attitudes"; Stephan and Finlay, "Role of Empathy"; Harrison, "Great Sum"; and Vezzali et al., "Greatest Magic of Harry Potter." For a parallel argument by a historian (on the power of the emergent novel to stoke readers' visceral emotions and produce empathy for working classes in eighteenth-century Europe), see Hunt, *Inventing Human Rights*, 35–69.
12. Perry, *More Beautiful and More Terrible*, 44–46.
13. On the latter, see Perry, 44–45; and Smith, *Less than Human*.

14. Adichie, "The Danger of a Single Story," mins. 9:17 and 10:03.

15. For example, Andrews, *Afro-Argentines*; Geler, *Andares negros*; Frigerio and Lamborghini, "Los afroargentinos"; Ko, "From Whiteness to Diversity."

16. Demos, "Afterword."

17. See, for example, Natalie Zemon Davis's "invention . . . held tightly in check by the voices of the past" (*The Return of Martin Guerre*, 5); Saidiya Hartman's "critical fabulation" ("Venus in Two Acts," 11); Tiya Miles's rejection of seamless narrative in constructing a visibly "quilted chronicle" (*Dawn of Detroit*, 14); and Paula Fass's "disciplined imagination," as interpreted and brought to bear on especially recalcitrant silences by LaKisha Simmons, *Crescent City Girls*, 10–11. On the creative methodological innovations of scholars of African American women's history who "combin[e] imagination and documentation," see Miles, *Ties That Bind*, 211–12.

18. Slotkin, "Fiction for the Purposes of History," 231.

19. Menton, *Latin America's New Historical Novel*, 22–24. Prominent examples of this kind of fiction include Alejo Carpentier, *El reino de este mundo* (1949) and *El arpa y la sombra* (1979); Gabriel García Márquez, *Cien años de soledad* (1967); Augusto Roa Bastos, *Yo, el supremo* (1974); and Mario Vargas Llosa, *La guerra del fin del mundo* (1981). The short stories in Jorge Luis Borges's *Ficciones* (1944) and *El Aleph* (1949) use these techniques for similar goals.

20. Hutcheon, *Poetics of Postmodernism*.

21. Bernal, *Black Athena*. On this other class, see Alberto and Mir, "History 101."

22. Juderías, *La leyenda negra de España*.

23. Gibson, *Black Legend*; Powell, *Tree of Hate*; Adelman, "Introduction." For Native critiques, see, e.g., Silver Moon and Ennis, "View of the Empire."

24. For further discussion of these "legends" and their political implications in contemporary Argentine historical fiction and public life, see the publication that emerged from teaching this material: Alberto, "Indias Blancas, Negros Febriles." On "racial democracy" and similar ideologies in hemispheric context, see Alberto and Hoffnung-Garskof, "'Racial Democracy' and Racial Inclusion."

25. On the useful distinction between *story* as an "event unit" (a relation of who, what, when, and where), and *narrative* as "a system of stories" related to one another through coherent themes, see Halverson, Goodall, and Corman, *Master Narratives of Islamist Extremism*.

26. See especially Mbembe, "Afropolitanism." For further discussion of this concept, see the other articles in this special issue and especially the editors' introduction.

27. Alberto, *Black Legend*.

28. Perry, *More Beautiful and More Terrible*, 48.

29. Slotkin, "Fiction for the Purposes of History," 231.

30. Perry, *More Beautiful and More Terrible*, 188.

31. Brazilian Institute of Geography and Statistics, "What Color Are You?"

32. Slotkin, "Fiction for the Purposes of History," 229.

33. Bennett, "Writing into a Void."

34. See, for example, Mbembe, "Afropolitanism"; Dabiri, "Pitfalls and Promises of Afropolitanism"; Miller, *Slaves to Fashion*; Powell, "Sartor Africanus"; Lewis, *Dandy Lion*; and the work of the *New York Times* critic Wesley Morris.

35. Kyoko Kishimoto defines "an anti-racist approach to teaching and course delivery" as one that seeks to: "(1) challenge assumptions and foster students' critical analytical skills; (2)

develop students' awareness of their social positions; (3) decenter authority in the classroom and have students take responsibility for their learning process; (4) empower students and apply theory to practice; and (5) create a sense of community in the classroom through collaborative learning" ("Anti-Racist Pedagogy," 546).

36.   Slotkin, "Fiction for the Purposes of History," 223.

References

Adelman, Jeremy. "Introduction." In *Colonial Legacies: The Problem of Persistence in Latin American History*, edited by Jeremy Adelman, 1–14. New York: Routledge, 1999.

Adichie, Chimamanda Ngozi. "The Danger of a Single Story." TEDGlobal, July 2009. https://www.ted.com/talks/chimamanda_ngozi_adichie_the_danger_of_a_single_story/transcript#t-190772.

Alberto, Paulina L. *Black Legend: The Many Lives of Raúl Grigera and the Power of Racial Storytelling in Argentina*. New York: Cambridge University Press, 2022.

Alberto, Paulina L. "Indias Blancas, Negros Febriles: Racial Stories and History-Making in Contemporary Argentine Fiction." In *Rethinking Race in Modern Argentina*, edited by Paulina L. Alberto and Eduardo Elena. Cambridge: Cambridge University Press, 2016.

Alberto, Paulina L., and Jesse Hoffnung-Garskof. "'Racial Democracy' and Racial Inclusion: Hemispheric Histories." In *Afro-Latin American Studies: An Introduction*, edited by George Reid Andrews and Alejandro de la Fuente, 264–316. Cambridge: Cambridge University Press, 2018.

Alberto, Paulina L., and Farina Mir. "History 101: What It Is and Why We Need It Now." *Perspectives on History* (April 2018). https://www.historians.org/publications-and-directories/perspectives-on-history/april-2018/history-101-what-it-is-and-why-we-need-it-now.

Andrews, George Reid. *The Afro-Argentines of Buenos Aires, 1800–1900*. Madison: University of Wisconsin Press, 1980.

Batson, C. Daniel, Marina P. Polycarpou, Eddie Harmon-Jones, Heidi J. Imhoff, Erin C. Mitchener, Lori L. Bednar, Tricia R. Klein, and Lori Highberger. "Empathy and Attitudes: Can Feeling for a Member of a Stigmatized Group Improve Feelings toward the Group?" *Journal of Personality and Social Psychology* 72, no. 1 (1997): 105–18.

Bennett, Herman L. "Writing into a Void: Representing Slavery and Freedom in the Narrative of Colonial Spanish America." *Social Text* 25, no. 4 (2007): 67–90.

Bernal, Martin. *The Fabrication of Ancient Greece*. Vol. 1 of *Black Athena: The Afroasiatic Roots of Classical Civilization*. New Brunswick, NJ: Rutgers University Press, 1987.

Brazilian Institute of Geography and Statistics. "What Color Are You?" In *The Brazil Reader: History, Culture, Politics*, edited by Robert M. Levine and John J. Crocitti, 386–90. Durham, NC: Duke University Press, 1999.

Brock, Timothy C., Melanie C. Green, and Jeffrey J. Strange. "Power beyond Reckoning: An Introduction to Narrative Impact." In *Narrative Impact: Social and Cognitive Foundations*, 1–16. New York: Psychology Press, 2002.

Citroën, Lida. *Control the Narrative: The Executive's Guide to Building, Pivoting, and Repairing Your Reputation*. London: Kogan Page, 2021.

Columbian. "Obama: Dems Have 'Better Story' to Tell Women." *Columbian*, March 5, 2012. https://www.columbian.com/news/2012/mar/05/obama-dems-have-better-story-to-tell-women/.

Dabiri, Emma. "The Pitfalls and Promises of Afropolitanism." In *Cosmopolitanisms*, edited by Bruce Robbins and Paulo Lemos Horta, with an afterword by Kwame Anthony Appiah, 201–11. New York: New York University Press, 2017.

Davis, Natalie Zemon. *The Return of Martin Guerre*. Cambridge, MA: Harvard University Press, 1983.

Demos, John. "Afterword: Notes from, and about, the History/Fiction Borderland." *Rethinking History* 9, nos. 2–3 (2005): 329–35.

Frigerio, Alejandro, and Eva Lamborghini. "Los afroargentinos: Formas de comunalización, creación de identidades colectivas y resistencia cultural y política." In *Aportes para el desarrollo humano en Argentina*, 1–51. Buenos Aires: PNUD, 2011.

Geler, Lea. *Andares negros, caminos blancos: Afroporteños, Estado y Nación Argentina a fines del siglo XIX*. Rosario, Argentina: Prohistoria, 2010.

Gervais, Michael. "Disrupt Your Own Narrative." *Harvard Business Review*, March 20, 2020. https://hbr.org/2020/03/disrupt-your-own-narrative.

Gibson, Charles. *The Black Legend: Anti-Spanish Attitudes in the Old World and the New*. New York: Random House, 1971.

Green, Melanie C., and Timothy C. Brock. "The Role of Transportation in the Persuasiveness of Public Narratives." *Journal of Personality and Social Psychology* 79, no. 5 (2000): 701–21.

Halverson, Jeffry, H. L. Goodall Jr., and Steven R. Corman. *Master Narratives of Islamist Extremism*. New York: Palgrave Macmillan, 2011.

Hannah-Jones, Nikole, Caitlin Roper, Ilena Silverman, and Jake Silverstein, eds. *The 1619 Project: A New Origin Story*. New York: One World, 2021.

Harrison, Mary-Catherine. "The Great Sum of Universal Anguish: Statistical Empathy in Victorian Social-Problem Literature." In *Rethinking Empathy through Literature*, edited by Meghan Marie Hammond and Sue J. Kim, 135–49. New York: Routledge, 2014.

Harrison, Mary-Catherine. "The Paradox of Fiction and the Ethics of Empathy: Reconceiving Dickens's Realism." *Narrative* 16, no. 3 (2008): 256–78.

Hartman, Saidiya. "Venus in Two Acts." *Small Axe: A Caribbean Journal of Criticism*, no. 26 (June 2008): 1–14.

Henricks, Thomas. "The Stories We Tell Ourselves." *Psychology Today*, June 21, 2019. https://www.psychologytoday.com/us/blog/the-pathways-experience/201906/the-stories-we-tell-ourselves-0.

Higginbotham, Evelyn Brooks. "African-American Women's History and the Metalanguage of Race." *Signs* 17, no. 2 (1992): 251–74.

Holloway, Richard. *Stories We Tell Ourselves: Making Meaning in a Meaningless Universe*. Edinburgh: Canongate Books, 2020.

Hunt, Lynn. *Inventing Human Rights: A History*. New York: W. W. Norton, 2008.

Hutcheon, Linda. *A Poetics of Postmodernism: History, Theory, Fiction*. New York: Routledge, 1988.

Juderías, Julián. *La leyenda negra de España*. Madrid: La esfera de los libros, 2014.

Kishimoto, Kyoko. "Anti-Racist Pedagogy: From Faculty's Self-Reflection to Organizing Within and Beyond the Classroom." *Race, Ethnicity and Education* 21, no. 4 (2018): 540–54.

Kleber, Claus. "Obama: We Have the Better Story." *ZDFHeute*, January 31, 2021. https://www.zdf.de/nachrichten/politik/obama-book-kleber-interview-100.html.

Ko, Chisu Teresa. "From Whiteness to Diversity: Crossing the Racial Threshold in Bicentennial Argentina." *Ethnic and Racial Studies* 37, no. 14 (2014): 2529–46.

Lewis, Shantrelle P. *Dandy Lion: The Black Dandy and Street Style*. New York: Aperture, 2017.

Mbembe, Achille. "Afropolitanism." In *Cosmopolitanisms*, edited by Bruce Robbins and Paulo Lemos Horta, with an afterword by Kwame Anthony Appiah, 102–7. New York: New York University Press, 2017.

Menton, Seymour. *Latin America's New Historical Novel*. Austin: University of Texas Press, 1993.

Miles, Tiya. *The Dawn of Detroit: A Chronicle of Slavery and Freedom in the City of the Straits*. New York: New Press, 2017.

Miles, Tiya. *Ties That Bind: The Story of an Afro-Cherokee Family in Slavery and Freedom*. Berkeley: University of California Press, 2005.

Miller, Monica L. *Slaves to Fashion: Black Dandyism and the Styling of Black Diasporic Identity*. Durham, NC: Duke University Press, 2009.

MSNBC. "Changing the Narrative, with Nikole Hannah-Jones." *Into America* (podcast), November 19, 2021. https://www.msnbc.com/podcast/nikole-hannah-jones-her-1619 -project-power-narrative-n1284204.

NPR. "Transcript: Obama's Speech at the 2018 Nelson Mandela Annual Lecture." NPR, July 17, 2018. https://www.npr.org/2018/07/17/629862434/transcript-obamas-speech-at-the-2018 -nelson-mandela-annual-lecture.

Perry, Imani. *More Beautiful and More Terrible: The Embrace and Transcendence of Racial Inequality in the United States*. New York: New York University Press, 2011.

Powell, Philip Wayne. *Tree of Hate; Propaganda and Prejudices Affecting United States Relations with the Hispanic World*. New York: Basic Books, 1971.

Powell, Richard. "Sartor Africanus." In *Dandies: Fashion and Finesse in Art and Culture*, edited by Susan Fillin-Yeh, 217–42. New York: New York University Press, 2001.

Schank, Roger C. *Dynamic Memory Revisited*. Cambridge: Cambridge University Press, 1999.

Shiller, Robert. "Narrative Economics." *Cowles Foundation Discussion Papers*, no. 2069 (January 2017).

Silver Moon, and Michael Ennis. "The View of the Empire from the Altepetl: Nahua Historical and Global Imagination." In *Rereading the Black Legend: The Discourses of Religious and Racial Difference in the Renaissance Empires*, edited by Margaret R. Greer, Walter Mignolo, and Maureen Quilligan, 150–66. Chicago: University of Chicago Press, 2007.

Simmons, LaKisha M. *Crescent City Girls: The Lives of Young Black Women in Segregated New Orleans*. Chapel Hill: University of North Carolina Press, 2015.

Slotkin, Richard. "Fiction for the Purposes of History." *Rethinking History* 9, nos. 2–3 (2005): 221–36.

Smith, David Livingstone. *Less than Human: Why We Demean, Enslave, and Exterminate Others*. New York: St. Martin's, 2011.

Stephan, Walter G., and Krystina Finlay. "The Role of Empathy in Improving Intergroup Relations." *Journal of Social Issues* 55, no. 4 (1999): 729–43.

Turner, Mark. *The Literary Mind*. Oxford: Oxford University Press, 1996.

US Department of the Army, Headquarters. *Insurgencies and Countering Insurgencies*. Field Manual 3-24, Marine Corps Warfighting Publication 3-33.5, May 13, 2014. Washington, DC. https://www.google.com/url?sa=t&rct=j&q=&esrc=s&source=web&cd=&cad=rja &uact=8&ved=2ahUKEwiIjL3brbL3AhXbIzQIHTsADI8QFnoECAUQAQ&url=https% 3A%2F%2Firp.fas.org%2Fdoddir%2Farmy%2Ffm3-24.pdf&usg=AOvVaw2hdSGoGA9 v2yMgMxi-LjFe.

Vezzali, Loris, Sofia Stathi, Dino Giovannini, Dora Capozza, and Elena Trifiletti. "The Greatest Magic of Harry Potter: Reducing Prejudice: Harry Potter and Attitudes toward Stigmatized Groups." *Journal of Applied Social Psychology* 45, no. 2 (2015): 105–21.

Vashambadzi

The Coast Walkers

David Schoenbrun

A Deeper History of Mobility for Afropolitanism

It is conventional to think people other than Africans explored and named the edged, continental place we know today as Africa. The financial, cultural, political, and familial interests of such "explorers" entered a dynamic interplay with African interests as Africans resisted, evaded, or cocreated them.[1] In the course of responding, Africans' understandings of their continent took shape. The implications of the forced migrations to involuntary slavery for the creation of African diasporas dominate this view. Historians understand the underlying political and economic dynamics behind forced migrations into slavery overseas to have emerged from sources outside the continent, even if African states were indispensable to the workings of that system. Those outside forces prompted erudite and transformational diasporic imaginings of African homelands.[2] A similar dynamic could be sketched for the effects of oceanic (Mediterranean, Atlantic, and Indian Ocean), imperial and colonial processes on histories of African self-awareness and self-fashioning.[3] Africans cocreated, resisted, and evaded imperial violence and colonial rule, shaping them in the process. But those were responses to forces issuing from historical dynamics rooted in other places. The "Africa" these historical processes produced necessarily derives from them, leaving Africans in a reactive position with respect to their understanding of "home."

Radical History Review
Issue 144 (October 2022)   DOI 10.1215/01636545-9847872
© 2022 by MARHO: The Radical Historians' Organization, Inc.

Considering mobility in maritime geographies resists a simple directionality in the discovery of a continental home. Paul Gilroy's black Atlantic is a zone of multidirectional movements of Black people and ideas to and from many locations on the sea's landward boundaries.[4] Although he said little about African continental historical processes, Gilroy's approach set aside Melville J. Herskovits's one-way links running from West Africa to the Caribbean, and Sidney Mintz and Richard Price's "cognitive orientations" and "creolization," but presaged J. Lorand Matory's "dialogues" connecting many sides of an Atlantic world upended by the violent mix of slavery and commodification and its afterlives.[5]

Recent scholarship has reframed these issues, largely in their landward forms.[6] But the hegemony of the paradigm just mentioned mutes the impacts of that scholarship, which engages themes handed to us from that very paradigm— state formation, commercial life, religions of the book, even race. Afropolitanism, in part, synthesizes and updates such struggles over naming and framing "Africa," shifting the subject to varieties of urban, literate, and mobile living, and exploring the ways in which race, gender, identity, and moral belonging inform a lexicon of Africa.[7] It is an overwhelmingly—at times explicitly—modernist project, hugely valuable for decentering without dissolving the burdens of naming and framing by foregrounding a blend of urbanism, literacy, and mobility, precisely what slavery, imperialism, and colonialism would deny Africans.[8]

The mobility binding enslavement and modernity has an earlier history. Before the fifteenth century, people crossed an array of boundaries exceeding the coastal, not driven by the commodification of people. Their movement altered the content of moral belonging, the forms inclusion and exclusion might take, to make the future better than the present. This deep history of unstable belonging and shifting geography refuses a presentist imagination in which continental and national geographies are the referents for modernist citizenships and belonging.

With such a narrative at hand, later instances of learning about, intruding into, and struggling over social, political, economic, and intellectual space look different. Afropolitan stories might sample such a narrative. Samples bring the past into the present, inviting listeners to reflect on their current salience.[9] Samples point to "narrative hinterlands" where the curious will find material for debating and assessing the sample's possible meanings in the present.[10] Afropolitan stories that sample past practices of mobility can revise the idea that Africa became an imaginary category only through its often, but not always or permanently, racialized continental edges.[11]

A few narratives exist of earlier mobile West African individuals—pilgrims, traders, miners—constructing and debating historical geographies of belonging in landscapes, prompted by places.[12] There are also very different narratives of Africans discovering a continent before it became the medievalist's, the early modernist's, the modernist's, or the Afropolitan's continent. They are stories of language dispersals, told in technical terms. Because many of these narratives sprawl over such vast tableaux of time and geography, many historians balk at the continuity of the assumptions driving the narrative.[13] The whole we need now—ordinary individual actors, whose lives are enmeshed in multigenerational relationships—is too often absent from earlier African history's archives.

It is time for another approach: a historical account, told as creative nonfiction, which translates abundant academic findings about the dynamics and concrete politics of mobility in shaping African life before the fifteenth century.[14] Mobility unfolded in rhythmed scales. Shifting agriculture, transhuman pastoralism, hunting itineraries, and seasonal fish work were durable examples. Tighter rhythms included travel to markets (regular and permanent), to shrines (evanescent and emplaced), into battle, to regular (seasonal rebuilding events) or impromptu (installations of political figures, mourning events) occasions hosted by elites in central places. Farmers seeking new land to work moved incrementally but not always contiguously. Traders, herders, hunters, and fishers tended toward the routinized out-and-back, balloon, or loop routes. A newly married person traveled to their spouse's natal area along a route that grew familiar. Travel into conflict risked the loss of control over one's itinerary.

Control lies at the core of mobility's importance. Loss or gain of control prompts memory work or history thinking—as in the disarticulations of diasporas. The dynamic interplay of movement, memory, and knowledge constitutes the core of "discovery." This essay explores contextual factors that converted rhythmed mobility—where the traveler largely determines the directionality and the timing of movement, summed up in the Shona word *vashambadzi*—into the one-way route of an enslaved person with no control over direction or timing.[15]

The stories blend historically specific forms of mobility, groupwork, and the creativity and discipline of labor. Seating mobility within groupwork and labor clarifies similarities and differences with other regions. Groupwork invites people to imagine they share common history but does not require they distinguish it from the history of other regions or groups.[16] Artisanal and other kinds of labor nourish mobility and groupwork, giving embodied, emplaced, and educational form to the values, practices, and intellectual orientations in a lexicon of living. Forced migrations, or the loss of control over one's movements, attach the pain of loss to the challenges of self-making and groupwork. Bringing them to life in the time before Atlantic worlds opened, through a moving story of named individuals in the fourteenth century, lends depth to Black Atlantic, imperial, colonial, and anthropocenic mobilities.

Is This Scholarship?

The stories bring existing knowledge—built from unconventional sources and amplified by affective novelistic prose concerning ordinary named individuals and threads of subjectivity—to a bigger scholarly audience for early African history. Footnoting tethers the historical imagination in the prose to formal source criticism applied to unusual archives like archaeological site reports, studies of rock art, or vocabulary items reconstructed through the comparative study of a set of related languages. Notes point readers to the "narrative hinterlands" found in those unusual archives, where they may refuse or revise the story's imaginative components by checking sources. The cited sources foster historical argument and restrain readers from simply projecting their own worlds into the distant past.

The dynamic interplay of racial slavery, violent mercantilism, imperialism, and statecraft largely omits subaltern lives from conventional archives. Bringing these lives into the present promises to disrupt dominant narratives formed without centering subaltern action and experience. That desire to conjure the absent provokes literary moves such as Saidiya Hartman's "critical fabulation" and "narrative restraint."[17] Stories are built with a sequence of events. Taken as a whole, that sequence is a story's fabula. Events have causes. People act, prices change, rain fails to fall. Hartman uses critical fabulation "to jeopardize the status of the event," to make counter-narratives that "displace the received or authorized account."[18] Hartman's practice makes "visible the production of disposable lives (in the Atlantic slave trade and, as well, in the discipline of history)" by listening "for the mutters and oaths and cries of the commodity." Her approach gives us a story of "the time of slavery as our present." In that spirit, this essay engages an altogether different set of archives: traces of the ordinary lives of small-scale farmers, hunters, ceramicists, weavers, healers, and so forth.[19] Such people discovered Africa. Telling a story of their discoveries displaces accounts that understand discovery as literally originating in fundamental ways from beyond the continent or as being driven by interests ("causes") originating from beyond the continent. The new account draws on a rich set of causal factors and moral imaginations with local and regional roots deeper than European involvement and sometimes crossing continental edges.

Hartman's counter-narratives are restrained by a "refusal to fill in the gaps and provide closure" and by "the imperative to respect black noise." Closure allows one to depart the experience cleanly, as if the entailments of a story do not continue. Yet the afterlives of displacement and mobility live with us today. Likewise, the "noise" Hartman calls on us to respect are "aspirations" that fall outside of or refuse hegemonic systems of their time or our present. For Hartman, those include capitalism and humanism. In this essay, I practice narrative restraint by leaving endings out of the stories, favoring strings of various departures. That choice respects a counter-hegemonic "noise"—the persistence of movement—which embraces and promotes moral imaginations usually examined in the settled life of village and town. Self-control, hard work, cultivation of skill, cooperation, families, participation, and accountability live on the road as they do in a village or a town. Africans on the move do not contradict settled Africans.

Traces of their lives include the patterning of material culture and spatial practice archaeologists unearth and interpret.[20] Or the sequences by which people speaking a language introduced new meanings into a given semantic domain, and made them stick, which historical linguists reconstruct.[21] Or the exegetical communities who, in debating the meanings of oral material, simultaneously altered them and made them stick in traditions with the "out-thereness" of written texts.[22] Art historians return social contexts to the objects and drawings made and used on the continent to understand what their makers and users did with them. Historical ecologists and landscape historians bring to life mutual influences of shifts in climate; animal (including human), fish, plant, and insect life; and what people did in the past.[23] Historians face distinct challenges of chronology and context when working with each of these sources. From climate ecology to art history, each kind of trace connects varying scales of historical action, from the region to the individual maker of an object or its beholder. The historical actors sent missing by modernity's founding violence, or overly abstracted from documents like a ship captain's log or a bill of lading, turn up in other archives, such as the archaeology of food production or reconstructed vocabulary for agriculture. Intentionally or otherwise, ordinary people used the things archaeologists unearth, and the ideas that the reconstructed vocabulary represents, as media to create and curate historical-geographical knowledge. Ordinary actors are ubiquitous in these archives, lending them a republican grain missing from archives of documents.

But historians must still address the absences and silences in this information that gender, status, and generational frictions exert. It is often impossible to gloss the vocabulary, material culture, and sociological dynamics of exegetical communities with the necessary grays of individual standing and intentionality. People argue over the meanings of story performances, reshaping or reinforcing their content. Often such exegetical communities were exclusive.[24]

Everyone uses language, if under different conditions of possibility. Yet the impact of a person's speech depended on the conventions of standing and biases of authority in place when they spoke. Everyone's living leaves traces on the landscape, patterned materially, if under different conditions of consequence. Yet the uneven effects of biochemical processes on the preservation of ancient objects favors some kinds of materiality (work in metals, building in stone or adobe) over others (wooden tools and buildings). Everyone interacts mutually with other-than-human beings, from water to termites, under different conditions of desire. Yet the assumptions of archaeologists and palaeoecologists about what is worth recognizing, as well as the uneven preservation of some life forms and not others, may erase key relationships (with termites or trees), privilege others (domestic animals or plants), and leave still other relationships (with fish) frustratingly undifferentiated. Exclusions, defeats, and vagueness of meaning in the past guarantee that historians need critical fabulation, practiced with narrative restraint, to create counter-narratives. The present case explores the *varieties* of mobility ordinary lives embodied, a variety often effaced by the interests and blind spots of the authors of documents.

A fourteenth-century story can explore regional historical-geographical practices in different parts of Africa. Recent work questions the influence of a supposed desire for exotic goods on the contours of Zambezian and Kalahari political economies. Scholars increasingly locate regional domestication of exotics inside older, more expansive economies of taste and standing. They paint a picture of a more participatory and mobile political culture than the one implied by framing exotics as prestige goods controlled by political elites who limited access to them to actors willing to assist in promoting elite interests.[25] People planned and acted with logics of value, place, and time rooted in far-flung but interacting communities in the interior of the continent, at a remove from the oceanic or desert edges conventionally linking Africa to elsewhere. Value emerges from tending to the dynamic interplay of individualisms and groupwork. Place uses the accumulations of the past in landscapes of groupwork—such as hilltop shrines; the fords, camps, and markets on trade routes; and the courtyards of leaders—to prompt critique, revise the value of tensions between individualisms and groupwork, and invest them with moral purpose oriented to the future. Critique and participation convert the intersections of value and emplaced assembly into media for balancing individualisms and groupwork. Time reshuffles or underscores the order of generational responsibilities to relations between value and place. Time is a social strategy constructed in part to uncover opportunities in a crisis and restore or control the flow of social life.[26] Group genealogies and heroic itineraries reflect this work. Competent speaking by hunters, spirit mediums, healers, imams, grandmothers, royals, and traders may reshuffle time—or reinvest in a particular temporal arrangement—to achieve critique and transformation. The latitude to do both creates durability. That latitude is a capacity to improvise on the contents of value, the varieties of place, and the forms of time, and to argue about their interrelations. Mobility is often a key means to accumulate that capacity.

To sum up, a scholarly journal welcomes the footnote, directing readers to the evidence restraining authorial voice in creative nonfiction. As Hartman explains, restraint lies at the core of the politics of representation.[27] Who can say what about whose inner worlds, why what they say should be taken seriously, and what saying it erases about the past—all rest on an unstable blend of authorial standing, historical evidence, and loss. Today's economies of authenticity in reckoning belonging to or exclusion from the groups touched by a creative nonfiction story such as "Vashambadzi" affect an author's standing in a reader's eyes. Current modes of belonging and exclusion based on race, gender, class, sexual orientation, and so forth echo in the writing, helping readers project themselves into the story. But an equally weighty dimension of representation lies in what counts as evidence. In most cases, the alternative sources informing the stories given below represent traces of a more republican cultural history than what one finds in contemporary documentary sources. Representation of past lives risks errors of omission and of emphasis, under any circumstance. While new sources disperse that risk across a broader range than the social experience and interests of the literate, they also reflect the workings of power and authority in the past. Adhering scrupulously to historical evidence should ease readers into thinking of the story as history inflected by struggle and inequality. The footnote balances the literary burdens of pointing, shading, character development, and presentism. Some notes lead readers to a cache of rich examples, some lead readers into a thicket of scholarly disagreements. Other notes stop readers to say, "This I have invented, do not take my invention and turn it into a fact, however tempting it might be to do so, in the present."

Plot, Character, Ground

Four events frame the plot. First, Bosutswe, a large town on the eastern edge of the Kalahari Desert, burns around the turn of the fourteenth century. The burning shows that random events prompt mobility. Second, the main characters, a young woman and a young man, choose to relocate to a new town, Danamombe, 250 kilometers northeast of Bosutswe. Eventually, their economic and social successes threaten a minor faction in Danamombe's political kaleidoscope. Third, they survive an accusation of blame in the death of a child from that faction. In its aftermath, they elect to leave. This shows that social events prompt mobility. One hundred kilometers east, in their new town, the ancient Great Zimbabwe, they join vashambadzi, skilled trader-travelers working routes between the northeastern edges of the Kalahari Desert and the Indian Ocean, choosing mobility. Lastly, at the coast, south of the mouth of River Nzambezi, a debt and a dip in the price of ivory leads to the woman's enslavement. As an enslaved woman, she loses control over her destination, and the bereft man has lost the way to family and standing the two of them were making together.

Mma, a young woman, and Tswan, a young man, form a romantic partnership that drives the story. Mma was born on the eastern edge of the Kalahari salt pans, one hundred kilometers northwest of Bosutswe. Tswan was born at Tsodilo Hills, five hundred kilometers northwest of Bosutswe. Both are multilingual, but their mother tongues belong to different language families. Tswan's maternal line includes an itinerant forager-hunter grandmother famed for her healing.[28] She gives Tswan some beads, a sphere made of copper at Tsodilo, and an index-finger-long hank of thick ostrich eggshell disks strung on a rigid line of dried sinew she received in that form from a family from Hungorob, six hundred kilometers west, on the far side of the Kalahari.[29] His paternal line includes a famous grandfather skilled at hunting the sitatunga, an antelope of the wetlands between the Zambezi and the Okavango.[30] Mma's maternal line runs deep in the eastern Kalahari's cattle-keeping and salt-farming lands. Her mother's family used that wealth to place her mother in the court of a trader-grandee at Bosutswe. Mma grows up there. Her court hosts belong to a social stratum that also ruled at the faded city Mapungubwe Hill, in the Shashe-Limpopo basin, some two hundred miles southeast of Bosutswe. At Bosutswe, Mma learns weaving as an apprentice to an older woman who is also a healer. Mma's father's people ran salt gardens in the Makgadikgadi Pans of the Kalahari. That easily convertible commodity made life comfortable in a village. Her father's skill at timing conversions rested in part on her mother's knowledge of the political fault lines converging at Bosutswe. Mma came to understand that economic success turned on the self-mastery required to elicit others' trust. Tswan's parents died when he was young. Mma's childhood and adolescence unfolded with less loss, giving her a sense of possibility as boundless as Tswan's but disciplined less by mastering the sting and risk of absent family. Both understood that admirable behavior nourished carefully chosen nodes in their networks.

The dynamic interplay of three themes grounds the story. Developing skills and joining networks is the first theme. It turns in part on the second theme, cultivating personal comportment to win the admiration of others. Success or failure—the limits of their personal and social power—in those domains is realized at the threshold between different scales of economic structures, the third theme.

Their families accept their companionate marriage. Exchanges of baskets of gifts entailed by Mma and Tswan's relationship expand the array of people interested in the couple's future. Bosutswe's burning separated them from many of those networks. As they move away from Bosutswe, they enter new networks largely as social outsiders, dangerously atomized. They know that excellence in hunting, healing, weaving, and transacting will best allow them to choose a home on their own terms. They seek opportunities to do so in the full knowledge that events could change their plans.

In Danamombe, Mma makes a place as a weaver. Tswan joins a group of elephant hunters, as a trailer, adding to his skills and taking him far afield of Danamombe. Mma exploits the cachet her Eastern Kalahari healing skills carry in Danamombe. Her clients grow in number, thickening her knowledge of Danamombe's social realities. A Danamombe family, whose scarce granaries limit their shows of hospitality, accuse the successful newcomer, Mma, of witchcraft. The senior man of the elephant hunters comes from another Danamombe family, with ties to Great Zimbabwe, a growing town to the southeast. The senior man, Lembeni, understands the costs and benefits of healthy relations with outsiders like Tswan and Mma. They represent new networks and new skills and knowledge but can threaten existing balances of power already susceptible to the vagaries of rainfall. As Tswan's patron and leader of Danamombe's senior house, Lembeni holds a trial and finds the evidence inconclusive. Tswan's performance in the trial avoids guilt. But a disapproving audience for his performance makes self-exile better than insisting their patron continue to protect him and Mma. Rather than return to a ruined Bosutswe, they set out from Danamombe, heading for Great Zimbabwe. There they meet a crew of itinerant traders—the vashambadzi—and walk with them to the Indian Ocean coast. Tswan knows a few of them from the elephant hunts.

Their journey ends in the town of Manyikeni, stone built in the Zimbabwe style, some one hundred kilometers southwest from the Indian Ocean coastal town of Chibuene. In Manyikeni they find a measure of stability by meeting the challenges of dislocation through skill, reputation, and reciprocal obligation. The time and place for children arrives. Mma joins an informal group of weavers in Manyikeni, some of whom are from the coast, others are from Madagascar. A few are like her, from far to the west. While they work, she translates the conceptual universe in which her healing power makes sense to weavers connected to Swahili and Malagasy towns. Her conversation with them about their homes recognizes common tropes of bigness and firstness expressing authority, precedence, and power. She marshals similar figures in whose footsteps she has walked. Their life histories of mobility express hers, explaining the circumstances of her accumulated skill in healing, which traffics in occult powers and exposes her to risks of counter-attack. She makes her healing knowledge appear both exotic and accessible, a renewable source of standing and influence. This tactic presages how she will survive the middle passage to Cairo and join communities of Africans in Cairo in the 1340s.

Up and down the coast, a glut of ivory drives down its price. They had used ivory as a down payment, with more promised, on a large quantity of cotton cloth purchased from a Manyikeni family hosting the representative of a merchant family based in Cairo, Aden, and India. The shrinking value of the ivory Tswan has planned on getting highlights the debtor part of their standing as artisanal vashambadzi.

As the social and economic circumstances turn against them, Mma and Tswan decide they should transform their cloth debt by pawning her to the merchant's representative. Tswan uses other goods, like tanned hides, to add to the ivory he scavenges in the river basin. Working under the cover of night, Mma weaves threads from the imported cloth into local cotton and sells this rewoven cloth to vashambadzi headed west. She uses the profits, realized in glass beads, to add value to Tswan's ivory. They plan to use this basket of things to redeem Mma before the dhows depart in April, ahead of the southwest monsoons.

But they are thwarted. Before they make up the difference in value between ivory and imported cotton cloth, the merchant-representative decides to convert the cloth debt into Mma's person. He thinks such a move will protect his Cairene patron from the unstable price of ivory with the stable value of Mma's weaving skill in Cairo, where a profound economic crisis has set in. Meeting local Cairene demand for a necessity like cotton cloth will ease frictions between his patron's house and others in the city. He has Mma enslaved by youths working for his host in Manyikeni. Enslaved and pregnant but possessing latitude with her skills as a weaver and a healer, Mma transits the Indian Ocean world of Kilwa, then Aden, stopping in Cairo.

The following stories sample this plot.[31]

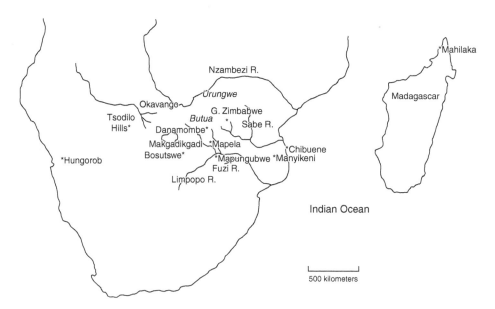

Figure 1. The Kalahari and Zambezia, the world of the Vashambadzi. Map created by the author.

Stories

Vashambadzi, the Coast Walkers

Everything happens at the same time.[32] The rest are stories, collected by a great moth who uses them to make cocoons.[33]

Bosutswe

Mma smells the burning grass behind the noisy water dropping into her calabash as she washes. She raises her head and pushes her chin out to listen. The water on her bright, round face slides down her neck.

Houses moan when they burn. The whistling air, its flecks of soot an urgent black against a grey winter sky, tells her this is a big fire.

Mma lives with her mother in one of the outer houses of the court, high on the central precinct of Bosutswe, a prominent flat-topped hill at the desert's edge. She goes out their front door, down a brief walkway hemmed in by neighbors' walls, and into the main street running atop the hill's subtle sloping spine with the sight line west. Behind her, the tall wall of the court blocks the sunrise view. Smoke from the smiths' quarter will soon reach their part of the town, just behind the fire jumping in the morning's breeze from grass-crowned house to grass-crowned house.[34]

People stand in the street, their cloths askew. Everyone thinks: time to get down to the flats.

Tswan sees the fire's glow beneath the morning cloud and knows people will soon flood into the low, open ground where his host's house sits below the hilltop town. Mma and he had planned that if fire came, they'd meet in the mopane trees at the edge of the River Lengele's floodplain north of the hilltop town.

The fire eats most of the town's buildings by late afternoon. Mma and her mother work from memory to find their house amid the hot, puddled mud walls. They find the wooden plank shelves burned, their pots fallen into a heap of shards. The woven gourd holders—and all their gourds—have burned away. The metal things remain, on the ground, shorn of their handles and butts. Outside, in their courtyard, the grain bin is a shadow of ash on a darker ground of hard, pounded mud and straw. In a lidded pot, the cache of *phane*—dried caterpillars minus their insides that Mma had collected from mopane and marula trees on a trip back from her father's place at the edge of the pans—and the two beads her father gave her have escaped the heat.[35] They collect the *phane*, beads, knife, hoe blades, and razors, wrap them in the second of the two lengths of brown cotton cloth Mma's mother grabbed before running, and turn back into the smoldering street. They are in the burned house in less time than Mma took to wash her face.

. . . . .

Bosutswe grows where the desert's edge meets the rise bearing rivers to the sea, a moon-long walk toward the sunrise. It is a big town full of cattle and fancy families with ties to other big towns, the kind of place people visit from near and far. The variety of lives and wealth in Bosutswe and the obvious connections between opportunity and travel helped Mma's mother show her that a woman's life could be more than marriage, craftwork, farming, and family if she brought the wisdoms of travel to the complexities of managing a household. A person can travel on foot or with words. Both ways helped Mma's mother learn many languages, including ones that crackled like a burning, pitchy log.[36] Mma knows some, too, learned from her mother. Her father speaks a few languages, but they are all quite similar. The salt buyers who came with beads from the direction of the sunrise to her father's place at the edge of the pans spoke them, so he learned them.[37] Mma's personality, smarts, and ambition put off some people, suitors and girlfriends alike. She moves between introspection and garrulous conversation. She learns things quickly. And she wants to walk a line between home and beyond. At the court in Bosutswe, Mma found weaving suited her blend of thoughtfulness and conversation. Many of the girls and boys she grew up with were quiet or talkative as youths. Few young people feel them both at once, twins lightly tapping from within, calling her third self to choose. Mma is the kind of person that people needed.

As Tswan got to know Mma during his visits to Bosutswe, those qualities—including her languages—drew him to her. His grandmother Hande also spoke many languages, including those that crackled. She was an itinerant trance healer from the Tsodilo Hills that rise above the desert, beyond the Okavango Delta, a moon's walk from Bosutswe toward the sunset.

Mma was two seasons from her first blood when she met Tswan in Bosutswe. She got to know the young hunter in the market on the flats where she'd go to buy bushmeat, hides, or a bone to grind for an awl. He spoke the crackling tongues too. She found him at ease, which let words flow. They soon began to share their hopes for the future. Each of them wanted to see the towns of stone up east, on the plateau. They wanted to smell the salty sunrise sea they'd been told lay below and beyond the uplands. When Bosutswe burned, that cold dry season, they had already chosen Danamombe as their destination. Mma had come to know quite a bit about it while serving Lembeni's people when they visited Bosutswe from Danamombe. Tswan knew of the new town from others in the bushmeat market. Elephant hunters told of large herds in the forested, narrow headwater valleys making the River Mzingwane, which ran through Danamombe. It was a good place to hunt.

. . . . .

Mma and her mother sit in the cooler shadows, out of the sun, spinning cotton thread and discussing how Mma can use her knowledge of Bosutswe's court life to travel east and grow their family.[38]

"Lembeni's people know you're not interested, but you've got to pretend so no one's embarrassed."

"Why do you think I keep my eyes on the whorl?"

Mma's mother pinches more brown cotton onto her thread.

"They're from the old town, Mapela," her mother says, "looking for people to back their move to the new one, Danamombe."

"I'll go," Mma says to her hands, "but not as a wife."

"A wife grows powerful from experience and learning. It takes time."

Mma lets her mother's words swish around in her mind before answering. A drop of blood blooms on Mma's finger. She lost sight of the black aloe needle against the dark basket holding her thread. Working late in the day and being prone to reverie has its risks.

"So, I'll move and learn, then choose?," she replies at last. But her mother has gone inside the courtyard gate to see if the beer pots are full. Visitors will soon arrive, thirsty and hungry for food and gossip.

. . . . .

The men from Danamombe have come to Bosutswe seeking partners. Their father's brother died at Mapela two moons ago, and they recently closed his death with a proper funeral, burial, and mourning. Now their people need a new place to take their problems. They are asking for a new person to listen, receive their gifts, and choose how and when to act with them in solving problems and taking advantage. The Danamombe men need others like Mma's family at their backs. For their ambition to work with a minimum of violence they want to tie the well-spun threads of families like Mma's into knots of power. Gathering the threads is the easy part. Each should emerge from a different place and bring a different skill to Danamombe. Tying the entangling knot is the hard part. One family's accomplishments can be another's losses. Threads that bind their pasts too tightly will close the knot of power. The trick is to knot the threads loosely enough to hold each to a common purpose without choking off the patience for listening to people's needs or the ambition to try something new to meet them.

A young girl brings another pot of sorghum beer into the courtyard. Many drinkers in the circle have slipped a clean filter onto the end of their long reed straws while waiting for the fresh supply to arrive. They poke the straw's protected end into the froth atop the new pot and pull silently.

Lembeni is the eldest of the Danamombe men, so he speaks first. Mma follows their banter from the eaves of the entryway house between the yard and the street. She just leans back into the curve of the inner room and lets her ear catch the conversation running along the wall. Adult talk interests her because of what they don't say. When she talks with the youths in the visitors' entourage, they speak less guardedly about life in Bosutswe and in the new town of Danamombe. That's how she knows that the elders leave things out of their exchanges.

"Young people should visit other towns. That way, when they settle, they'll know what's possible and can decide who to trust," Lembeni says.

"Yes, but if they go too far away or for too long, we lose them. They should move only among the towns of our House where people who know us can teach them." A thin grimace crosses Fanamanga's face as he speaks.

"Travel is fine," he continues, "but a valued person can just move on. You, you will return to Danamombe because you like solving problems. You didn't learn to like that by traveling. You discovered your skill by sitting around your father's courtyard, watching and listening."

It's a long speech for him. The subject stirs him. As a youth he loved to travel. He had been to Tsodilo and the big waters in and around Okavango. But his father and mother died just after he'd married. As the elder of their sons and someone who found peace in his obligations to others, when people asked him to stay put and learn Bosutswe's place in the world from his many uncles, he found he could not refuse.

Lembeni's people talk about their ancestors, inviting Fanamanga and other wealthy hosts at Bosutswe to join in. They create a story tying their ambitions for Danamombe to the actions of a departed ancestor both of their people have claimed to share as descendants of an ancient group patronized by a spirit who manifests today as a crocodile.[39] Today, aunts and daughters in both their families sometimes get possessed by a crocodile spirit or they encounter a crocodile at an unexpected time or place. Just three moons ago, Fanamanga's sister met a crocodile at a spring below a high jumble of boulders, in the rising hills east of Bosutswe more than a day's walk from the gathering streams of River Limpopo. For Lembeni and

Fanamanga, crocodiles out of place are ancestors asking them for something. They're both pretty sure the crocodile Fanamanga's sister met wants them to figure out how to make Danamombe a place sending power into its hinterlands. It is well known that a crocodile will jealously protect its home in a river or a stretch of shore along a lake or a swamp. Only drought—or a stronger crocodile—will make it leave.

Family representatives and their followers introduce the figures from their past, and their deeds, into the story. They argue about the past by taking for granted a minimum set of characters and actions. Ngwena, the crocodile ancestor, is one. Of the many sons claiming descent from Ngwena, Lembeni's great-great-grandfather Shoko was the son of Fanamanga's great-great-grandfather Kgabo. Fanamanga's house was closer to Ngwena; that's why when Lembeni crossed the River Limpopo to visit Fanamanga at Bosutswe, he did so as the small crocodile. If they succeed in making Danamombe stand up to rival houses from Great Zimbabwe, Lembeni will still be the small crocodile. The crocodile of his time will only lose its smallness as generations of young men go off into Danamombe's hinterlands and make families.

Visiting back and forth, over the last years of trading and marrying between the two towns, Fanamanga and Lembeni obsessed about matters of shared—or not shared—history. Mma's mother explains that this is the work of politics. By talking about only a small number of them, you weave a shared past from the many versions of crocodile history Ngwena's numerous sons had made. Claiming particular sons of Ngwena as one's own ancestors meant taking up the responsibilities of extending their accomplishments. That way, the storytellers and the audience shared obligations to grow the families. They would share the future made possible by promoting Danamombe's preeminence against interference from Great Zimbabwe. The seniority of families, the breadth of their ties to distant places, and the variety of skills members of each possessed or were willing to learn specifies who risks, who supports, and who stands aside, in reserve. The work is tiring, even with the beer. Lembeni's people arrived more than a half moon ago and still argue over which crocodile-protected elder planted the first millet and sorghum in the flats beneath Danamombe Hill, which of her brothers brought the first cows to the edge of town, who, therefore, will be responsible for pulling the rain down should it refuse to fall next rainy season, and all of that.

Mma catches the names of all the hills and springs they mention as stopping places and the river crossings between them, as the crocodile sons, brothers, and sisters made their way to Danamombe. She knows that the weight of each stop and river ford along the way magnifies a crocodile ancestor's accomplishments. The expansive distance their travels encompassed does the same in the minds of listeners who know the places mentioned. Their journeys are like strings of different kinds of beads. The opaque blue-black glass beads come from the lands of the sunrise. The pale grey disks made from the giant land snail come from home.[40] The shiny white disks ground from ostrich eggshell belong to the sunset deserts. Whether you wore them around the waist, for a lover, or around your neck or ankles for all to see, or you put them on a person for burial, all these pretty beads point to the far corners of the world and the layers of life it held. Where her elders worry over the symbolism of all of those stops in ancestral travels, she wants to see the actual places for herself. She wants to climb Mapela Hill, watch the cranes mass along a rain-swollen River Shashe, and feel the humidity rising as she descends to the sunrise sea.

. . . . .

The antelope fat Tswan worked into his heels in the morning is gone now, leaving thirsty cracks. On the last day of walking, fingers of stony ground began to rise more often between expanses of sand until the hard ground won. The sand made his calves ache, but the stones could cut into dry soles.

Tswan naps in the deep shade pooled at the base of the mopane tree's straight bole. He wakens when he senses the two boys. They stand in the dappled sun, staring at him. Shaking the sleep off, he realizes they've come to take him up onto Bosutswe's impressive hill. Several winters have passed since his first visit with his father's people. Things have changed.

Tswan pleases his hosts with smoked sitatunga meat. The rich people living atop the hill town love the smoky flavor of the tiny antelope from the big water across the desert.[41] When they serve it, the distinctive aroma reveals the long reach of their wealth. It took Tswan nearly a moon to walk from Okavango to Bosutswe.

He has less of the game than he'd come with because he traded some for a ball of arrow-poison. Bosutswe's bushmeat market often had some of the most potent, long-lasting arrow poisons he ever used. A lump of fine, resinous poison worked into the barbs on an arrow's head could be the difference between finding the swamp antelope you'd hit or losing track of it in the maze of thin trails between patches of lily-covered open water. Tswan tucked the tiny gourd of arrow poison under his arm, at the outer edge of his ribs, and turned toward the hill to see if he could remember where the path up started.

Danamombe

Tswan and Mma recognize Danamombe's freshly cut stone platforms. Tswan had seen some stone walls in the pans, a rambling set of tentacles running from huge baobabs on a low rise down to the edge of the salt pan. Mma had heard people tell of such places when she visited her grandmother's house at Bosutswe. Danamombe fit the description, but they chose it because it was a new town.[42] Its leaders would need followers to stand up to the competition for people, animals, and things at places like Great Zimbabwe. They could help each other.

In the dim time before dawn Tswan couldn't see the details in the painting, but he figured he knew the gist of it. His grandmother had shown him a lot of them, back at Tsodilo. She had told him about such paintings on the roof walls of caves, lit only briefly by a sun setting or rising.[43] These weren't meant for ordinary people. They communicated secrets and they communicated secretly. Others, like this one, out in the open, were about familiar things, like hunting.[44]

Youths loved to look at the paintings in the open. These paintings showed the personalities and characters from the stories their parents and grandparents told them. The paintings let you think privately about their meaning in your life. The personalities in the pictures become your comrades, your adversaries, your sense of the present collapsing into hopes for your future. The images teach a landscape of helpers and enemies, they entertain but also provoke. They remind you that people are one among many beings. That the world is rich but full of risks.

Tswan loved the paintings of flying termites, their nests, and the mushrooms that grew atop the nests, which the termites ate. He felt a clear and powerful charge from the mushroom-encrusted edges of the termite nest that disgorged its winged riches. His grandmother told him those paintings made her think of life and death as a whirlpool in a river. Old people willing to talk about where they were in the pool's spiral said they'd worked their whole lives to earn the immortality of being remembered by the living. They could not control what the living would do with stories about them. After all, they themselves had argued about the fame and failings of people from before. The point was to have a place in a story of the present, not to control what the living did with their stories of the past.

The painting in front of him tells how to gather the ability to hunt, it does not show a strategy for hunting an elephant. A family of elephants is separated by a flowing river of impalas flecked with a few taller figures, with bows. The changing afternoon light infuses the scene with motion. A field of black and red and white, purpled with age, says "the herd lasts because one elephant risks standing apart."[45] A hunter's creative bravery helps larger groups of people live.

Actual elephant hunting bore only a vague similarity to the scene Tswan studies. Boredom weighs on hunters awaiting an elephant's fall into the prepared pit; it alternates with rushes of adrenalin. Running leads directly to the heavy work of finishing or butchering. Or it leads to another long wait, back at the blind. Joints grown stiff from crouching then had to carry you out into the open, racing to a fallen animal. Close, coordinated work as a team becomes a rush to reach the giant before anyone else. The winner might earn a gift from the lead hunter: a choice joint or an expanse of hide to work, or the tail's powerful hairs. If there were tusks, you might receive a hank of arm bangles, worked back at Danamombe.

This painting starts a discussion about grandmothers and grandfathers with the power to sniff out a transgressor hiding in a herd and put the animals at ease.[46] Tswan heard stories like that at Tsodilo, told by visitors from Hungorob at the far edge of the deserts, toward the sunset sea. It doesn't surprise him to hear a version here. Tswan thought that every herd hid a rebel. So, when they have an elephant, he and his companions leave filets of meat, cut from the part of the animal hit by the arrows or spears, in thanks.[47] It is wise to give something to those who had come before in return for their knowledge.

. . . . .

"You should go with them when they try for elephant next," Mma told Tswan while she razored off the fibers dangling from an aloe's sharp tip and used an awl to make an eye in a needle. "It's not like waiting for the water antelope." She wondered what kept Tswan from Lembeni's elephant-hunting group, soon headed north toward Nzambezi, on the other side of the high country.[48]

"Yes," he says absentmindedly from across the yard bright with the late morning sun. Tswan struggles to wrap a wet, slippery sinew as tightly as he can around the haft slats at the head of a spear body. "The sitatunga taps the lily pads like a child testing the chief's drum, the elephant beats the ground like the drum's maker." His father's proverb reminds Tswan that the things beings shared in the world did not cancel their differences. Calm can turn the contrariness of the world to your purpose. That's why Tswan loves to hunt swamp antelope. It teaches him that patience is the path to a chance to outwit them. With elephant, the challenge is as much about gauging the elusive motives of other people as those of the elephants. Below Danamombe, on the River Shashe, he learns to convert his skill at waiting into the patience to navigate the large group it took to track, encircle, bring down, and butcher an elephant.[49]

Nzambezi

After walking for a half moon they are well below the Nzambezi's crashing falls. Elephants favor this place.[50] Back in Danamombe, Lembeni had chosen to use spears with heavy points and butts and a balance suited to piercing elephant skin. From their camp, smaller groups scouted various elephant families, choosing the ones to stalk and considering promising terrain for encirclement and the number of tuskers. Over a period of days, the hunters learned the paths the elephants preferred as they moved between forest and river. They prepared the medicines to give their dogs, to wear themselves, and to put on their spears. Now it was time to give something to the spirits of the hunting place, the ones who had brought the elephants. So far from home, this was a risky proposition.

Tswan's ambition to work with brave patience weakened his lingering doubts about hunting so far from home. Success meant the wealth of the elephant and the stories his colleagues would tell back at Danamombe. With both, he and Mma could hope for Lembeni's gift of land in Danamombe, where they could stay and start their family.

Lembeni and his hunting group had decided to hunt here, far from Danamombe, to dip into the trade running again along River Nzambezi's famed elephant hunting grounds, drawing copper ingots onto the Zimbabwe plateau. The ingots are easier than ivory to carry—their makers shaped them into crosses so that the weight spread evenly over one's back. Their rarity made them easier than ivory to convert. These qualities of copper bars drove elephant-hunting teams in one region to compete against those of another region to create a market for trade in elephant products with towns in Urungwe, Butua, beyond the Shashe-Limpopo.[51] Success means choices in conversion, once the leading house got its tusk. Tswan plans to trade his part of the hide for one of the copper cross ingots that Urungwe's smiths make.

Ordeal

"Are you sleeping, Mma, or can't you move?" Chana broke the silence.

Sunrise lit the tallest hump of treeless granite above Mma's place in the line of women waiting to fill their water gourds from the spring.[52] Even on the coldest mornings, the water line was a lively place to share news and enjoy the salty taste of a fresh rumor. Mma, her hand at her sternum, absent-mindedly fingered the two beads from Bosutswe hanging there. No one but Chana had dared engage Mma even a month after the drama at Lembeni's court.

She and Tswan avoided Vadzvi's jealousy because Lembeni had not cut a judgment about Vadzvi's accusation that Mma's Kalahari medicines had caused the sudden death of Vadzvi's daughter.[53] Instead of a public stand on the question, Lembeni had chosen to test whether or not they'd been involved in that sad death by having Tswan drink the poison ordeal on their behalf. The narcotic brew made Tswan stumble toward the rope strung between the two cut tree branches that one of Lembeni's sons had dug into the soil. When Tswan cleared the rope, the crowd had mostly stamped their feet in approval at the innocence his steps proclaimed. Vadzvi's family and friends stood by, heads downcast, feet frozen to the earth.

Despite having lived in Danamombe for less than two farming seasons, Mma and Tswan have friends. It impresses Lembeni. But friendship has limits. Even in the glow of release from suspicion, Mma and Tswan each know that their time in the city has ended. Vadzvi's people will come at them again. How long could good stories, a healing hand, help in the chase, and patience with the spinning whorl, aloe needle, and handloom keep them from the bottomless well of an ambitious family's insecurities?

Great Zimbabwe

Katete, last son of the man Ndoro and the woman Tsitsi, was the first ruler to live in the western parts of the Great Enclosure, from the 1280s to 1300. Katete's open ears, sharp eyes, and generosity brought them a rich network of knowledge and wealth. Tsitsi's wit and shrewdness brought her own followers to the courtyard in the complex of buildings they called home. Skilled masons expressed their respect for his and her standing by building out the massive walls of the Great Enclosure in a striking new style of stonework. Not only did they cut each granite block to fine, squared edges, they fitted them together into interlocking courses, shrinking their widths incrementally as they laid one course on top of the other. This arrangement dispersed the granite weight downward in an even flow, stabilizing the wall and increasing its life span.[54]

Katete's many daughters with Anodiwa had been part of his success; they had drawn the threads that spun in-laws into networks of tight knots that Katete and Anodiwa could tie and untie as they saw fit. Though he had sons of his own, none was a man whom others wanted to serve and support. Rusvinga's ears were closed. He took no counsel. Mucheri soon tired of balancing contentious requests and too often relieved his boredom by choosing to cultivate the respect of disloyal people. Katete's daughters had grown a vast network of allies. But neither Rusvinga nor Mucheri could make knots of respect and wisdom, like Lembeni, out of the houses living at the town. They could not retain Katete's followers, let alone draw new ones committed to his rule. Tswan and Mma saw the new stone wall on their way to the camp outside town and suspected a big house might be trying hard to keep its walls standing. If so, they knew the period of tension that followed, as other houses positioned themselves to tie a new knot of rule with their family's threads of power, meant openings for them. Contending houses needed all the followers they could get. Two well-traveled young adults, skilled in making things people needed, would have some choices if they learned who was who.

The heart of the town lay between the high hill, where the founders had lived, and a growing clutch of homes in the Great Enclosure of stone in the valley below. When Tswan and Mma arrived, they saw masons working on the ellipse's massive walls, three times the height of a man and as thick across as a well-fed man's sleeping form.[55] In each neighborhood, walls connected the six or seven houses belonging to an extended family and their dependents.

New neighborhoods were being built down the gentle slope of the valley, toward the sunrise. Beyond that, the valley tightened and dipped off the plateau, making the start of River Chiredzi. They knew from stories that one could follow that river to River Runde, then River Sabe, all the way to the endless sunrise water of salt. The feeling of a great gate that opened on to the unknown intoxicated them both with the possibilities. It filled them with fear as well, for they knew the basket of people whose love kept them ahead of life's risks would shrink to the two of them, even in a group of vashambadzi—coast walkers—who would have them.

In Lembeni's town, you kept your words from an unintended ear by whispering or lighting a crackling fire or putting the door into the house's doorway. Here, in the great *muzinda* of Zimbabwe, stone walls separated inside from the outside.[56] Many ruling houses were here. It was an important place, on the lips of others. Mma had heard of it at Bosutswe. Wealth and power were on full display here. Poor rulers lived alongside ordinary people grown rich in metals, cloth, and beads that they attracted by hard work and ingenuity. Proximity was a good reason for privacy.

Opportunities for wealth and standing attracted vashambadzi, the men and women who walked great distances, trading.[57] Ordinary people clustered their skills in a great *muzinda* like this, their homes of stone built among the treeless humps of granite and spread across the open flats nearby. Their sinuous lines mimicked the round forms of rock that made the hills above. Duties of rule clung to individual houses, drawing outsiders to those families to seek entrance by marriage. Commoner houses enjoyed the latitude afforded them by their ordinary standing. Mma and Tswan, set loose on the land by twists of fortune, envy, and jealousy, could find in this *muzinda* a way to keep their ambitions alive.

"Let's find some of Lembeni's people and see if they're expecting us."

"It's a start," said Mma, "but I think we were faster on the road than his messenger."

"If you're right, Lembeni's people here will only have gossip about the ordeal."

"They're probably down at the end of the valley, where the newer houses stand."

They walked through dust kicked up by a herd of cattle returning from a day's grazing beyond the town and headed down the valley. They could get some sense there of where they stood.

Vashambadzi

Hot and tired from the road, Mma and Tswan say little as they think of preparing an ephemeral camp at the end of the day. A few others head into the floodplain below the ridgeline they have walked all morning. Mma goes down with them, looking for the promise of water offered by a baobab tree. After a quarter moon of walking, she was tired of the road, anxious to begin finding a place in a city where she knew no one.

"Where's Dzandzi? I haven't seen him since morning," says a familiar voice from behind her. Shende, the group's leader and guide, asked no one in particular. Dzandzi, a youth about the same age as Mma's youngest brother, had latched on to them at Pafuzi, a village of cattle keepers and hunters where River Fuzi joined River Limpopo.[58] Mma and Tswan left the busy dusty town of Great Zimbabwe with a group of traders. They followed a road into the headwaters of River Chiredzi, which gathered, an hour of walking away from the city, at the edge of the plateau. The road descended into the warmer, drier world below the plateau, which they reached at midday the second day out. Dzandzi was a son of Shende's mother's people. Dzandzi's parents had asked Shende to take him along so he could learn how to travel, make friends, and trade safely as an adult. His calm, helpful way boded well for a future with vashambadzi, the coast walkers.

On her way to the spring, Mma notices Dzandzi, facing a large boulder, his back turned to the baobab and the otherwise thin forest. The unmistakable motions of eating draw her eye. Crouching, pulling at something, studying the bit taken, then jabbing it toward his mouth, a small woven bag at his feet. He is an unassuming member of their group. Food has been scarce on the way down from the high country to the sea, but not so scarce as to eat alone, she thought.

Plashing water pushes thoughts of food from Mma's mind as she swings the gourd from her back to her belly, runs her hand up its leather strap and passes the gourd over her head as she kneels at the base of a stream of water falling from a lip of stone. The gourd's fluted mouth catches most of the spray the river's warm breath combs into the steady rill of water. The solitude of this spring reminds her of the noisy gatherings of neighbors at Bosutswe's spring, toward sunset, far away on the other side of the hills where River Limpopo starts. If someone told stories of travel while they all waited their turns for water, everyone listened. She wonders now, just a few days out from the Great Zimbabwe, if she can cultivate a similar audience at Manyikeni, when she hears the shouts.

After days of birdsong, animal calls, and the sounds of their own voices, the shout raining down from the cliff above the river scares the travelers. The shouter is too far away to understand, and he and his comrades quickly back away from the cliff edge. By drawing attention to themselves they signal they are not to be feared. Tswan and a few others make their way into the floodplain and head for a promontory at one of the river's bends. They wait there to see what will happen next. Mma and the rest of their group stay on the road, under a huge baobab tree, out of the sun, grateful for a chance to cool down and rest. Now that they're close to the sunrise sea, the air has become humid.

"Take the ridge top the rest of the way. Down the road from here, until the road to Manyikeni, it is not safe." A wiry man with a scrim of gray hairs on his chin and upper lip leans on a long walking pole, with one leg bent at the knee, the foot resting inside the other leg's knee. He stops talking, stretches his neck out slowly and spits a stream of juice from between a gap in his front teeth.

"Many elephants are in the river's valley."

Chamai, one of Tswan's group of travelers who is older and from Great Zimbabwe, knows the spitter and calls him by name across the low roar of the river. They have traveled together on this road before.

"Dunje, did you start from Manyikeni or Chibuene?"

"Manyikeni. In Chibuene the big families are squabbling over who will host which of the visitors from the ships. The winds began to change last month. Already people from the north are arriving in their boats."[59]

Dunje spits again. He seems uncomfortable speaking so loudly in order to be heard over the flowing water.

"Thank you." Chamai says.

"Do you need food?" The muscles along Dunje's jawline work.

"We have dried meat and phane. Thank you. Do you need food?"

Dunje drops his bent leg, turns, and says no as he walks into the trees away from the river. Chamai thinks it's odd to be generous and rude at the same time. Then he realizes that the offer of food could have been a trick to see if the group was hungry and vulnerable at the close of a long journey. Might get the better of any exchange.

Manyikeni

Mma finishes her story about the tall healer who could cross open desert with short-statured people in the traveling group.[60] A woman weaver, from the big Island, asks a question in the coast language.

"Do short friends help because you give them something? Or do they help so you will give them something?"

"It depends. Like here it is good to share when we can because we can't always share. Friendship helps us keep things moving."

Silence drops on the veranda where they work. Each woman thinks to herself what she's given up on the way here, what she'll give up to stay or go. None allows their feelings to show on their face. They keep their eyes on their work or they look off down the lane toward the sea.

They know the risk of accepting such a large amount of cloth for what's left of the ivory Tswan scavenged on the road from Great Zimbabwe. His ivory represents only a portion of the value of the cloth. They must make up the remainder before Khassim sails in a moon's time or less. But it is a good risk. Mma can unweave the cloth to get the colored threads and reweave them with the brown and tan thread she can spin from African cotton. This will multiply the value of her cloth up River Sabe and beyond. Time is not the only thing pressing them. Ivory has become common recently. It buys less, making Tswan's plan harder.

"In Mahilaka, my home, ivory no longer buys you anything you want. Now, ivory is common."

The Merchant Changes the Terms

"I don't want the tusks. I want the weaver woman," Khassim says to himself. "She knows how to make cloth and that will provide reliable income in Al-Qahira. I can't trust ivory. Abou will be pleased."

Khassim cannot go to Manyikeni, but Maawo, his patron, and Maawo's people can. They know the way. They know the leading houses in the town. They want his patron to return in the future and accept their hospitality.

They work together across these thresholds. Khassim keeps Abou's counsel. Maawo keeps Khassim's counsel. The houses of Manyikeni keep their counsel. It is the young men who move between them, carrying and kidnapping for them and marrying for themselves, who might pass on what they overhear in one courtyard. In the street you hear a lot of things. Dzandzi knows he must trust Maawo's nephew. It is a good way into his house.

Khassim wonders if he's making the right choice. He eases his doubts by remembering the unforgiving fall in what ivory will buy in each of the ports he visited on the way from Aden. The glut has affected the entire western sea, showing no signs of relenting. Abou will know this, too, from his other representatives in Aden. It is no secret.

Tswan and Mma Plan

"I can find more," Tswan says. "I can go back up into the river's floodplain to scavenge. If I work alone, I won't have to share what I find." If he succeeds quickly enough, they can stay ahead of the debt.

"I can add the threads in a length of Khassim's cloth to threads I spin from my cotton and make Khassim's cloth go a very long way trading from Manyikeni to River Sabe and the great towns on the high country."

Each has doubts. But they discuss only one option. Can they take roads other than the ones between Tsodilo and Chibuene? What about the big island? What about this place called Kilwa? Their hearts are not in such possibilities. It would take too long to weave friendships and patronage. And the child will not wait. Their plans have brought them here, now, in this home. The cloth debt is the lump of risk they had to eat.

Now it is just work.

Taken

Twice in the night, Mma's dreams of Bosutswe awaken her with doubts about their plan. She talks herself back to sleep after the first dream by revisiting the logic in the plan. If they work fast, they can stay ahead. The second time, she realizes she needs to work rather than sleep. So she slips out of her cloth coverlet and wraps herself in its second piece against the cold of early morning. She splashes water into a wooden bowl, puts down the ladle, and comes all the way into consciousness with several palmfuls of water thrown over her head.

She goes to the veranda to work. A lamp of sheep's fat burns on a windowsill above her seated form. She works alone in the small pool of light. Bent over the piece she started two days earlier, Mma doesn't see the three young men until they are upon her. As soon as she senses their presence, she knows what will happen, and she screams very loudly. One knocks the awl from her hand. Another tries to pin her arms against her side. The third throws a loop of rough rope awkwardly over her head. She sees, then, that Dzandzi, now a grown man, has thrown the rope and holds it. A part of the loop catches on her shoulder, and the rest of it falls down her left side toward her waist, held up by the other two men's arms pinning hers. Before she can struggle out of their grasp, one pulls the remainder of the loop off her shoulder and the third man pulls it taut around her still-seated figure. She is caught, but her screams have drawn people's attention. A small crowd gathers.

David Schoenbrun (Northwestern University) has been learning, teaching, and writing about Africa since 1978. His latest book, *The Names of the Python: Belonging in East Africa, 900–1930* (2021), puts ethnic African history in its place by nesting it in broader forms of belonging, including those made with shrines, states, and print cultures. He is the coexecutive producer of two films on glass beads.

Notes

1. Thornton, *Africa and Africans*; Cooper, *Africa in the World*; Green, *Fistful of Shells*.
2. Home need not be in Africa or conceived of through a metaphor of family and descent; see Hanchard, "Afro-Modernity." As a lexeme touching Africa, *diaspora* has a history that opens after World War II; see Edwards, "Uses of Diaspora." As a simile likening African dispersions to those of Jews and as a component of Pan-Africanist thought, *diaspora* has a history that opens in the later nineteenth century; see Gilroy, *Black Atlantic*, 205–12; Shepperson, "African Diaspora"; Hanretta, "River of Salvation." For forced movements within Africa as diasporic, see Larson, *History and Memory*; and Ede, "Afropolitan Genealogies."
3. For critique, see Sweet, "Reimagining the African-Atlantic Archive," 147–57. On the Atlantic world from North America, see Cohen, "Amerindian Atlantic?"; and Weaver, *Red Atlantic*, 1–34.
4. Gilroy, *Black Atlantic*, 15–17; Edwards, *Practice of Diaspora*. On a Malagasy Afro-Indian Ocean, see Larson, *Ocean of Letters*.
5. Herskovits, *Myth of the Negro Past*; Mintz and Price, *Birth of African-American Culture*; Bastide, *African Religions of Brazil*. Recent scholars show people moving back and forth between both sides of the Atlantic, cocreating its modernities; Verger, *Flux et reflux*; Thornton, *Africa and Africans*; Matory, *Black Atlantic Religion*; Apter, *Oduduwa's Chain*. Historical archaeologists of the Atlantic World have pursued similar ends; see Monroe and Ogundiran, *Power and Landscape*; and Ogundiran and Saunders, *Materialities of Ritual*.
6. Ware, *Walking Qur'an*; Fauvelle, *Golden Rhinoceros*; Gomez, *African Dominion*; Ogundiran, *The Yorùbá*; Chirikure, *Great Zimbabwe*; Bennett, *African Kings and Black Slaves*; d'Avignon, *Ritual Geology*.
7. Eze, "Rethinking African Culture and Identity," 234–47.
8. Achille Mbembe mentions ongoing African discoveries of geography, but Africans move in an already edged continent; Mbembe, "Afropolitanism," 26–30; Mbembe and Balakrishnan, "Pan-African Legacies," 31.
9. Barber, *I Could Speak until Tomorrow*, 25–34.
10. Barber, *Anthropology of Texts, Persons, and Publics*, 84.
11. Lewis and Wigen, *Myth of Continents*, 120–23. See also Pearson, "Littoral Society"; Land, "Tidal Waves"; and Lovejoy et al., "Defining Regions of Pre-colonial Africa."
12. Farias, *Arabic Medieval Inscriptions*; Gomez, *African Dominion*, 38–39, 92–143; d'Avignon, *Ritual Geology*, chapter 2.
13. For a vast example, see Bantu language expansions; Grollemund, Schoenbrun, and Vansina, "Moving Histories." More modest scales accommodate the play of contingency;

see Stephens, *African Motherhood*, 20–26; de Luna, *Collecting Food*, 41–60; and Ogundiran, *The Yorùbá*, 31–62.

14. Ashley, Antonites, and Fredriksen, "Mobility and African Archaeology," 417–34.
15. Schoenbrun, *Lexicon*, RN 224.1.
16. Schoenbrun, *Names of the Python*, 7–13.
17. Hartman, "Venus in Two Acts," 11 (critical fabulation), 12 (narrative restraint). Hartman describes this here: https://www.macfound.org/fellows/class-of-2019/saidiya -hartman.
18. Hartman, "Venus in Two Acts," 11 (quote).
19. Elite, named central Africans show up in sixteenth- and seventeenth-century documents; Thornton, *History of West Central Africa*.
20. Baumanova and Smejda, "Space as Material Culture," 82–92; Wynne-Jones, *A Material Culture*.
21. Schoenbrun, "Early African Pasts," 10–17, 25–30.
22. Barber, *Anthropology of Texts*, 100.
23. Schoenbrun, "Early African Pasts," 7–30. On "exegetical communities," see Barber, *Anthropology of Texts*, 84–97. For historical linguistic archives, see Schoenbrun, *Historical Reconstruction*, and Schoenbrun, *Lexicon*.
24. Barber, *Anthropology of Texts*, 92–102.
25. Wilmsen, "Hills and the Brilliance of Beads"; Moffett and Chirikure, "Exotica in Context"; Chirikure, "New Perspectives."
26. For other purposes, see Birth, *Time Blind*.
27. Hartman, "Venus in Two Acts," 4, 6–7, 12–14.
28. Kinahan, "The Solitary Shaman"; Eastwood, "Networks of Supernatural Potency."
29. Miller, *Tsodilo Jewelry*; Kinahan, "Ritual Assemblage," 53 (Hungorob sinew strings).
30. De Luna, *Collecting Food, Cultivating People*, 191 (sitatunga as Kalahari trade item).
31. The story follows her sons (Sehande, with Tswan, and Ghamal, with her Cairene owner) into the Saharan book trade running from the Middle Nile to Gao-Kukiya, on the River Niger in West Africa, during the 1370s. The story ends with the life of Ghamal's daughter Falaba, born in the 1380s in Gao-Kukiya. Falaba left Gao-Kukiya as a young girl and grew up in Tada, on the lower River Niger. In the first decades of the 1400s, Tada was a border town joining the Nupe state and the collapsing cultural and economic hegemony of the Yorùbá city of Ilé-Ifè.
32. Erdrich, *The Night Watchman*, 267.
33. The emperor moth (*Saturniidae*; #-*cònjá* and #-*pánè*, in S-group Bantu) is a central personality in the oral texts of Southern Africa's desert-dwelling herders, hunters, and gatherers; Schoenbrun, *Lexicon*, RN 211.1 and 211.2. Threatened adult *Saturniidae* fully open their wings, revealing a pattern that mimics the staring eyes of a much larger being, giving would-be predators pause. They fly at night, in straight lines. Their spun cocoons are long-lived and used in healing work. Their camouflage, confident night flight, and protected transformation guide people through the guesswork of living. See Kinahan, "A Ritual Assemblage," 48–57.
34. Denbow et al., "Archaeological Excavations at Bosutswe," 466 (burning event).
35. Reid and Segobye, "Politics, Society, and Trade," 63 (marula nuts, phane); Klehm, "Local Dynamics," 608; Denbow et al., "Archaeological Excavations at Bosutswe," 369; Antonites, "Glass Beads," 418–19.
36. Some phonemes in Khoekhoen and Ju languages are pronounced with a variety of clicks. Bantu languages of the S-Group, like IsiZulu or AmaXhosa, and some Southwestern

Bantu languages, like Fwe, adopted some of those clicks as consonants. A second group of Bantu languages, including Northern S-Group members, has so-called marginal clicks, which don't operate at a phonemic level to distinguish lexical meaning. Still other Bantu languages in the S Group and beyond do not have clicks in their phonological inventories. In the first instance, the presence of clicks reflects the legacy of the kinds of relationships Hande lived, a high-status San-speaking woman raising children with a Southwestern Bantu-speaking man. In the second instance, the presence of clicks represents the kind of relationships Mma's mother lived, a Khoe-speaking woman raising children with a high-status speaker of northern S-Group Bantu languages; see Pakendorf et al., "Bantu-Khoisan Language Contact," 6–11, 26–29.

37. Klehm, "Local Dynamics," 608, 616 (salt and conversion).
38. Denbow et al., "Archaeological Excavations at Bosutswe," 469 (weaving); Antonites, "Fiber Spinning," 107 (weaving).
39. Landau, *Popular Politics*, 70–72.
40. Moffett, Hall, and Chirikure, "Crafting Power."
41. Denbow et al., "Archaeological Excavations at Bosutswe," 470 (sitatunga metatarsals at Bosutswe).
42. Machiridza, "Landscapes and Ethnicity," 656–62, 666.
43. Kinahan, "The Solitary Shaman," 555–57.
44. Mguni, "A New Iconographic Understanding," 38; Mguni, *Termites of the Gods*.
45. Garlake, *The Hunter's Vision*, 123–28 (elephants, hunting).
46. Wylie, *Death and Compassion*.
47. Coulson, Segadika, and Walker, "Ritual in the Hunter-Gatherer/Early Pastoralist Period," 212–13.
48. Chirikure, "New Perspectives," 157–58 (hunting specializations). Scavenging ivory from dead animals was common; Carruthers et al., "The Elephant in South Africa," 24–25; Forssman, Page, and Selier, "How Important"; Huffman, "Mapungubwe and Great Zimbabwe," 37–38.
49. Forssman, "An Archaeological Contribution," 25.
50. De Luna, *Collecting Food, Cultivating People*, 182, on elephant populations below Victoria Falls; de Luna, "Hunting Reputations," 279–99, on elephant hunting terms. For new dating of Ingombe Ilede, see McIntosh and Fagan, "Re-dating," 1069–77; Killick, "Ingombe Ilede's Trade Connections," 1087–88; and de Luna, "Ingombe Ilede and Its Hinterland," 1089–91.
51. De Luna, "Collecting Food, Cultivating Persons," RN 824, 594–96; and *Collecting Food, Cultivating Persons*, 211–17, here, 216 on *nkombalume* (and *sinyanga*) elephant hunter-leaders.
52. In twentieth-century Zezuru Shona, *dàná* could be glossed as "a hill without trees or rocks"; see Hannan, *Standard Shona Dictionary*, 108.
53. Feierman, "Ethnographic Regions," 185–96 (power of exotic medicines).
54. So-called Q-style walls built in this manner appear in Great Zimbabwe early in the fourteenth century. They were fresh when Tswan and Mma visited the city; see Chirikure and Pikirayi, "Inside and Outside."
55. Chirikure and Pikirayi, "Inside and Outside," 980.
56. Chirikure et al., "Elites and Commoners," 1072.
57. Mudenge, *Political History of Munhumutapa*; Moffett and Chirikure, "Exotica in Context," 349 (vashambadzi); Schoenbrun, *Lexicon*, RN 224.1 (°-shambadzi).

58. Plug, "Iron Age Fauna from the Limpopo Valley," 118 (location), 120 (cattle).
59. Macamo, *Privileged Places*. Chibuene was reoccupied in the fourteenth century after three centuries of senescence; the broken glass on the ground evoked a wealthy past from the seventh through the tenth centuries; see Sinclair, Ekblom, and Wood, "Trade and Society," 726.
60. Beaujard, *The Worlds of the Indian Ocean*, 412–15 (size and firstness in Imerina and Malaysia).

References

Antonites, Alexander. "Fiber Spinning during the Mapungubwe Period of Southern Africa: Regional Specialism in the Hinterland." *African Archaeological Review* 36 (2019): 105–17.

Antonites, Alexander. "Glass Beads from Mutamba: Patterns of Consumption in Thirteenth-Century Southern Africa," *Azania: Archaeological Research in Africa* 49, no. 3 (2014): 411–28.

Apter, Andrew. *Oduduwa's Chain: Locations of Culture in the Yoruba Atlantic*. Chicago: University of Chicago Press, 2018.

Ashley, Ceri Z., Alexander Antonites, and Per Ditlef Fredriksen. "Mobility and African Archaeology: An Introduction." *Azania: Archaeological Research in Africa* 51, no. 4 (2016): 417–34.

Barber, Karin. *The Anthropology of Texts, Persons, and Publics: Oral and Written Culture in Africa and beyond*. Cambridge: Cambridge University Press, 2007.

Barber, Karin. *I Could Speak until Tomorrow: Oríkì, Women, and the Past in a Yorùbá Town*. Edinburgh: Edinburgh University Press, 1991.

Bastide, Roger. *The African Religions of Brazil: Toward a Sociology of the Interpenetration of Civilizations*, translated by Helen Sebba. Baltimore, MD: Johns Hopkins University Press, 1978.

Baumanova, Monica, and Ladislav Smejda. "Space as Material Culture." *South African Archaeological Bulletin* 73, no. 208 (2018): 82–92.

Beaujard, Philippe. *From the Seventh Century to the Fifteenth Century CE*. Vol. 2 of *The Worlds of the Indian Ocean: A Global History*. Cambridge: Cambridge University Press, 2019.

Bennett, Herman. *African Kings and Black Slaves: Sovereignty and Dispossession in the Early Modern Atlantic*. Philadelphia: University of Pennsylvania Press, 2018.

Birth, Kevin. *Time Blind: Problems in Perceiving Other Temporalities*. Cham: Palgrave Macmillan, 2017.

Carruthers, Jane, André Boshoff, Rob Slotow, Harry C. Biggs, Graham Avery, and Wayne Matthews. "The Elephant in South Africa: History and Distribution." In *Elephant Management: A Scientific Assessment for South Africa*, edited by R. J. Scholes and K. G. Mennell, 23–83. Johannesburg: Witwatersrand University Press, 2008.

Chirikure, Shadreck. *Great Zimbabwe: Reclaiming a "Confiscated" Past*. New York: Routledge, 2020.

Chirikure, Shadreck. "New Perspectives on the Political Economy of Great Zimbabwe." *Journal of Archaeological Research* 28 (2020): 139–86.

Chirikure, Shadreck, Robert Nyamushosho, Foreman Bandama, and Collet Dandara. "Elites and Commoners at Great Zimbabwe: Archaeological and Ethnographic Insights on Social Power." *Antiquity* 92, no. 364 (2018): 1056–75.

Chirikure, Shadreck, and Innocent Pikirayi. "Inside and Outside the Dry Stone Walls: Revisiting the Material Culture of Great Zimbabwe." *Antiquity* 82, no. 318 (2008): 976–93.

Cohen, Paul. "Was There an Amerindian Atlantic? Reflections on the Limits of a Historiographical Concept." *Journal of the History of European Ideas* 34, no. 4 (2008): 388–410.

Cooper, Fredrick. *Africa in the World: Capitalism, Empire, Nation-State*. Cambridge, MA: Harvard University Press, 2014.

Coulson, Sheila, Phillip Segadika, and Nick Walker. "Ritual in the Hunter-Gatherer/Early Pastoralist Period: Evidence from Tsodilo Hills, Botswana." *African Archaeological Review* 33 (2016): 205–222.

D'Avignon, Robyn. *A Ritual Geology: Gold and Subterranean Knowledge in Savannah West Africa*. Durham, NC: Duke University Press, 2022.

De Luna, Kathryn M. *Collecting Food, Cultivating People: Subsistence and Society in Central Africa*. New Haven, CT: Yale University Press, 2016.

De Luna, Kathryn M. "Collecting Food, Cultivating Persons: Wild Resource Use in Central African Political Culture, c. 1000 B.C.E. to c. 1900 C.E." PhD diss., Northwestern University, 2008.

De Luna, Kathryn M. "Hunting Reputations: Talent, Individuals, and Community in Precolonial South-Central Africa." *Journal of African History* 53, no. 3 (2012): 279–99.

De Luna, Kathryn M. "Rethinking Ingombe Ilede and Its Hinterland." *Antiquity* 91, no. 358 (2017): 1089–91.

Denbow, James, Jeannette Smith, Nonofho Mathibidi Ndobochani, Kirsten Atwood, and Duncan Miller. "Archaeological Excavations at Bosutswe, Botswana." *Journal of Archaeological Science* 35, no. 2 (2008): 459–80.

Eastwood, Edward B. "Networks of Supernatural Potency: San Rock Paintings of Loincloths and Aprons in the Central Limpopo Basin." *South African Archaeological Bulletin* 68, no. 188 (2008): 130–43.

Ede, Amatoritsero. "Afropolitan Genealogies." *African Diaspora* 11, nos. 1–2 (2018): 35–52.

Edwards, Brent Hayes. *The Practice of Diaspora: Literature, Translation, and the Rise of Black Internationalism*. Cambridge, MA: Harvard University Press, 2003.

Edwards, Brent Hayes. "The Uses of Diaspora." *Social Text* 66/19, no. 1 (2001): 45–73.

Erdrich, Louise. *The Night Watchman*. New York: Harper Collins, 2020.

Eze, Chielozona. "Rethinking African Culture and Identity: The Afropolitan Model." *Journal of African Cultural Studies* 26, no. 2 (2014): 234–47.

Farias, Paulo F. de Moraes. *Arabic Medieval Inscriptions from the Republic of Mali: Epigraphy, Chronicles, and Songhay-Tuareg History*. Oxford: Oxford University Press, 2001.

Fauvelle, François-Xavier. *The Golden Rhinoceros: Histories of the African Middle Ages*. Princeton, NJ: Princeton University Press, 2018.

Feierman, Steven. "Ethnographic Regions—Healing, Power, and History." In *Borders and Healers*, edited by Tracy J. Luedke and Harry G. West, 185–96. Bloomington: Indiana University Press, 2006.

Forssman, Tim. "An Archaeological Contribution to the Kalahari Debate from the Middle Limpopo Valley, Southern Africa." *Journal of Archaeological Research* (2021). https://doi .org.turing.library.northwestern.edu/10.1007/s10814-021-09166-0.

Forssman, Tim, Bruce Page, and Jeanetta Selier. "How Important Was the Presence of Elephants as a Determinant of the Zhizo Settlement of the Greater Mapungubwe Landscape?" *Journal of African Archaeology* 12, no. 1 (2014): 75–87.

Garlake, Peter S. *The Hunter's Vision: The Prehistoric Art of Zimbabwe*. London: British Museum Press, 1995.

Gilroy, Paul. *The Black Atlantic: Modernity and Double Consciousness*. Cambridge, MA: Harvard University Press, 1993.

Gomez, Michael. *African Dominion: A New History of Empire in Early and Medieval West Africa*. Princeton, NJ: Princeton University Press, 2018.

Green, Toby. *A Fistful of Shells: West Africa from the Rise of the Slave Trade to the Age of Revolution*. Chicago: University of Chicago Press, 2019.

Grollemund, Rebecca, David Schoenbrun, and Jan Vansina. "Moving Histories: An Authoritative Phylogeny of the Bantu Languages Parsed with Histories of Mobility and Eclectic Foodways." *Journal of African History*, forthcoming.

Hanchard, Michael. "Afro-Modernity: Temporality, Politics, and the African Diaspora." *Public Culture* 11, no. 1 (1999): 245–68.

Hannan, Michael. *Standard Shona Dictionary*, 2nd ed. Salisbury: Rhodesia Literature Bureau, 1974.

Hanretta, Sean. "The River of Salvation Flows through Africa: Edward Wilmot Blyden, Raphael Armattoe, and the Redemption of the Culture Concept." In *Indigenous Visions: Rediscovering the World of Franz Boas*, edited by Ned Blackhawk and Isaiah Lorado Wilner, 279–315. New Haven, CT: Yale University Press, 2018.

Hartman, Saidiya. "Venus in Two Acts." *Small Axe* 12, no. 2 (2008): 1–14.

Herskovits, Melville J. *The Myth of the Negro Past*. New York: Harper and Brothers, 1941.

Huffman, Thomas N. "Mapungubwe and Great Zimbabwe." *Journal of Anthropological Archaeology* 28 (2009): 37–54.

Killick, David. "Tracing Ingombe Ilede's Trade Connections." *Antiquity* 91, no. 358 (2017): 1087–88.

Kinahan, John. "A Ritual Assemblage from the Third Millennium BC in the Namib Desert and Its Implications for the Archaeology and Rock Art of Shamanic Performances." *Azania: Archaeological Research in Africa* 53, no. 1 (2018): 40–62.

Kinahan, John. "The Solitary Shaman: Itinerant Healers and Ritual Seclusion in the Namib Desert during the Second Millennium A.D." *Cambridge Archaeological Journal* 27, no. 3 (2017): 553–69.

Klehm, Carla. "Local Dynamics and the Emergence of Social Inequality in Iron Age Botswana." *Current Anthropology* 58, no. 5 (2017): 604–33.

Land, Isaac. "Tidal Waves: The New Coastal History." *Journal of Social History* 40, no. 3 (2007): 731–43.

Landau, Paul S. *Popular Politics in the History of South Africa, 1400–1948*. New York: Cambridge University Press, 2010.

Larson, Pier. *History and Memory in the Age of Enslavement*. Portsmouth, NH: Heinemann Publishers, 2000.

Larson, Pier. *Ocean of Letters: Language and Creolization in an Indian Ocean Diaspora*. New York: Cambridge University Press, 2009.

Lewis, Martin W., and Karen E. Wigen. *The Myth of Continents: A Critique of Metageography*. Berkeley: University of California Press, 1997.

Lovejoy, Henry B., Paul E. Lovejoy, Walter Hawthorne, Edward A. Alpers, Mariana Candido, Matthew S. Hopper, Ghislaine Lydon, Colleen E. Kriger, and John Thornton. "Defining Regions of Pre-colonial Africa: A Controlled Vocabulary for Linking Open-Source Data in Digital History Projects." *History in Africa* 48 (2021): 1–26.

Macamo, Solange. *Privileged Places in South Central Mozambique: The Archaeology of Manyikeni, Niamara, Songo, and Degue-Mufa*. Uppsala: Afrikansk och jämförande arkeologi, 2005.

Machiridza, Lesley Hatipone. "Landscapes and Ethnicity: An Historical Archaeology of Khami-Phase Sites in Southwestern Zimbabwe." *Historical Archaeology* 54 (2020): 647–75.

Matory, J. Lorand. *Black Atlantic Religion: Tradition, Transnationalism, and Modernity in the Afro-Brazilian Candomblé*. Princeton, NJ: Princeton University Press, 2005.

Mbembe, Achille. "Afropolitanism." In *Africa Remix: Contemporary Art of a Continent*, edited by Simon Njami, 26–30. Johannesburg: Johannesburg Art Gallery, 2007.

Mbembe, Achille, and Sarah Balakrishnan. "Pan-African Legacies, Afropolitan Futures." *Transition: An International Review*, no. 120 (2016): 28–37.

McIntosh, Susan Keech, and Brian M. Fagan. "Re-dating the Ingombe Ilede Burials." *Antiquity* 91, no. 358 (2017): 1069–77.

Mguni, Siyakha. "A New Iconographic Understanding of Formlings, a Pervasive Motif in Zimbabwean Rock Art." *South African Archaeological Society Goodwin Series* 9 (2005): 33–44.

Mguni, Siyakha. *Termites of the Gods*. Johannesburg: Witwatersrand University Press, 2015.

Miller, Duncan. *The Tsodilo Jewelry: Metal Work from Northern Botswana*. Rondebosch, South Africa: University of Cape Town Press, 1996.

Mintz, Sidney W., and Richard Price, *The Birth of African-American Culture: An Anthropological Perspective*. Boston: Beacon Press, 1979.

Moffett, Abigail Joy, and Shadreck Chirikure. "Exotica in Context: Reconfiguring Prestige, Power and Wealth in the Southern African Iron Age." *Journal of World Prehistory* 29, no. 4 (2016): 337–82.

Moffett, Abigail Joy, Simon Hall, and Shadreck Chirikure. "Crafting Power: New Perspectives on the Political Economy of Southern Africa, 900–1300." *Journal of Anthropological Archaeology* 59 (2020): 101–180.

Monroe, J. Cameron, and Akinwumi Ogundiran, eds. *Power and Landscape in Atlantic West Africa and the Atlantic World*. New York: Cambridge University Press.

Mudenge, Stanley I. *A Political History of Munhumutapa: c. 1400–1902*. London: James Currey, 1988.

Ogundiran, Akinwumi. *The Yorùbá: A New History*. Bloomington: Indiana University Press, 2020.

Ogundiran, Akinwumi, and Paula Saunders, eds. *Materialities of Ritual in the Black Atlantic*. New York: Cambridge University Press, 2014.

Pakendorf, Brigitte, Hilde Gunnink, Bonny Sands, and Koen Bostoen. "Prehistoric Bantu-Khoisan Language Contact." *Language Dynamics and Change* 7 (2017): 1–46.

Pearson, Michael N. "Littoral Society: The Concept and the Problems." *Journal of World History* 17, no. 4 (2006): 354–73.

Plug, Ina. "Overview of Iron Age Fauna from the Limpopo Valley." *South African Archaeological Society Goodwin Series* 8 (2000): 117–26.

Reid, Andrew, and Alinah Segobye. "Politics, Society, and Trade on the Eastern Margins of the Kalahari." *South African Archaeological Society Goodwin Series* 8 (2000): 58–68.

Schoenbrun, David L. "Early African Pasts: Sources, Interpretations, and Meaning." In *Oxford Encyclopedia of African Historiography: Methods and Sources*, edited by Thomas Spear, 1:7–44. Oxford: Oxford University Press, 2019.

Schoenbrun, David L. *The Historical Reconstruction of Great Lakes Bantu Cultural Vocabulary: Etymologies and Distributions*. Köln: Rüdiger Köppe Press, 1997.

Schoenbrun, David L. "A Lexicon of Affect, Violence, Vulnerability, and Belonging in Eastern Bantu: Semantics and Distributions." Unpublished manuscript.

Schoenbrun, David L. *The Names of the Python: Belonging in East Africa, 900–1930*. Madison: University of Wisconsin Press, 2021.

Shepperson, George. "African Diaspora: Concept and Context." In *Global Dimensions of the African Diaspora*, edited by Joseph E. Harris, 46–53. Washington, DC: Howard University Press, 1982.

Sinclair, Paul, Anneli Ekblom, and Marilee Wood. "Trade and Society on the South-East African Coast in the Later First Millennium AD: The Case of Chibuene." *Antiquity* 86, no. 333 (2012): 723–37.

Stephens, Rhiannon. *A History of African Motherhood: The Case of Uganda, 700–1900*. New York: Cambridge University Press, 2013.

Sweet, James H. "Reimagining the African-Atlantic Archive: Method, Concept, Epistemology, Ontology." *Journal of African History* 55, no. 2 (2014): 147–57.

Thornton, John K. *Africa and Africans in the Making of the Atlantic World, 1400–1800*. 2nd ed. New York: Cambridge University Press, 2012.

Thornton, John K. *A History of West Central Africa to 1850*. New York: Cambridge University Press, 2020.

Verger, Pierre F. *Flux et reflux de l traite des nègres entre le Golfe de Bénin et Bahia de Todos os Santos du XVIIe au XIXe siècle*. Paris: Mouton, 1968.

Ware, Rudolph T., III. *The Walking Qur'an: Islamic Education, Embodied Knowledge, and History in West Africa*. Chapel Hill: University of North Carolina Press, 2014.

Weaver, Jace. *The Red Atlantic: American Indigenes and the Making of the Modern World, 1000–1927*. Chapel Hill: University of North Carolina Press, 2014.

Wilmsen, Ed. "Hills and the Brilliance of Beads: Myths and the Interpretation of Iron Age Sites in Southern Africa." *South African Humanities Journal* 21 (2009): 263–74.

Wylie, Dan. *Death and Compassion: The Elephant in Southern African Literature*. Johannesburg: Witwatersrand University Press, 2018.

Wynne-Jones, Stephanie. *A Material Culture: Consumption and Materiality on the Coast of Precolonial East Africa*. Oxford: Oxford University Press, 2016.

A Needle in the Desert

Héctor Mediavilla

Sidahmed Seidnaly, now known as Alphadi as well as the "Magician of the Desert," is a renowned fashion designer from Niger who had a vision to create an international fashion festival in the heart of Africa. The first edition of the International Fashion Festival in Africa (Festival International de la Mode en Afrique, FIMA) took place in 1998 at the base of the cliffs of Tiguidit in Niger, on the outskirts of the Sahara Desert. Alphadi's first action was to bring together African designers and handicraft makers from across the continent alongside their international counterparts to promote African cultures, encourage investment, and advance economic and social development. The theme of the festival was "Culture, Peace, and Development."

Alphadi is a globe-trotter whose permanent residence is still in Niamey, Niger. Born in Timbuktu, in Mali, he moved to Niger with his family when he was a child. A graduate of the Atelier Chardon Savard, a Parisian school of fashion and design, he presented his first "haute couture" collection in 1988. His talent was quickly recognized by legendary designers, including Yves Saint Laurent, Kenzo Takada, and Paco Rabanne. Since then, he has participated in the Paris and New York Fashion Weeks on multiple occasions, and his creations have been paraded across the globe. In 2016, Alphadi was designated UNESCO's Artist for Peace, a title given by the institution in recognition of his commitment to culture and development in the service of peace, respect, and human dignity, as well as for his contribution to promoting tolerance and his dedication to UNESCO's ideals.

Radical History Review
Issue 144 (October 2022)   DOI 10.1215/01636545-9847886
© 2022 by Héctor Mediavilla

Alphadi's four children, all born in Niger, have grown up and studied in different parts of the world: Niger, the United States, and France. It is a family with multiple and complex interests and identities, rich in nuances. Alphadi's eldest daughter, Lalla Doe, who collaborates with her father to organize the festival, explained to me in a telephone conversation we had in August 2021: "I am who I am. I belong everywhere I want to belong, not to a fixed place but to what I feel in my heart. I find home in people who feel like me, we are children of the world." Her observations resonate with the literary scholar Chielozona Eze's comments on the concept of the Afropolitan: "We are Afropolitans not because we move from one city to another, but because we are capable of occupying several cultural spaces and relations from which we define who we are. Our self-definition does not seek to exclude; rather it seeks to include . . . one only needs to cross the psychic boundaries erected by nativism, autochthony, heritage and other mythologies of authenticity."[1]

However, the second edition of FIMA, held in 2000, supported in part by the United Nations Development Program and held on the banks of the Niger River, became very controversial. In spite of Alphadi's work to create jobs, attract tourism, and raise money for Nigerien development, the festival also offered a feminized and sexualized image of a new modern Africa, which perhaps underestimated the degree to which Islamist sentiments had been on the rise in Niger. Religious figures expressed their opposition to the festival as contrary to the tenets of Islam. Muslim activists held anti-FIMA meetings in mosques, denounced the festival in sermons, and marched in protest.[2]

Now, after thirteen editions, generally scheduled every two years, FIMA has become one of the most important cultural events in Niger. It exhibits the creativity and expertise of African designers and stylists and bestows respect and recognition on African fashion in the context of the global economy. During the festival week, in addition to the fashion shows and competitions, professional talks and debates take place. It is an ideal space for exchange, where new talents of the African fashion industry establish relationships with more prestigious designers from the continent or the diaspora. New networks emerge among people of different nationalities. The same applies to fashion models, stylists, and other fashion-related craftspeople. Sometimes evoking or reinterpreting African modes, styles, and elements, as a collective these African creators construct a space where new ideas, proposals, and creations are shared to shape a wider world.

I first landed in Niamey, Niger, in December 2013 for FIMA's ninth edition and have since returned two more times. At that time, the festival had to leave the open spaces of previous years to take place in a secure area in the country's capital, Niamey, because of recent terrorist activity. FIMA's 2015 edition was cancelled at the last minute, even though quite a few participant designers, models, and members of the press had already landed in Niamey. The following year, in 2016, the festival moved to Agadez, Niger, for its tenth edition. It was held simultaneously with other cultural events such as the Ténéré marathon and the enthronement of the Sultan de l'Aïr, in an attempt to demonstrate that Agadez, a city that for almost a decade had disappeared due to regional instability, was once again safe for tourism. In 2018, the festival was held in Dakhla, a disputed territory of the Western Sahara claimed by Morocco. In spite of all these difficulties, the festival continues its forward-facing vision and adapts to the economic and sociopolitical circumstances of the moment.

Lauren Ekué, a French-born writer of Togolese descent and a good friend of mine, first told me about this event. She knew I would be very interested because, as an artist, I am motivated to develop audiovisual projects related to the construction of identity in unique human groups, including their relationship with the environment. I was intrigued by and wanted to experience firsthand the apparent contradiction of a high fashion and cultural event in a country usually ranked last in the United Nations' Human Development Index. I had previously developed long-term projects in Africa and other parts of the world that had global, transnational, and migratory elements, such as my exhibits and book on Congolese *sapeurs* in Brazzaville, Congo.[3] Sapeurs are a heritage from a colonial past who reinterpret the elegance and manners of the colonizers in a unique way. Supported by the respect and admiration of their community, today's sapeurs consider themselves artists. They add a touch of glamour to their humble environment through their refined manners and impeccable dressing styles. They all share the same dream: to go to Paris and return to Brazzaville as the ambassadors of supreme elegance.

My main interest in the FIMA festival was the idea of an initiative put forth by a country in the Global South that not only challenged the development model imposed by Global North countries but also the country's cultural and religious status quo. Thus I approached this project in phases. First, in a video piece, I contrasted the "bubble" of the festival with the everyday street life of Niamey and Agadez. My photography focused on behind-the-scenes elements of the festival, where glamour coexists with precariousness. I also followed some local models in their everyday life away from the catwalk to understand their fit in the traditional Nigerian society and their aspirations as young women. Here I worked with the Abdou Salèye sisters, who started their modeling careers at the ages of fifteen and sixteen at the FIMA festival. They came from a Christian middle-class family, though Christians count for less than 5 percent of Niger's population. I also followed twenty-three-year-old Haoua Ide, who was born in a traditional Muslim family and for whom fashion opened the possibility of expanding her world and perspectives in life. She now lives in France with her husband and her two-year-old son, Noah. She presented her new clothing brand Waye Bi last June in Niamey.

I connect my experiences at the FIMA festival to the concept of the Afropolitan even though the concept still seems complex to me due to the different perspectives and debate among scholars. But I believe the disagreement and apparent contradictions in the term are part of the dualistic nature of reality and that we all need to accept them if we want to move forward together. Reality cannot be framed in a fixed structure no matter how much more comfort doing so confers. The world keeps on spinning. As Eze remarks, "We, Afropolitans, believe in the ever expanding universe in which we are the centres; we are the centres of the world because in each of us there is a space big enough to contain apparent contradictions and oddities: We are not half this or half that; we are this and that."[4] This expansive conceptualization is what I see in the work of Alphadi and many of the artists who participate in FIMA.

Héctor Mediavilla (1970, Barcelona) is a storyteller who uses different audiovisual media to share his questioning of the human being and his identity as a social, cultural, spiritual, and political fact. He is a photographer, director, educator, and manager of participatory photography projects. He has been awarded in international competitions both as a photographer and director. He has created photographic essays in Africa, the Americas, and Europe, which have been published in a range of international media and exhibited internationally, including at the Guggenheim in Bilbao and the French Institute in Kinshasa and Brazzaville. He has also designed and conducted workshops for young African photographers in Africa. He holds a degree in economics and an MBA, and he is currently completing a postgraduate degree on "Photographic Creation and Reflection," which is expanding his questioning of how reality is visually represented in new territories. He can be reached at hello@hectormediavilla.com.

Notes

1. Chielozona Eze, "We, Afropolitans," *Journal of African Cultural Studies* 28, no. 1 (2016): 117.
2. Barbara M. Cooper, "Anatomy of a Riot: The Social Imaginary, Single Women, and Religious Violence in Niger," *Canadian Journal of African Studies/Revue canadienne des études africaines* 37, nos. 2–3 (2003): 467–512, https://doi.org.10.1080/00083968.2003 .10751276.
3. Héctor Mediavilla, *S.A.P.E.* (Paris: Éditions Intervalles, 2013).
4. Eze, "We, Afropolitans," 117.

CURATED SPACES provides a focus on visual culture in relation to social, historical, or political subject matter.

Figure 1. Fashion shoot on the banks of the Niger River. Image courtesy of Héctor Mediavilla.

Figure 2. Miriam Abdou Salèye (second from the left) and four other models are almost ready for a fashion photo shoot in the old town of Agadez, near the great mosque. They are dressed in the new collection of Modeste Ba from Ivory Coast, who is helping one of the models. Image courtesy of Héctor Mediavilla.

Figure 3. Her elder brother is driving Miriam Abdou Salèye to the BCEO center, where the 2013 FIMA is taking place. She was sixteen at that moment and about to fulfill her greatest dream since childhood: to become a fashion model. As time has gone by, she has developed a successful career in Africa and was awarded Miss Niger 2020. Image courtesy of Héctor Mediavilla.

Figure 4. Preparations and rehearsals in the secured area in Agadez, the wrestling stadium, where the tenth edition of the FIMA festival is taking place. Image courtesy of Héctor Mediavilla.

Figure 5. Backstage at midday. Temperatures are almost 40 degrees Celsius, but there is no air conditioning available, just a few fans. Image courtesy of Héctor Mediavilla.

Figure 6. A model tries on the makeup she will use for tonight's fashion show. Image courtesy of Héctor Mediavilla.

Figure 7. Detail of golden embroidery. During the hours before the fashion show there is a lot of movement backstage finalizing details for a perfect show. Image courtesy of Héctor Mediavilla.

Figure 8. Nadia Abdou Salèye and other models are being styled backstage before going to the catwalk. Image courtesy of Héctor Mediavilla.

Figure 9. Generators are used in order to ensure the power supply during the show. The army and local police also secure the festival area to prevent any incident, in particular any terrorist attack. Image courtesy of Héctor Mediavilla.

Figure 10. Haoua Ide is ready to go on the catwalk for tonight's main show. Image courtesy of Héctor Mediavilla.

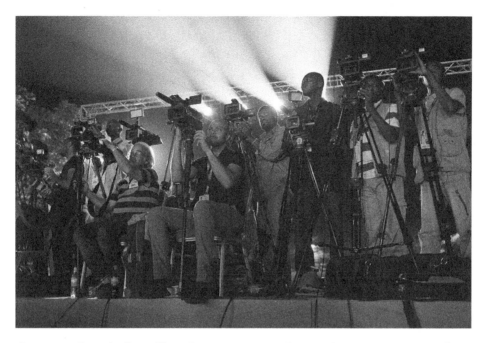

Figure 11. Media coming from Africa and some Western countries cover the event. Image courtesy of Héctor Mediavilla.

Figure 12. Final parade of one of the most acclaimed designers of the tenth edition of FIMA. Image courtesy of Héctor Mediavilla.

Figure 13. Alphadi observes the evolution of the show from backstage. Image courtesy of Héctor Mediavilla.

Figure 14. Habib Sangaré, a fashion designer from Ivory Coast, leaves the catwalk with his models after the show. Image courtesy of Héctor Mediavilla.

Figure 15. Mercy Ashie poses for a photo shoot Sunday early in the morning with a Kennedy Nana Kofi Ansah dress. Image courtesy of Héctor Mediavilla.

An Afropolitan in South Asia

Encounters between Postcolonial Subjects

Emeka Okereke and Mathangi Krishnamurthy

Figure 1. Participants of the Trans-Bangladeshi road trip look into India from the borders in Bangladesh. © Emeka Okereke, courtesy of Invisible Borders Trans-African Project, 2019.

Radical History Review
Issue 144 (October 2022)   DOI 10.1215/01636545-9847900
© 2022 by MARHO: The Radical Historians' Organization, Inc.

Emeka Okereke: Since 2009, the Invisible Borders Trans-African Project has brought together African artists—photographers, writers, filmmakers—to make road trips across the African continent. In the process, the artists create works inspired by their encounters and stories of being on the road. At the heart of the project is the urge to articulate, understand, and consequently generate knowledge about the operative nature of borders. In essence, it is a questioning of the colonially imposed cartography that became perhaps the most contested fixture of the twenty-first century. Thus, I often note that such a project represents a response to the volatile negotiation between the past and present, which is a strong determinant of the reality of our time. As the cofounder, artistic director, and fellow artist, I have been a participant of this project since its inception.

In 2019, we made the first attempt at bringing the Invisible Borders Trans-African Project to South Asia. The project took a slightly different approach, in the sense that we joined forces with Bangladeshi photographers from the Drik Network. We formed an African–South Asian team and traveled within Bangladesh for five weeks. Initially, we had planned to travel from Bangladesh into India. Unfortunately, we could not overcome the grueling bureaucracy before the scheduled event. Thus, we decided to journey within Bangladesh while making stops in five towns where Bangladesh borders India.

Dhaka, as with Chennai or Lagos, is a city of peoples. Life happens explicitly and in public spaces. Encounters are a common occurrence. Intimacy can be spurred by the tiniest of moments. I know this feeling because I have been on the road, journeying across African cities and towns, for over a decade. When you are in such spaces, you are compelled to be alive where this means constant movement and bumping into each other—literally and metaphorically. Yet much of my presence in Bangladesh was marked by an insistent reference to the fact that we (mainly the Nigerians) were an aberration to the norm. There was a certain intensified visibility foregrounding much of our encounter. It was always obvious that we have brought our bodies to parts that, naturally, they have no business being in. Over the years, we have come to understand that as we employ our bodies in the remapping of borders, they operate as "objects of useful agitation." In this sense, my first thought was: What can I make of an encounter that, although full of warmth and hospitality, tends to present itself as something which deflects intimacy? As a result, my body of work was titled "In Search of Intimacy."

Mathangi Krishnamurthy: *Emeka, you and I met as fellow cosmopolitans, if you will, in Chennai. And here we are, talking about intimacy and encounters in Bangladesh.*

I remember thinking, when first meeting you, as to how instant connection was possible, even though we do not share any countries or cities, and even as we may have traveled through many of the other's habitats. You in Lagos, Berlin, Paris, Amsterdam, and I in Chennai, Mumbai, Pune, Austin, Madison. Between

Figure 2. A photograph is worth a thousand eyes. © Emeka Okereke, courtesy of Invisible Borders Trans-African Project, 2019.

the two of us, we may be poster children for cosmopolitanism. And yet, we also are not. Brownness, Blackness, and gender complicate everything.

And when we met, the ferment was also quite interesting. An anthropologist of Asia meets a photographer moving across borders in Africa.

What might you and I be able to say, then, about the nature of encounter between kindred Asiapolitans, if you will, and Afropolitans?

Emeka: I love your diligent attempt to encapsulate our convoluted displacement in the world and subsequent encounter in the most befitting isms. Yet, one can already sense it is much more than any category can contain. This is how I felt when our paths crossed in Chennai. In hindsight, it is the best of human stories. As you have rightly alluded to, there were things we shared in common which served as a connecting thread. Before I get carried away, I must be careful not to take for granted the catalytic quality of our common grounds.

It is not abstract but rather a tangible fixture in the effervescent, malleable nature of our relation. First, as an anthropologist and a photographer, our relationship is set in stone which both disciplines carved out of the need to understand and articulate human relations. Over time, much of this has devolved into ossified identity politics for which photography and anthropology played a significant role in making into a fixed image/gaze. What I felt with our encounter was: here are two conscious people looking to affirm a "presencing" fluttering at the fringes of inherited

Figure 3. Asif and mother. © Emeka Okereke, courtesy of Invisible Borders Trans-African Project, 2019.

limitations without disavowing what lies within and beyond our inherent frontiers. I believe this has kept us connected to each other, both as friends and colleagues, to the point that the former and latter are complementary to each other. It has also allowed us to dance to (or around) the blues-like unrhythmic disparity between presence and proximity.

Mathangi: *When I see these photographs, I am intrigued mostly by the nature of both presence and absence. The photographs are defined by subjects who do not see the camera. You are a quiet, perhaps even hiding presence. You are there, present, but may not be recognized if your subject sees you. You, yourself, will become an object of curiosity, easily named but not easily understood by your photographic subjects. What do we call such intimacy?*

Emeka: Lately, I have been reflecting on how almost all border crossings simultaneously invoke a paradox. When I speak of the unrhythmic disparity between presence and proximity, in a way, I speak of a frame of reality made up of presumed contradictions looking for resolution in flows rather than conflict. What kind of intimacy can be found in a situation where appearance, visual recognition, and named gaze are relegated to a secondary consideration? Intimacy is evidence of mutual communication, and resonance amongst beings and entities. I was looking for an intimacy that is paradoxical to the many configurations of identity by which we delineate the self. If we should entertain, even as utopia, the thought that all those tropes of identity politics do not exist, it is also likely that borders will not exist. Our bodies will move, flow, and find themselves in places on a whim. Encounters will not be burdened by the weight of named gaze. You spoke of my quietness and a hiding presence. Every time I photographed, I was looking for moments that are most evident of presence beyond a bodily connotation. The body has a language. But I am more interested in *how* it remembers. In other words, how it calls forth its language in its *presencing* as it displaces from one place to the other.

Figure 4. A casual shoulder. © Emeka Okereke, courtesy of Invisible Borders Trans-African Project, 2019.

Figure 5. Friendship parade at the India-Bangladesh border post. © Emeka Okereke, courtesy of Invisible Borders Trans-African Project, 2019.

Figure 6. A bird will serve as a milestone. © Emeka Okereke, courtesy of Invisible Borders Trans-African Project, 2019.

I think of the photograph titled "A bird will serve as a milestone." The central figure is a leg behind which sprawls a shadow cast by its full body. Veering off the edge, a bird is perched on a stone. This photograph represents one of the many moments I was intuitively conscious of capturing something of an ungraspable presence. It was a moment that *revealed* itself as if it was looking to uniquely harmonize with my disposition—like a measure of my presence and distance in relation to other persons sharing the same space with me. It brings to mind the popular Igbo concept of duality: "Where one thing stands, something else stands beside it."

Intimacy relies on this sort of corollary interplay between the visible and the invisible, between what is seen and what is revealed. In other words, absence always foreshadows presence, and vice versa. At the crevices of these binaries, one finds the experience of intimacy in an encounter.

For as long as I can remember, I have carried this way of thinking of encounters (and intimacy) as I cross borders from one place to another. I tend to think that no matter where we go, we always carry our own "presence" with us. It is ingrained in one's unique way of navigating, measuring, or taking up space. The encounter is a by-product of letting ourselves experience the myriad ways our presence enters into relation. At every point in time, the photographic moment was preceded by a visceral one which needn't result in a photographic image, more than that it could have urged a quiet smile of inward acknowledgment.

So, Mathangi, what prompted our selection of these photographs is your reference to the idea of "non-encounter" as constitutive of intimacy, especially when deprived of the privilege of accustomed familiarity, as was my case with meeting you for the first time in Chennai, but also me traveling through Bangladesh making these photographs. I am curious as to how you think of the relationship between encounter and non-encounter in this context.

Mathangi: *I suppose part of my curiosity was invoked by our own encounters when traveling through Chennai and what I think of something that has become quite a buzzword in my own intellectual/academic circle: South-South collaboration. It speaks to my own sense of heightened awareness as well when we were flaneurs through Chennai: me a Brown woman, you a Black man, and what kind of gaze you, I, and we were subjected to. It also spoke to me about a general awareness of racism and casteism, not only in the Indian subcontinent but anywhere vis-à-vis Blackness and Brownness and asymmetrical histories of collaboration, co-optation, deceit, enslavement, and/or shared subjugation. We know these differences across the continent of Africa and the former metropole. Add to this the history of southern India and its own racialization in relation to northern India, plus Chennai's history of being colonial India's first modern city, and you have yourself quite the potent mix. As you and I floated through the city, we were most definitely watched. And yet, there is no clear distinction in my mind between encounter and non-encounter. The city itself demands oblivion of a certain kind, and a South Asian postcolonial city even more so. The mere materiality of noise, crowd, sights, and cacophony from vehicle horns means that we were constantly encountered and dismissed. Such a situation is, in my mind, rife for both relationality and moving beyond. If you remember, the temple priest anointed your forehead with ash, something that is a practice marked by caste, and yet, in the moment it was also an inclusive act, one of encounter and non-encounter. You took photographs in the precincts of the temple—of various people including me—going about their worship oblivious to your gaze. Or at the least, they may have been peripherally aware. This to me was also the hyphen between* non *and* encounter.*

Is this Afropolitanism also?, therefore I ask.*

And it would be great if you could use my reflections to speak about some of your photographs in Bangladesh and if there might be any resonance in your travels with the kind of affective charge I speak about.

Emeka: I remember that one of the remarkable thoughts of my time in Chennai was how much the reality of racism and casteism is so complex and layered. In a way, it had the effect of quelling the rate at which I come to conclusions about otherness. My time at the temple in Chennai was heavily mediated by your presence. You made it familiar, amiable, and something I wanted to partake in, while being blissfully

Figure 7. History in progress. © Emeka Okereke, courtesy of Invisible Borders Trans-African Project, 2019.

oblivious to any possible problematics. Also, I was very taken by the fact that you too went into the temple to observe a certain part of the ritual, even though you have not done so for quite a long time. There is something about those moments that offered us a portal of transcendence, if you may. And I believe this is one of the offerings of the hyphenated spaces you and I embodied throughout our interactions with Chennai.

I may have carried something of this "calm criticality" with me to Bangladesh. I guess searching for intimacy through my photographs was searching for this portal of transcendence, a hyphenated space. This is captured succinctly in a text about the photographs: *In Search of Intimacy* preempts a space of negotiation, of exchange, of sharing (give-and-receive) between me and the many persons I have met and photographed in the course of the journey across Bangladesh. It is my story weaved with theirs, and mine in theirs. This story is also our fate, our path and, in hindsight, our pact. It carries things that could not be worded. Questions that could not be answered. Misgivings that could be forgiven. Exchanges that are untranslatable.

Yet, it is not so much about anything as an attempt to speak from within something; from within a place.

A place where, if ever there is an end, my heart will fall into. Where perhaps one day, I will become all the encounters of my journey.

A place of needful utopia.

Figure 8. You will know me when you hold me. © Emeka Okereke, courtesy of Invisible Borders Trans-African Project, 2019.

Figure 9. Further down the road. © Emeka Okereke, courtesy of Invisible Borders Trans-African Project, 2019.

Figure 10. Twin tomb. © Emeka Okereke, courtesy of Invisible Borders Trans-African Project, 2019.

So to answer your question: Is this Afropolitanism? I would say, yes, Afropolitanism is a place of needful utopia.

Mathangi Krishnamurthy is associate professor of anthropology at the Indian Institute of Technology Madras, India. She holds a PhD in anthropology from The University of Texas at Austin and was an Andrew W. Mellon Postdoctoral Fellow at the University of Wisconsin, Madison. Her areas of interest include the anthropology of work and gender, urban studies, globalization, and affective labor. Her book *1–800-Worlds: The Making of the Indian Call Centre Economy* (2018) chronicles the labor practices, lifeworlds, and media atmospheres of Indian call center workers.

Emeka Okereke is a Nigerian visual artist, writer, filmmaker, and DJ who lives and works between Lagos and Berlin. He holds a master's degree from the École Nationale Supérieure des Beaux-Arts in Paris. In 2015, his work was exhibited at the Fifty-Sixth Venice Biennale. Okereke is the founder and artistic director of the Invisible Borders Trans-African Project. He is also the founder and host of the Nkata Podcast Station. Okereke has served as guest/visiting lecturer in several art platforms and learning institutions, notably Hartford University's MFA program in photography; Summer Academy of Fine Arts, Salzburg Austria; and Sandberg Institute, Amsterdam. In 2018, he was named Chevalier dans l'Ordre des Arts et des Lettres by the Ministry of Culture of France in recognition of his contribution to the discourse on art in Africa, France, and the world at large.

CURATED SPACES provides a focus on visual culture in relation to social, historical, or political subject matter.

Does Afropolitanism Apply to the Americas?

Aniova Prandy

The term *Afropolitanism* is new to me and unknown in the Dominican Republic. Yet it feels very old, too. Conceptually, we have always been Afropolitans, because there is no better example of "worlds in movements" than what has happened in the Caribbean since 1492. I am using the term as an intervention, because now the term is in my head and I will start using it to name, define, and describe concrete practices in Santo Domingo.

I can conceive my latest work, *The Sugar Maafa*, as an Afropolitan practice. *Maafa* is a Swahili term to describe a big disaster or a great tragedy, in this case resulting from the capitalization of sugar production. The work is born from the need in the Dominican Republic to visibilize and generate discussion in contemporary art of the slave trade of the sixteenth, seventeenth, and eighteenth centuries. In this work, I propose to debate the concept of cultural patrimony based on the mercantilization of people, from a decolonial perspective.

The piece has fourteen silk cushions to approximate the millions of African women, children, and men who were traded as slaves in the Americas. All of them are set in a perfect line to simulate the movement of thousands of ships across the Atlantic. Each cushion is filled with brown sugar, and on each sits a collar and a mountain of white sugar.

The Sugar Maafa encloses and hides bags of sugar in an allegorical manner: millions of pounds of the sweet product and millions of individuals enslaved to produce it.

Radical History Review
Issue 144 (October 2022)   DOI 10.1215/01636545-9847914
© 2022 by MARHO: The Radical Historians' Organization, Inc.

The movement of people across the Atlantic supported European economies and monarchies. The cushion mimics the way that crowns were presented to the monarchs and evokes comfort and luxury. Cushions always function to provide comfort to heads, knees, buttocks. In this case, the cushions support iron collars that interrupt the comfort and instead emphasize the human costs of sugar.

In *The Sugar Maafa*, the cushions display iron collars to signify torture and death. The iron collars represent the void of a name, of a woman, a man, a girl, an ethnicity, a culture.

The Sugar Maafa also talks about agency and creativity. All the collars, except one, are open, evoking the breaking of chains. The shape of the white sugar on the cushions represents the mountains where Africans escaped to claim freedom. *Cimarrones* were the first Afropolitans. They had to invent themselves on a new soil. They had to use the usurper's language to construct dissidence. They had to adapt and adopt different African customs and traditions to create a new world. They had to negotiate with European monarchs, find new ways of fighting, and form new societies. *Cimarrones* were in constant need of renovation in order to survive. *Cimarrones* were constantly renovating themselves out of necessity. Surviving was a creative motor.

Thus the term *Afropolitan* is automatically decolonial because it rewrites history. It is a synthesis of all the political struggles, of all that has been achieved and studied. It is a practice of affirmation. The Afropolitan person assumes herself as such.

Aniova Prandy, visual artist and performer, is the winner of the Twenty-Ninth National Visual Arts Biennial organized by the Ministry of Culture of the Dominican Republic (2021).

Translated by Rosa Elena Carrasquillo.

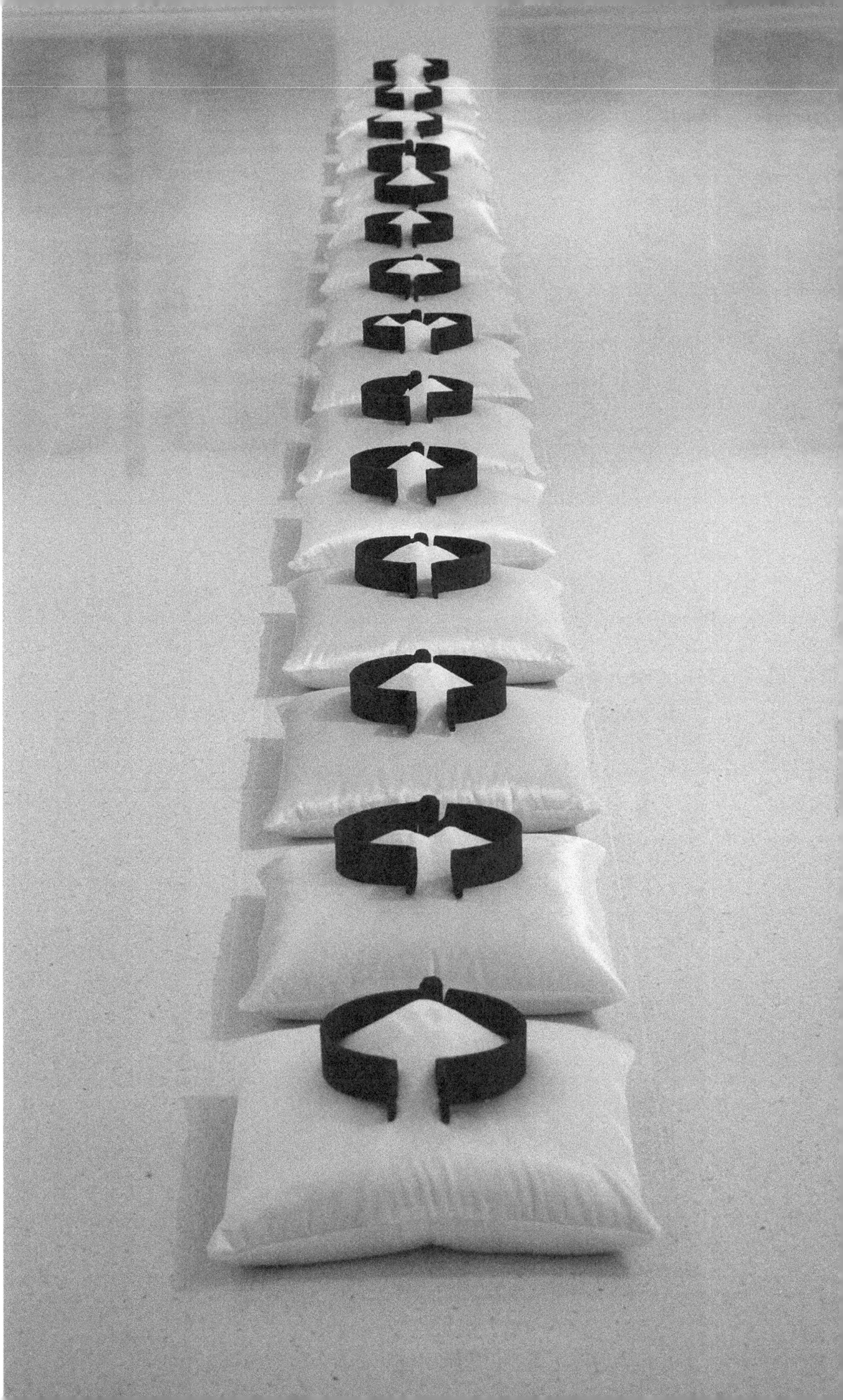

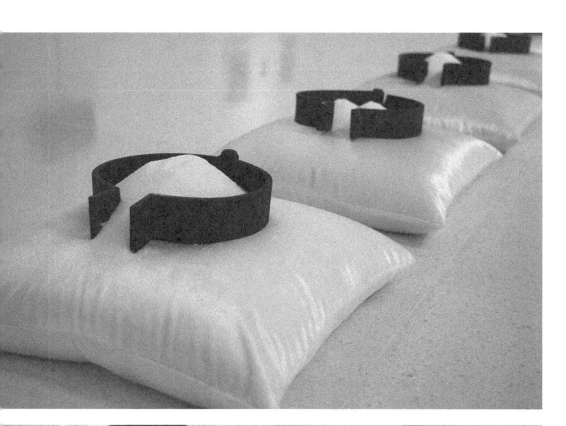

Keep up to date on new scholarship

Issue alerts are a great way to stay current on all the cutting-edge scholarship from your favorite Duke University Press journals. This free service delivers tables of contents directly to your inbox, informing you of the latest groundbreaking work as soon as it is published.

To sign up for issue alerts:

1. Visit **dukeu.press/register** and register for an account. You do not need to provide a customer number.

2. After registering, visit **dukeu.press/alerts**.

3. Go to "Latest Issue Alerts" and click on "Add Alerts."

4. Select as many publications as you would like from the pop-up window and click "Add Alerts."

read.dukeupress.edu/journals